STATIONS & STRUCTURES
—— OF THE ——
SETTLE & CARLISLE
RAILWAY

including Track Layouts,
Signalling Diagrams & Illustrations

Frontispiece: The one single structure that for most people symbolises the Settle and Carlisle Railway is Ribblehead Viaduct, seen here in the course of construction in a view looking south towards Ingleborough across Batty Moss. The abutment and seven of the stone piers have been completed and the centring has been positioned for turning the arch rings in brick. The extensive use of timber scaffolding and platforms can be remarked upon, a common feature of mid-Victorian construction.

BR Area Civil Engineer, Preston

STATIONS & STRUCTURES
—— OF THE ——
SETTLE & CARLISLE
RAILWAY

V.R. ANDERSON & G.K. FOX

Oxford Publishing Company

An imprint of Ian Allan Publishing

First published 1986
Reprinted 2000
This second edition first published 2014

ISBN 978 0 86093 662 6

© V. R. Anderson and G. K. Fox 1986
Colour art section © 2014

Published by Oxford Publishing Co

an imprint of Ian Allan Publishing Ltd, Hersham, Surrey KT12 4RG.
Printed in England.

Visit the Ian Allan Publishing website at www.ianallanpublishing.com

Front cover: LMS 'Black Five' No 5305 approaches Ribblehead on 8 March 1986. Whernside is in the background. *W. A. Sharman*

Back cover: SR No 850 *Lord Nelson* crosses Ais Gill Viaduct on 3 August 1982. *J. H. Cooper-Smith*

Acknowledgements

We gratefully acknowledge the kind help and assistance of the numerous people who have made this publication possible.

Our sincere thanks to Mr R. J. Coon, C. Eng., FICE, SCIT, former Regional Civil Engineer BR (LMR), Mr P. J. White, C. Eng., FICE, former Area Civil Engineer, Manchester BR (LMR) and Mr S. D. Duncan, B.Sc., C. Eng., MICE, Area Civil Engineer, Preston.

In order to prepare this book we have called on the assistance of many people, and whether they have been able to show one photograph or a collection, or whether their word has provided one sentence or pages of text, their help has been our inspiration. In alphabetical order they are A. Austin, P. E. Baughan, G. Biddle, O. F. Carter, J. M. Hammond, D. Ibbotson, D. Jenkinson, R. Leslie, G. Nicol, D. F. Tee, D. Thompson, M. S. Welch, P. Weston, J. White and N. Wilkinson.

To our wives we give our thanks for continuing to withstand the onslaught of rolls of drawings and boxes of photographs.

Introduction

The opening to the public, on 1st May 1876, of the Settle to Carlisle route of the Midland Railway saw the culmination of a struggle for freedom that had occupied the minds of the Midland Railway Board of Directors for almost twenty years. From that date Midland traffic could be carried as far as Carlisle, without recourse to the whims of rival companies.

Few lines have captured the imagination of the railway enthusiast as has the Settle & Carlisle. Numerous books and papers have been written on the subject, but this work is intended as a sequential survey of the 72 miles 1,728 yards of the route from Settle Junction to Petteril Bridge Junction. Included are maps, diagrams, plans of the track layout at the stations, junctions and sidings. In addition, line drawings detail the structures. As well as photographically illustrating the buildings to be found at stations, we have tried as far as possible to include pictures of signal boxes, tunnels, major viaducts and a representative selection of the many bridges.

Although a brief outline of the events leading to the conception of the line is included, this is not a full and frank discussion of the socio and economic factors affecting history, development and management of the Settle to Carlisle route. Nor do we pretend to document the locomotives, rolling stock and train workings; we leave all these to the more erudite commentators in the proliferation of writings about this line. We hope the inclusion of train pictures will not detract from our survey of structures and track.

In order to get the complete background information, we would recommend the reader to the following works:

North of Leeds by Peter Baughan. This fully documents the history and development of the line and the background history concerning the Midland Railway's bid to reach Scotland.

The Midland Railway, its rise and progress by F. S. Williams. This contains an absorbing account written at the time the line was being constructed.

Rails in the Fells by David Jenkinson. This fully covers the social, economic and geographical factors affecting the railway.

The Scenic Settle Carlisle by Donald Binns. This book is of general interest.

In addition to these, many interesting books have been published by the Dalesman Company.

In its quest to carry traffic from the Midlands towards Scotland, the Midland Railway had acquired control of the Leeds and Bradford Railway by Act of Parliament in July 1851. By working the Little North Western Railway from 1852, with eventual take over in 1871, Midland trains could reach Lancaster for onward transmission of passengers or freight over the Lancaster and Carlisle Railway to be handed over to one of the Scottish companies.

It had been intended that the main line of the Little North Western should pass through Ingleton and on to the Lancaster and Carlisle Railway near Tebay, but economies dictated that the section north of Ingleton be abandoned in favour of connections to Lancaster and Morecambe. It was left to the LNWR as successors to the L&C to construct the line from Lowgill to Ingleton. The Midland hoped to send any Scottish traffic over this more direct route, opened in 1861, but difficulties and delays were experienced and no through running of Midland trains was permitted.

Breakdown of negotiations between the LNWR and Midland Railway over the latter's access to Carlisle, and over the Lancaster and Carlisle route, left the Midland seeking an alternative solution. An unexpected opportunity arose when a Bill was presented to Parliament in 1865 for the North of England Union Railway to build a line from Settle to Hawes and Leyburn, to connect with lines to Darlington, with branches to Clapham and Sedbergh. Although the Bill was approved by the Commons, the Midland Railway were able to step in before it was passed to the Lords. Modified, it was reintroduced in the 1866 session by the Midland company for a direct main line from Settle to Carlisle with a branch to Hawes. In spite of strong opposition from the LNWR, the Bill received Royal assent on 16th July 1866. This Act included running powers over the North Eastern Railway from Petteril Bridge Junction into Carlisle (Citadel) Station.

Having been beaten in attempts to keep the Midland out of Carlisle, the LNWR offered the Midland company easier access to Scotland over the Lancaster and Carlisle line, via Ingleton and Low Gill. In view of the expensive expansion policies of the Midland at that time, the company was sufficiently encouraged by these new proposals from the LNWR to consider abandonment of the Settle to Carlisle venture. However this did not meet with Parliamentary approval, due to opposition from the North British Railway and the Glasgow & South Western Railway who hoped to benefit by handling the Midland Railway's Scottish traffic, and by the Lancashire & Yorkshire Railway who needed access to Scotland independent of the LNWR.

When the abandonment Bill was rejected on 16th April 1869, operations recommenced after laying idle for a couple of years. Tenders were invited for four contracts for the main line and one for the branch to Hawes. Workmen moved into the Ribblehead area in autumn 1869, although the official cutting of the first sod was at Anley, near Settle, in November 1869.

John Sidney Crossley, who had been appointed Chief Engineer of the Midland Railway in 1858 to succeed Charles Liddell, was due to retire, but agreed to remain in office to supervise construction of the Settle to Carlisle line. Sharland, a Tasmanian engineer, was appointed to work out the route and gradients to the general plan instigated in 1865 by Mr Crossley, with the approval of the Midland Railway's General Manager, Mr James Allport.

The chosen route made use of the valley of the Ribble, passing through the shoulder of the massive bulk of Whernside at Blea Moor, skirting the valley of the Dee, under the fells of Rise Hill to the valley of Garsdale, over the watershed to a summit at Aisgill, before dropping down the valley of the Eden towards Carlisle.

Contract No. 1 from Settle Junction to Denthead, 17 miles 18 chains, was awarded on 14th September 1869 to John Ashwell of Kentish Town. The Midland appointed two resident engineers for this contract, R. E. Wilson for the first part, and E. O. Ferguson for the second. Contract No. 2 from Arten Gill to near Kirkby Stephen, about 17 miles, was let in November 1869 to Benton and Woodiwiss. John Storey was to be resident engineer with James Hay acting as contractor's agent.

For contract No. 3, covering the next 14½ miles, a tender was accepted from Joseph Firbank in March 1870. The resident engineer was Jesse Drage, with J. Throstle as agent. On 23rd April 1870, Eckersley and Bayliss were awarded the No. 4 contract for the final length to Petteril Bridge. For this stretch, two engineers were chosen, John Allen and Samuel S. Paine, and two agents, J. Lambert and S. Williams.

The fifth contract for the branch line to Hawes was not let until 1871, when the Benton and Woodiwiss offer was accepted. Frank Lynde became the resident engineer.

When accepting work, none of the contractors appreciated just how ferocious the weather conditions could be on the Northern Fells. Indeed, even Mr Crossley himself was not cognisant of this fact. Delays caused by rain, snow and frost during the time of construction caused the Midland Railway to petition Parliament three times for extension of the time granted to complete the railway. Only contract No. 4 seemed to proceed normally, situated as it was in the more temperate Eden Valley.

Contracts Nos. 1 and 2 were particularly affected by extremes of climate (Cite with prolonged periods of rain, measurably greater than normally encountered. Areas of clay, usually rock-hard would turn to impassable quagmires, tunnel workings became flooded holding up work for long periods, and boulder clay which needed blasting with explosives one minute would turn into a glutinous slurry in the tipping cart.

By mid-1871, John Ashwell was finding No. 1 contract too great a burden. His contract was relinquished by an Agreement dated 26th October 1871, and was taken over by the Midland Railway, who appointed a Mr W. H. Ashwell as its agent. Work and management of this section quickly improved.

In October 1872, Messrs Crossley, Allport and Kirtley (the Locomotive Superintendent) presented a report to the construction committee listing the proposed sites and sizes of engine sheds and stations. Small stations were suggested for Settle Junction, Horton in Ribblesdale, Selside, Hawes Junction, Hawes, Asby, New Biggin, Cumwhinton and Scotby, each with suitable facilities for coal and livestock traffic, but only Hawes was scheduled to receive a goods warehouse.

Larger stations were proposed for Settle, Kirkby Stephen, Crosby Garrett, Appleby, Long Marton, Langwathby, Lazonby and Armathwaite. Each of these was to have a goods warehouse, although the size varied for each location.

At this time it was thought that a decision about a station at Little Salkeld could be deferred, and that it might be found necessary to construct a station for Dentdale. No mention was made for any facilities at Culgaith or Ribblehead, although it does seem that this latter did take over the Selside proposal. The station for Asby was actually built at Ormside.

With regard to locomotive facilities, the committee were asked to sanction sheds for 24 engines at Hawes Junction and at Petteril, near Carlisle, and a shed for 2 engines at Hawes. Additional watering was suggested at Appleby and Lazonby.

At all stations and locomotive sites, cottages for the employees and houses for the stationmasters were to be built as appropriate.

In 1873 Messrs Allport, Crossley and Johnson (replacing Matthew Kirtley who had died) made a further report confirming the locomotive facilities. Hawes Junction shed was cut by half, and water tanks, each with pumping engine, and a cottage for the man in attendance were asked for at Hawes Junction (36,000 gallons), Appleby (20,000 gallons) and Lazonby (12,000 gallons). A shed for 24 engines, 25 cottages, and a 36,000 gallon water tank were needed at Carlisle.

In the event, no locomotive shed was built at Hawes, and the one that did appear at Hawes Junction was a small structure for North Eastern engines working on the branch.

Station designs by the Company Architect, Mr J. H. Sanders, were approved by the construction committee. John Holloway Sanders (1826-1884) was elected Fellow of the RIBA in 1872. He was perhaps best-known for the Midland station at Bath (1870) and for the joint station at Ilkley (1865).

Tenders for the building of the stations were received in mid-1874. J. Thornton of Bradford successfully tendered for stations at Settle Junction, Settle, Horton and Helwith Bridge.

Benton and Woodiwiss agreed to build stations at Kirkby Stephen and Arten Gill. This was the first positive mention of a station for this area, but the site for this Dentdale station had still not been finalised. The John Bayliss tender for a locomotive shed and fitting shops at Carlisle was accepted. Firbank agreed to construct the stations on the No. 3 contract.

George Black of Carlisle obtained contracts for Scotby, Cumwhinton, Armathwaite, Lazonby, Little Salkeld, Langwathby, and Duncowfold. The latter was a late addition in connection with a large plaster works being erected in the parish of Wetheral. It was named High Stand Gill during construction, known as Knot Mill for a time, but finally named Cotehill.

The problems of the station at Culgaith, which did not open until 1880, will be seen later. More will emerge about designs, construction and facilities as we journey along the line. Three designs of building for stations emerged, and some of the suggested large stations did actually receive a medium-sized building.

During the period of construction of the line, up to 7,000 men were employed at any one time, but there was a constantly-changing labour force; many left during bad weather and others were attracted to agricultural work during the summer and autumn. By the end of 1874, Crossley fell ill, and his work was taken over by John Underwood. Although Crossley would have liked to retire, the Midland Railway agreed on condition that he returned and remained in office until completion of the line.

After six long years of construction, goods trains finally ran over the whole length of the line in August 1875 but, even then, 21 miles of the route was not in a final state of completion.

At 10.30a.m. on 1st May 1876, without any ceremony at all, the first Midland Railway express to Scotland left St. Pancras Station to run over the Settle & Carlisle route, before being handed over to the Glasgow & South Western Railway and to North British Company locomotives for passage to Glasgow and Edinburgh respectively.

Construction of the Hawes branch continued for another couple of years, but it was not opened for Midland traffic until 1st August 1878, four days before Crossley died at the age of 65.

The Settle & Carlisle line forms a tangible memorial to John Crossley, and to the thousands of men who worked upon it.

The whole line is, structurally, not very different from when built, apart from the strengthening and subsequent reconstruction of a few girder bridges. The station buildings have fulfilled their function without significant alteration or addition. This must be unique to this line, compared with any other main line in Britain.

Notes on Drawings

Track Layouts — All track layout plans are reproduced to a scale of 2 chains (132ft. = 1in.) an acknowledged and commonly used scale for the recording of railway surveys before the adoption of 1:1250. A scale bar is included on all track diagrams.

Signalling Diagrams — All the signalling diagrams are reproduced in 'schematic' form and do not conform to any particular scale. The term 'signalling diagram' has been used throughout as a simplification of information extracted from signal box diagrams, working sketches, locking sketches, etc.

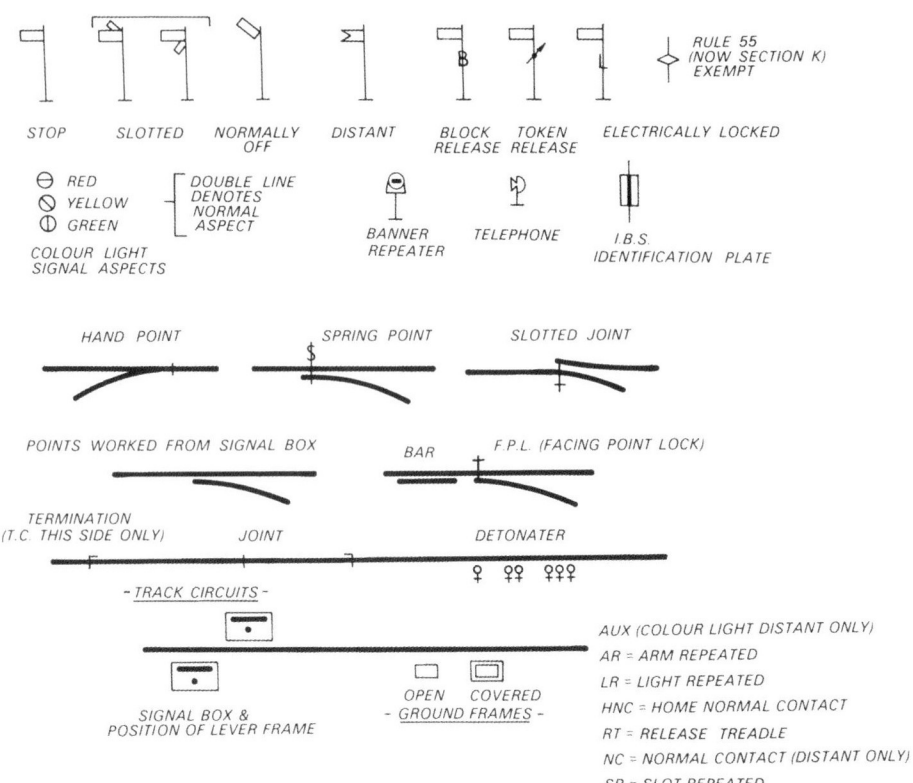

KEY TO SIGNALLING SYMBOLS

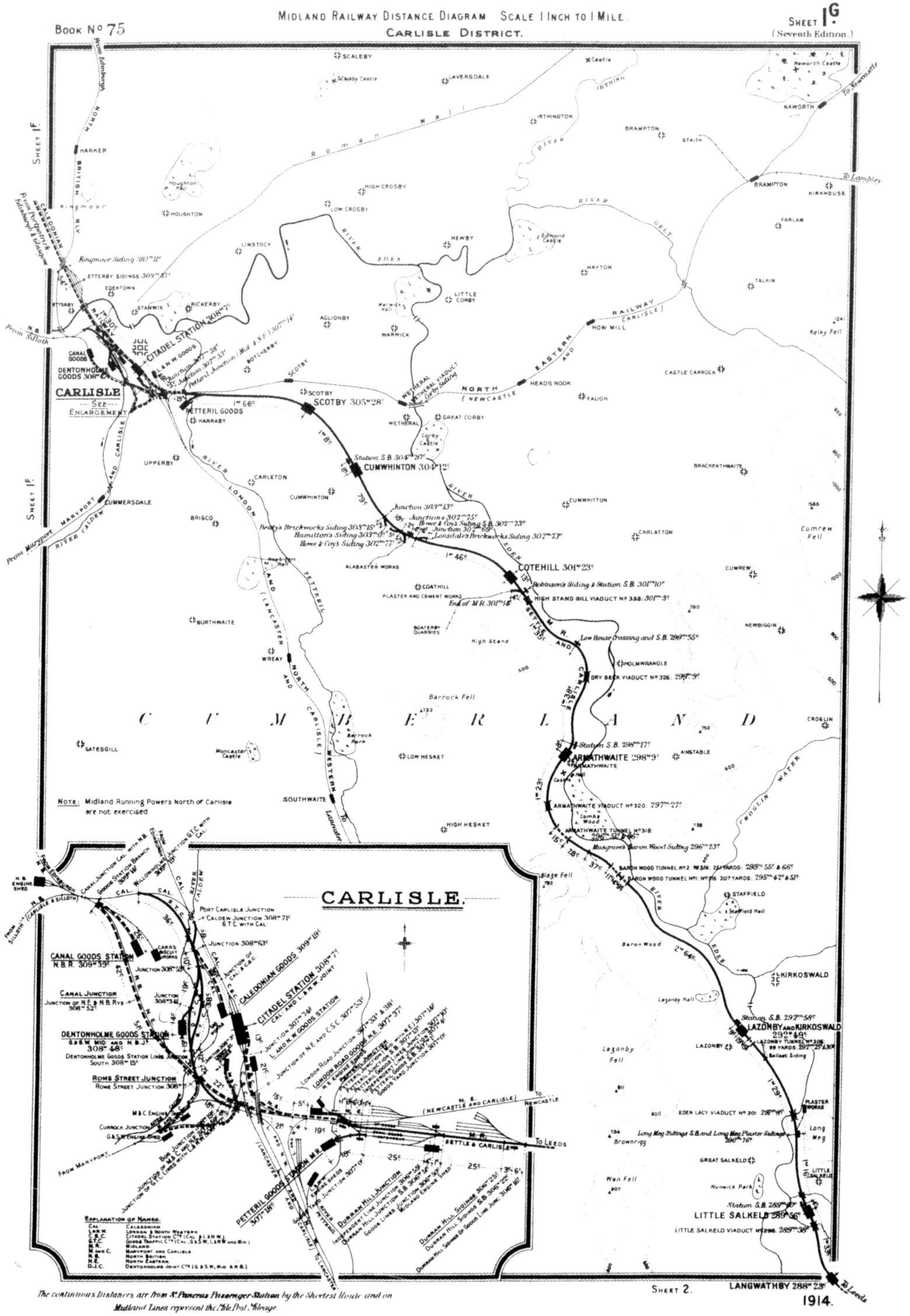

Book Nº 75

MIDLAND RAILWAY DISTANCE DIAGRAM   SCALE 1 INCH TO 1 MILE.
CARLISLE DISTRICT.

SHEET 1G
(Seventh Edition.)

Carlisle — Langwathby

CARLISLE

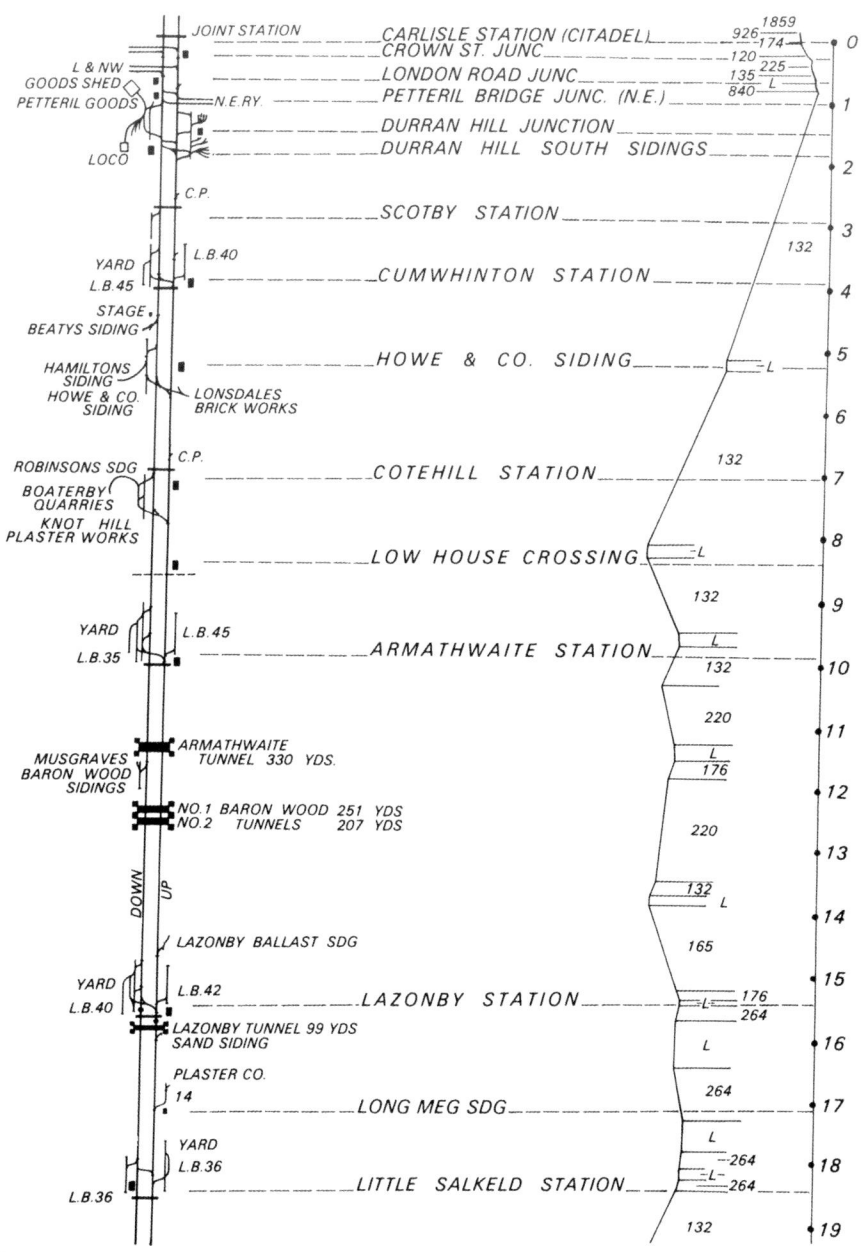

NOTE: Midland Running Powers North of Carlisle are not exercised.

CARLISLE.
See Enlargement.

The continuous Distances are from St. Pancras Passenger Station by the Shortest Route and on Midland Lines represent the Mile Post Mileage.

SHEET 2.

1914.

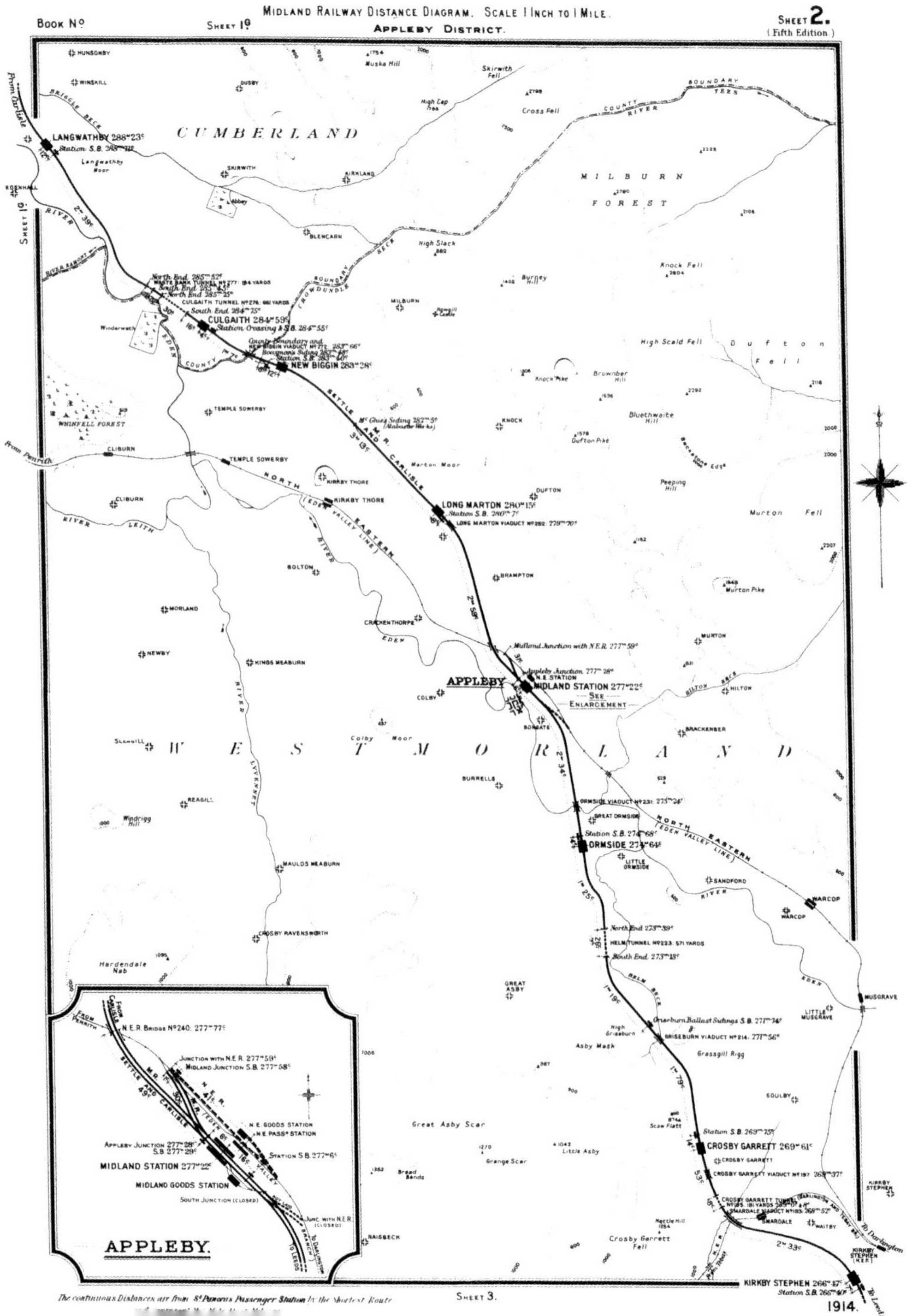

Langwathby — Kirkby Stephen

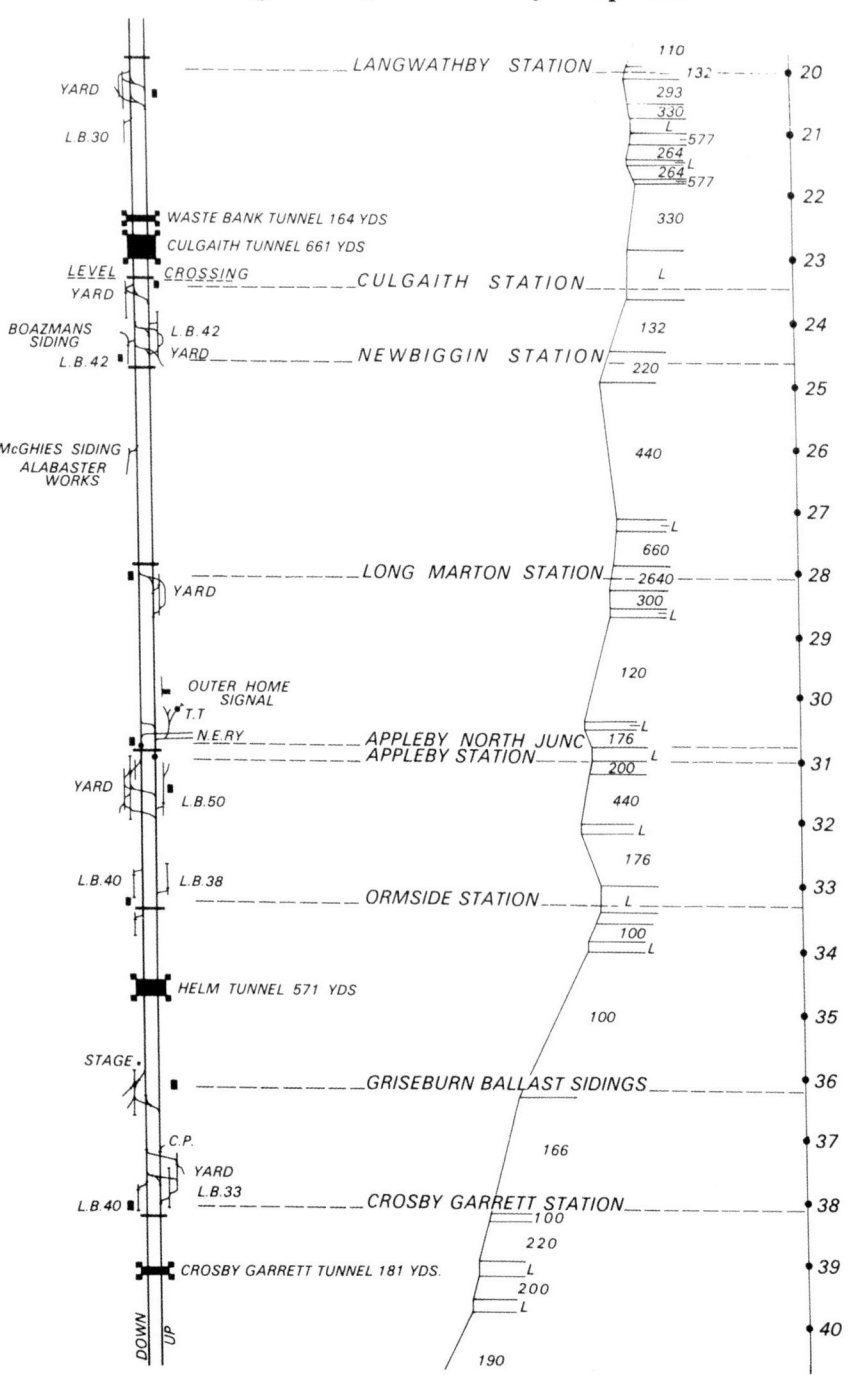

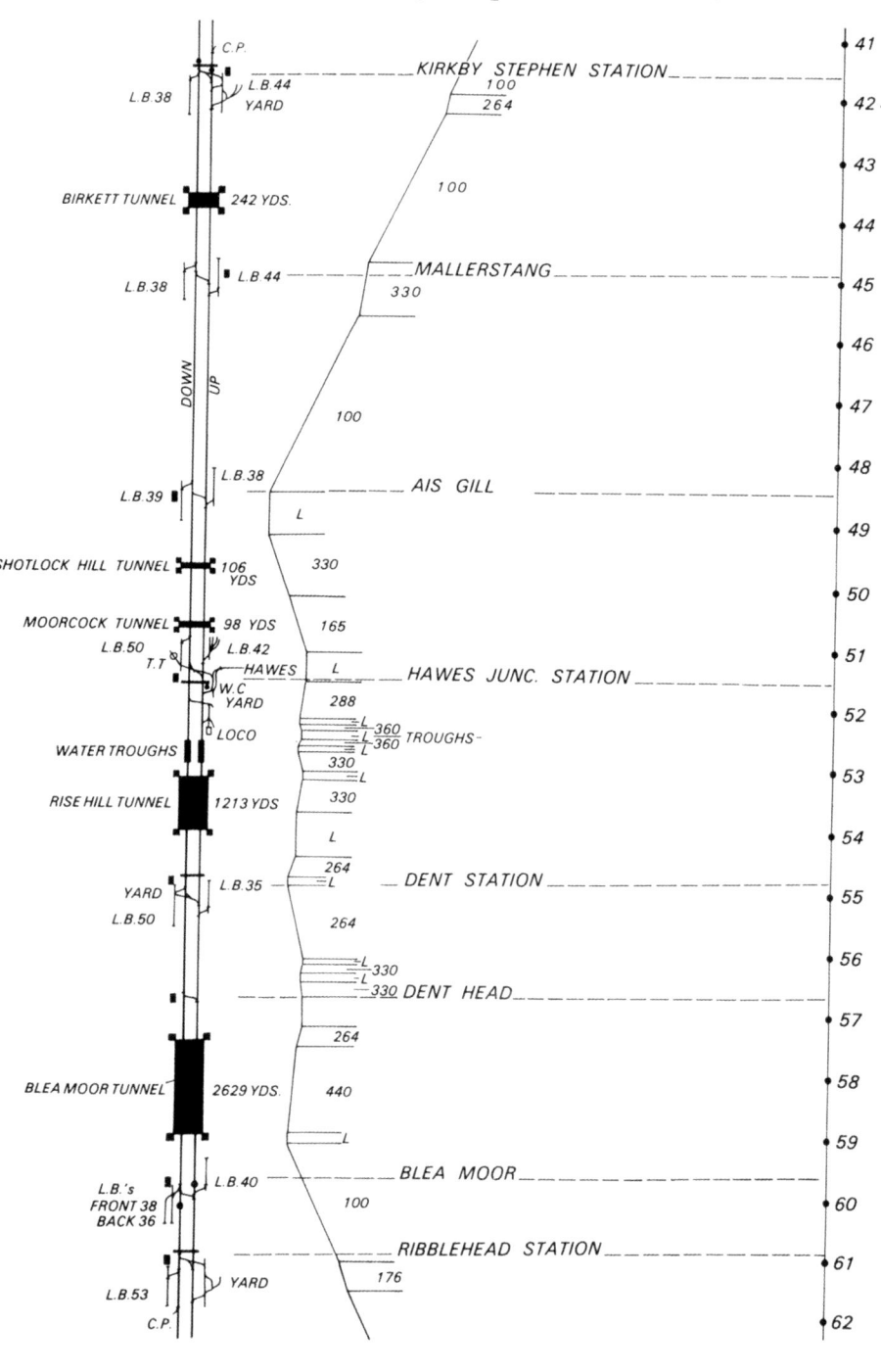

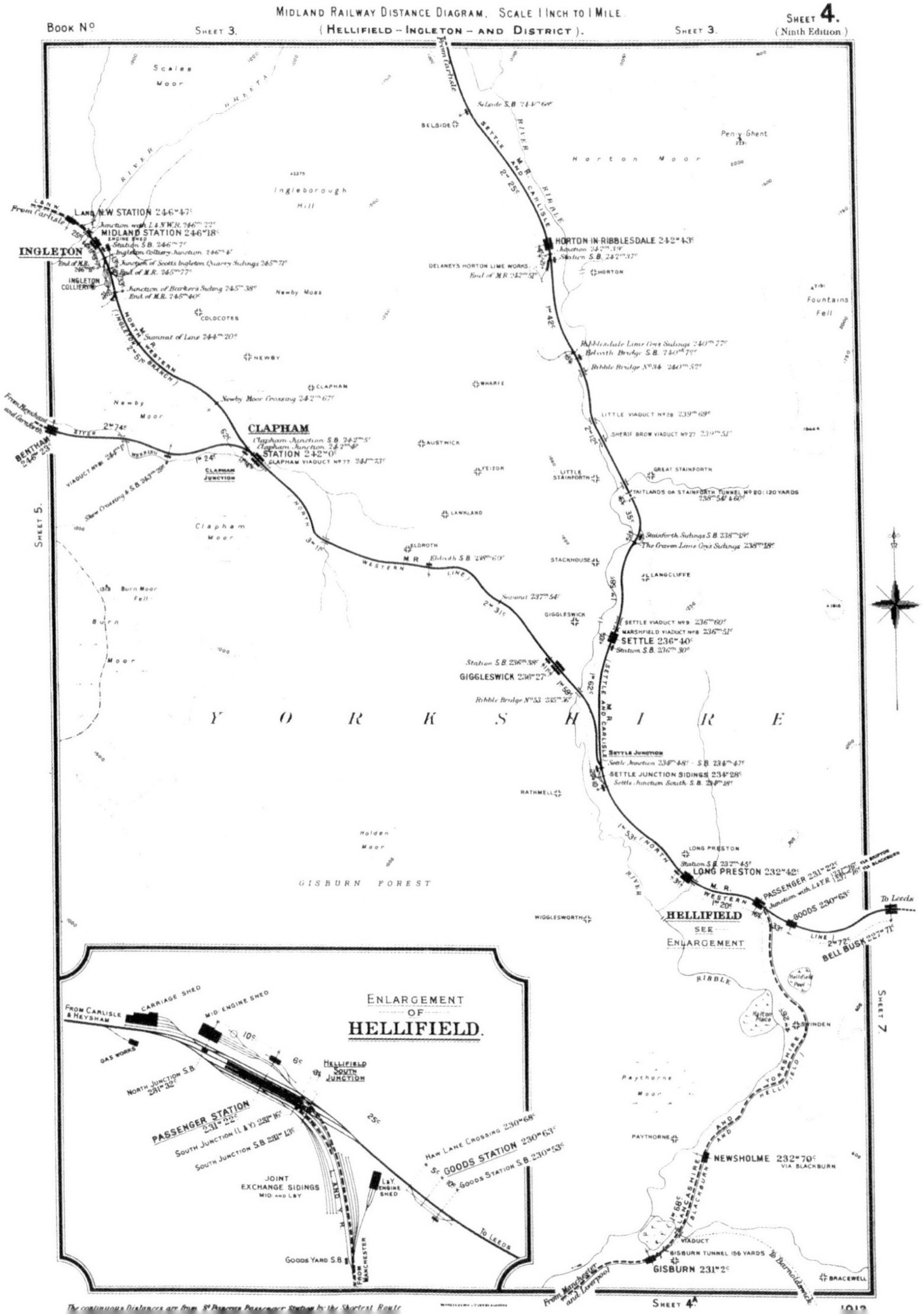

Selside — Settle — Hellifield

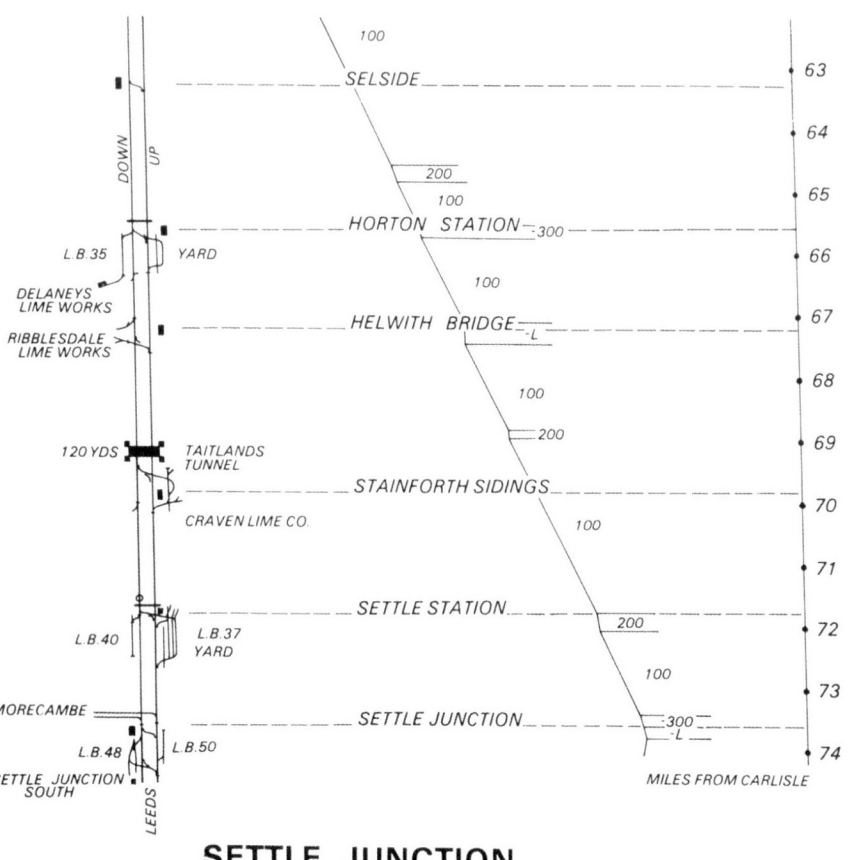

SETTLE JUNCTION

On this and the preceding three pages, the maps are taken from those used by the Midland Railway as their distance diagrams. The mileage given is that recorded before the 1914 reassessment. The diagrams are based upon those used by the LMS to record mileages and gradients. These also show the position of any sidings, and the wagon capacities of the sidings and goods yards.

SETTLE JUNCTION

Plate 1: Settle Junction area, photographed from Settle Junction South signal box, circa 1914. The milepost to the right, on the 'up' side, indicates 234¾ miles from St. Pancras, and results from the 'remileage' of the system in 1914. Evidence suggests that Settle Junction South box was instituted in 1874 and renewed in 1894 (Way and Works Committee Minute No. 13865). To the left are the Settle Junction Sidings. Late in 1922, instructions were given to remove the signal box, and the siding connections and crossover road seen here in the right foreground. The two sidings remained in use as lie bys' (see signalling diagram). In the centre of the photograph, adjacent to the locomotive smoke, is Settle Junction Station which by this time had been closed for a number of years. The traffic committee decided, in May 1872, that a passenger station, together with exchange sidings, would be a useful adjunct to deal with any traffic from the Skipton to Morecambe line. The station opened in November 1876 giving a total of three stations to serve Settle; Settle (Old) which was renamed Giggleswick in November 1877, Settle (New), near the town, which opened with the Settle to Carlisle line in 1876, and this one. However, by November 1877, Settle Junction passenger station closed, making it perhaps one of the shortest-lived Midland stations.

Plate 2: The photographer has strolled along the track towards Settle Junction to photograph the weighing machine and office (described officially as a weighhouse) which is situated on the 'up' siding. Connection to this siding from the 'down' main line in the vicinity of the former station was removed in 1913 at the time of junction alteration. This would make the weighing facility of uncertain value, but we have no information as to when this was withdrawn. Note the inside-keyed track still in use for the siding. This siding was finally recovered in 1968.

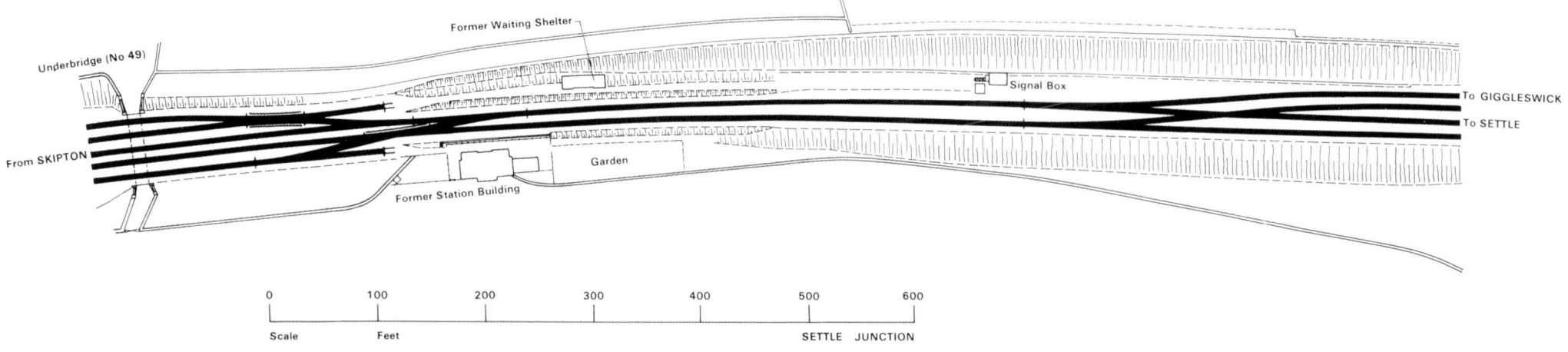

Figure 1: This illustrates the remodelling of Settle Junction, commenced in 1895, involving the easing of the alignment in favour of the Carlisle line. The location of the signal box had moved to the position shown on this plan in 1895 (Way and Works Committee Minute No. 12414, 3/6/1892) and renewed at a cost of £537. Considerable alteration to this layout occurred in 1913. The crossover and connection to the 'up' siding from the 'down' main line were removed to allow the junction to be moved some 140yds. nearer to Skipton. Another new signal box was then provided for the new junction.

Plate 3: Settle Junction Station building, photographed in 1939. After the station closure, the building eventually was converted into a ganger's house. This is one of the smaller type of station buildings to be discussed at length later.

N. Wilkinson

Plate 4: Settle Junction and the signal box in 1938. The Morecambe line falls away to the left. This signal box was built in 1913 and contained the original 25 lever Midland Tappet (6in. centre) frame.

N. Wilkinson

Plate 5: The Settle Junction signal box, photographed in 1972. In 1960, the lever frame had been replaced by a standard 1943 pattern one of 31 levers. Externally, the box remained the same, measuring 21ft. 6in. x 11ft. 6in. with the floor 8ft. above rail height. Note the original MR nameboard of 6in. cast letters screwed on to a 9in. board. The sleeper-built coal bunker was a Midland feature, but the concrete toilet was of LMS design.

Plate 6: Bridge No. 2 at Anley (235 miles 27 chains from St. Pancras) carries the Settle to Carlisle Railway over the A65 road. This conventional structure, constructed in 1871 using wrought iron for the main members, was not of a type associated with the line, although the relieving arches in the wing walls and abutments feature regularly as one travels north. Strengthening of the bridge took place in 1903 by the addition of a steel centre girder. This strengthening was associated with general line capacity improvements carried out at this time.

Figure 2: Settle Junction signalling diagram, based upon information for 1967.

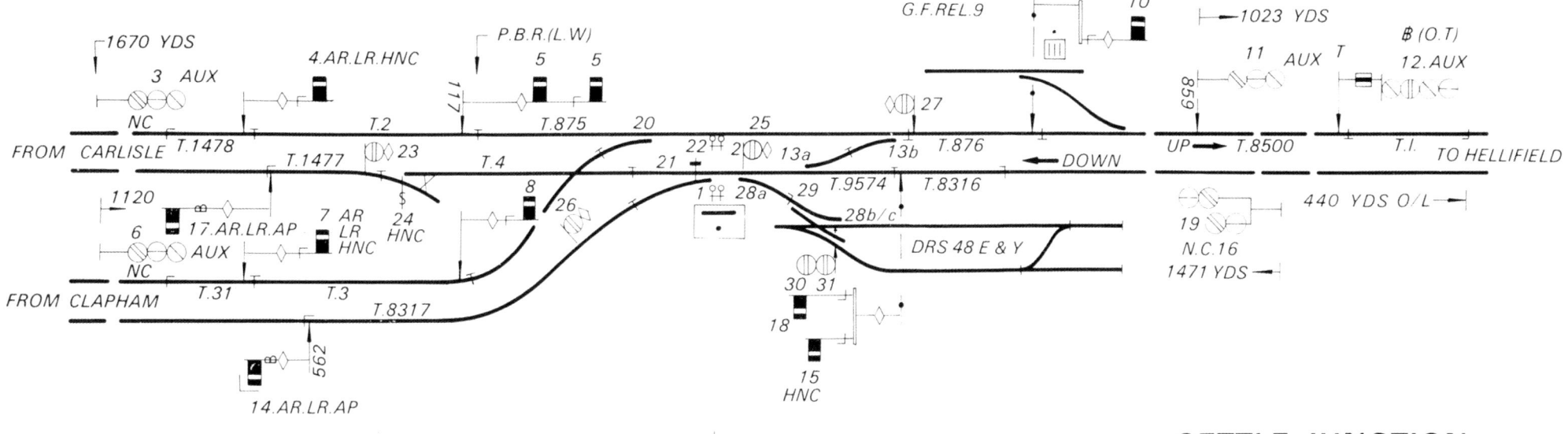

SETTLE JUNCTION

SETTLE

Plate 7: Settle, circa 1925. An unidentified superheated Class 700 4-4-0 locomotive heads an 'up' express through Settle Station. The station building is one of the three larger types used at the market towns situated near the line. This No. 1 (large) style is distinguished by a third small gable facing the platform, but more of this later. Attractive fretted bargeboards feature on all gables of the Settle & Carlisle buildings, although many were replaced in later years. On the right-hand extension of the building can be seen a recently-installed poster board bearing the legend 'London Midland and Scottish Railway'; one suspects that the timetable board with 'LMS' fixed on it is an updated Midland version. The tall 'up' home signal, behind the train, was replaced in November 1937 by a lattice steel post upper quadrant signal. When bridge No. 7, just north of the station, was renewed in 1955, it was found necessary to relocate this signal 8yds. further south to allow uninterrupted operation of the steam crane.

D. F. Tee Collection

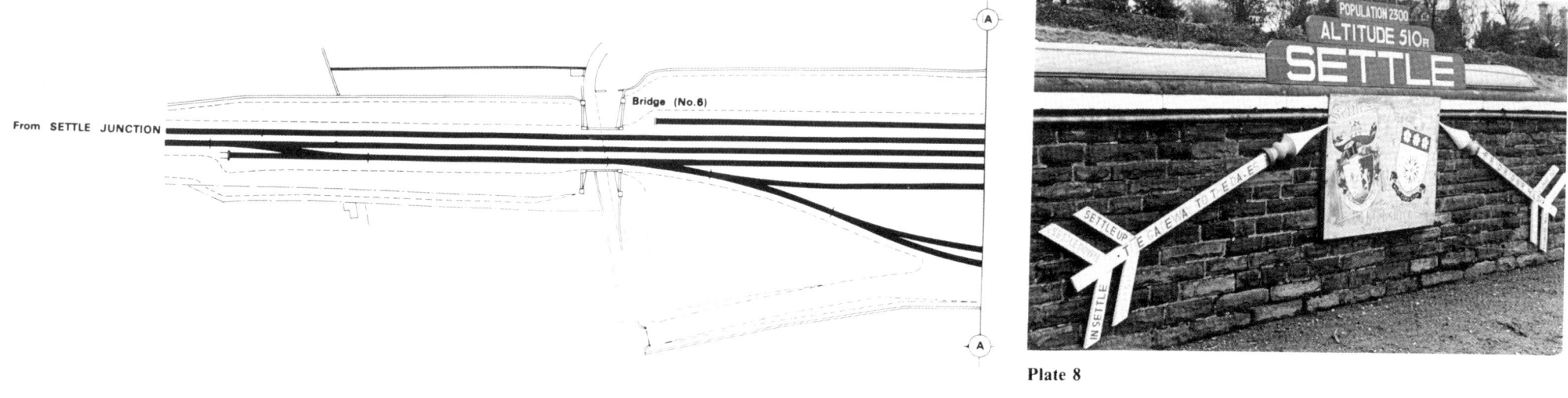

From SETTLE JUNCTION

Bridge (No.6)

Plate 8

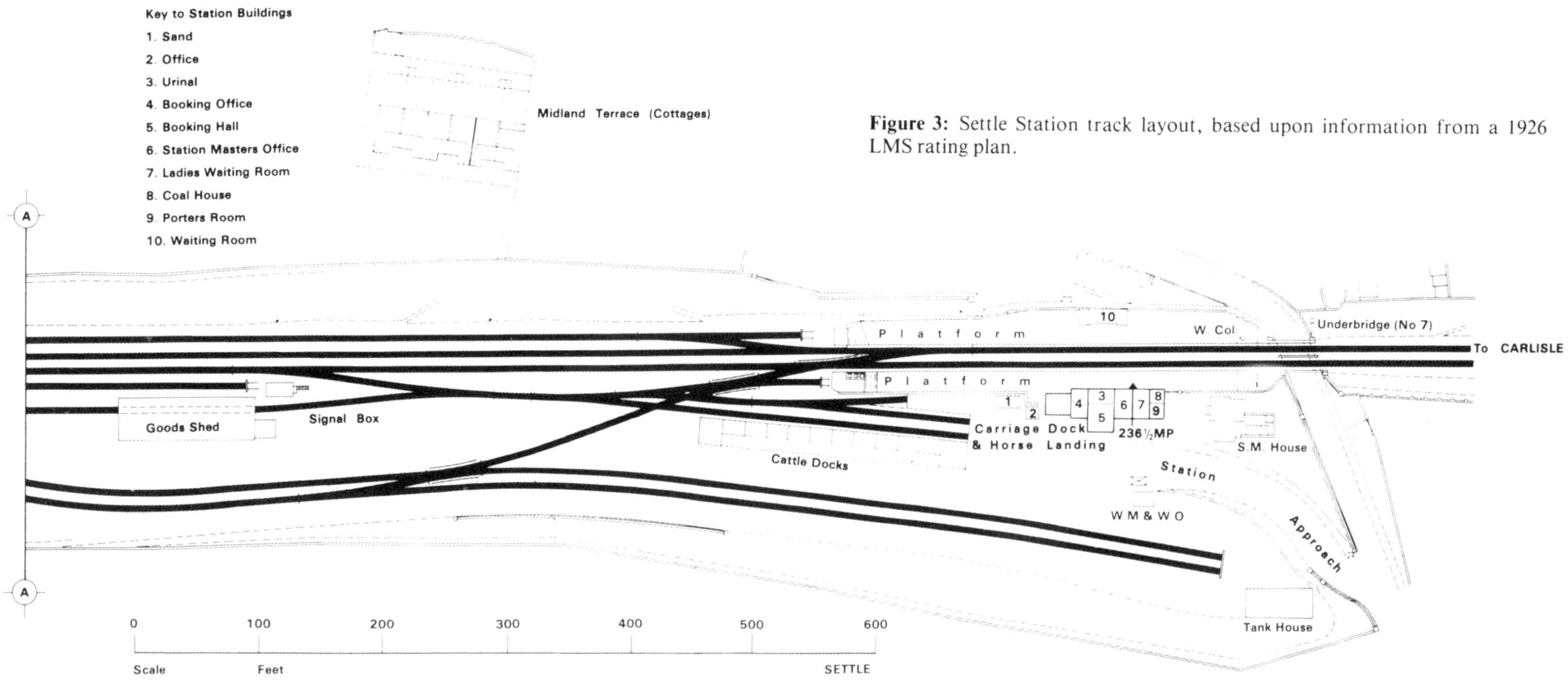

Key to Station Buildings

1. Sand
2. Office
3. Urinal
4. Booking Office
5. Booking Hall
6. Station Masters Office
7. Ladies Waiting Room
8. Coal House
9. Porters Room
10. Waiting Room

Midland Terrace (Cottages)

Figure 3: Settle Station track layout, based upon information from a 1926 LMS rating plan.

Goods Shed

Signal Box

Carriage Dock & Horse Landing

Cattle Docks

WM & WO

Platform

Platform

10

W Col

Underbridge (No 7)

To CARLISLE

236½MP

Station

Approach

S.M. House

Tank House

| 0 | 100 | 200 | 300 | 400 | 500 | 600 |

Scale   Feet

SETTLE

Plate 9: Settle, looking south, 1963.   *D. F. Tee*   **Plate 10:** Settle, looking north, 1939.   *N. Wilkinson*

Plates 9 & 10: These views portray, at different periods, the southern end of Settle Station. Over a period of 25 years, the most significant change has been the replacement of Midland lower quadrant signals. The 1872 report to the Construction Committee anticipated large traffic at Settle, and so suggested ample siding accommodation, a goods shed for five wagons (seen in the middle of **Plate 9**) and the cattle dock for twelve trucks (seen to the right of **Plate 10**). Goods facilities were withdrawn from Settle on 12th October 1970.

Plate 11: Settle, 1939, showing part of the extensive goods yard. The principle features here are the water tank (which did not figure in the report of 1873) and the weigh office, which although built of stone was of a typical Midland design *(compare Plate 616 in the OPC publication LMS Architecture)*. The rear of the station building can be seen on the left. The first indications of the rigours of the Northern Fells are evident in the background behind the town of Settle.

N. Wilkinson

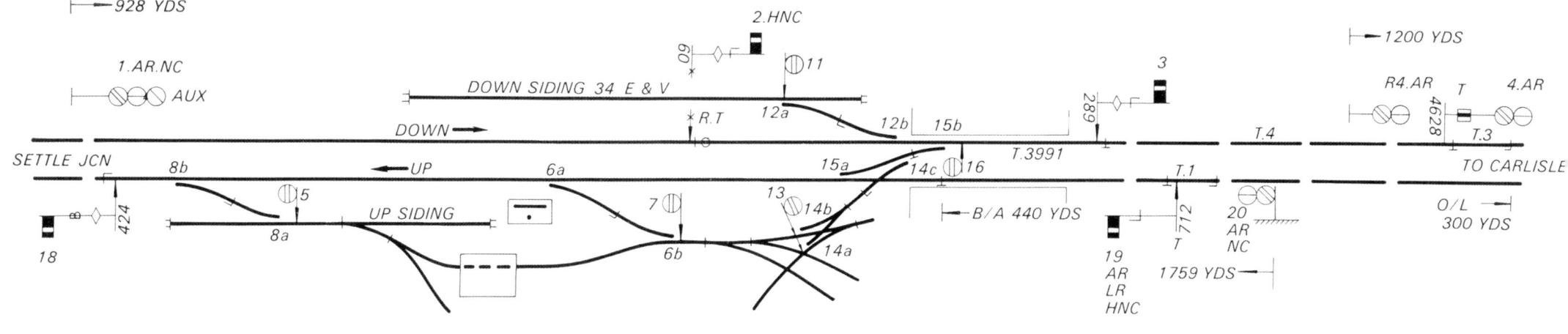

928 YDS

2.HNC

1.AR.NC · AUX

DOWN SIDING 34 E & V

1200 YDS

R4.AR · T · 4.AR

DOWN →

SETTLE JCN

← UP

TO CARLISLE

B/A 440 YDS

UP SIDING

O/L 300 YDS

18

19 AR LR HNC

20 AR NC

1759 YDS

SETTLE JUNCTION 1M.1386 YDS ← → HELWITH BRIDGE 4M 924 YDS

SETTLE STATION

Figure 4: A signalling diagram for Settle Station, based upon information available for 1963.

Plate 12: Settle, showing a closer view of the goods shed and signal box seen in the distance in **Plate 9**. This signal box, 21ft. 6in. x 11ft. 6in. x 8ft., of wood construction, was built in 1891 containing a 20 lever tumbler frame (Way and Works Committee Minute No. 10508 2/5/1890) sanctioned at a renewal cost of £235. Closure occurred on 1st May 1984. The goods shed is of a design specified for this railway but contained features common to Midland practice elsewhere (compare **Figure 62** at Langwathby). The timber porch protecting the entrance to the office indicates that adverse weather conditions could be expected. Note the chequered plate to the left of the shed doors indicating a limited clearance, and which was a feature commonly found on Settle & Carlisle structures.

N. Wilkinson

Plate 13: Settle waiting shelter, 1984. The first example on the line of the stone-built waiting shelter (compare **Figure 77** at Armathwaite). The rusticated seats, a well-known feature of the Midland station scene, are of a type which originated from the foundry of Andrew Handyside. These were used by many railways but are generally accepted as a Midland artefact. The electric lighting is a relatively recent addition to the station.

This is perhaps a suitable point at which to introduce some general notes on the architecture of the station buildings. The basic concept followed the practice typical of Midland building at that time, using a style introduced by Mr Crossley for a single storey building incorporating gabled pavilions, usually two but sometimes three. For the Settle & Carlisle, Mr Sanders, the Company Architect, prepared three designs with subtle differences, making them unique to this line. The three variants allowed for accommodation to suit the expected traffic and were numbered 1 (large), 2 (medium) and 3 (small).

All the stations, excepting Culgaith and Hawes Junction, have a common design feature in the pair of identical gables to the platform elevation and a single gable at the opposite side. Fretted bargeboards adorned all the gables and a stone device, in the form of a trefoil or quatrefoil, decorated each of the front gables. The pitch of the roof was much steeper than employed at other locations, and proved more suitable for the extreme weather conditions of the Northern Fells.

Outlining the variants in reverse order, No. 3, the smallest, was built at Settle Junction, Horton, Ribblehead, Dent, Hawes, Ormside, New Biggin, Little Salkeld and Cotehill. The gables projected some 7ft. beyond the main platform frontage and were set 14ft. apart to flank a glazed porch. In order to cover this waiting area it was necessary to flatten the roof pitch between the gables. A distinctive feature in the gables was a large window with a pointed head, the only vaguely Gothic feature beyond the steeply-pitched roofs to appear in the design. Porters' rooms and toilets found accommodation in a small adjunct projecting to the left of the main building. The roadside projection, as well as adding balance to the design, served to acommodate the large central booking hall.

The No. 2 style was larger and more imposing, and had no Gothic features. The pair of identical gables to the platform side projected barely a few inches beyond the main frontage. Again, a glass-fronted porch was used, giving entry to a spacious booking hall. Another extension to the right-hand end housed stores and toilets. Due to the shallow projection of the platform gables, it was possible to simply continue the same roof pitch to cover the glass-fronted waiting space. These were found at Crosby Garrett, Long Marton, Langwathby, Lazonby, Armathwaite, Cumwhinton and Scotby.

The largest, No. 1, design was reserved for three market towns bordering the line; namely Settle, Kirkby Stephen and Appleby. Although essentially similar to the type 2, the staff rooms to the left-hand end of the platform frontage are simply an extension of the main building, and not a reduced height adjunct. To this extension a third, but lesser span, gable was added. The roadside gabled projection for the No. 1 and No. 2 styles formed the passenger entrance to the booking hall.

Local materials were used for construction. For the intermediate stations between Scotby and Langwathby, Eden Valley red sandstone was chosen. At New Biggin, a change to a local golden-coloured freestone was made, but with red sandstone used for the plinth, quoins and window surrounds. Local dark red brick and sandstone dressing appeared at Long Marton and Appleby. Between Ormside and Settle, golden freestone again predominated.

Plate 14: A view of Settle, looking north from the 'down' platform in 1961, giving the overall impression of the platform elevation of 'station buildings No. 1' at Settle. It has been found necessary to replace much of the fretted bargeboarding on the gables. The lattice post signal and the bridge at the end of the platform are referred to in **Plate 7**.

G. Biddle Collection

Plate 15: Settle in 1961, looking at the northern end of the building, and detailing the difference between the No. 1 and No. 2 buildings, showing the addition of a third smaller gable. Note that the trefoil device usually decorating the gables is absent from the end of the building. Instead, an embrasure-like ventilator is provided, repeated on the roadside gable. The varied assortment of chimney pots were not indicated on the original drawings and, indeed, many buildings along the line received chimney modifications.

D. Jenkinson

Elevation drawings are shown for each type of station building, and are included against suitable locations, commencing here with **Figure 5**, illustrating Settle.

On the platform opposite the main building a smaller waiting shelter was usually to be found, built either in the same material as the main building or, in a few cases, timber was used.

Plate 16: Detail of the platform entrance to the booking hall at Settle in 1961, showing the screen with its window tracery cast support columns and filigree brackets. The stone infill beneath the windows of the screen has replaced an original timber panel with diagonal match boarding *(cf. Midland Architecture, Figure 14 and Plate 133 for Appleby).*

D. Jenkinson

Plate 17: Settle in 1968, showing the southern end of the road side of the larger type of building from the goods yard. In the background can be seen the stationmaster's house (cf. **Figure 88** at Cumwhinton).

D. F. Tee

Plate 18: Settle, circa 1950. A view of the northern end, from the station approach road.

N. Wilkinson

MR — **SETTLE** ᴛᴏ **CARLISLE** —
— **DRAWING** ꜰᴏʀ **STATION BUILDINGS** — Nº 1

— ELEVATION ɴᴇxᴛ PLATFORM —

— ELEVATION ɴᴇxᴛ APPROACH ROAD —

SCALE   FEET

Figure 5: A drawing of the No. 1 (large) type of building for Settle & Carlisle Railway stations.   For the end elevations see **Figure 76.**

Plate 19: Church Viaduct, Settle, circa 1900.

Plate 20: Church Viaduct, Settle, 1984.

Plates 19 & 20: After leaving Settle Station, the railway crosses Marshfield Viaduct (236 miles 51 chains), a structure of four arches, each being of 29ft. 9in. span. Nine chains later, the second Settle viaduct, known locally as Church, crosses the A65 road. This viaduct has six openings, five of 30ft. span and one 37ft. 8in. skew span, bridging the main road. Both viaducts were constructed in 1871. The view east, towards the town can be seen in **Plate 19** and the view west in **Plate 20** which also illustrates the square and skew spans of the viaduct.

STAINFORTH SIDINGS

Plate 21: Stainforth Siding in April 1955, looking north. During relaying operations, the saloon of the Engineer, Lancaster, has transported a party of schoolboys for a career trip, and waits at the Settle end of Stainforth Siding. The signal box is an LMS pattern all-timber box, constructed in 1950.

M.S. Welch

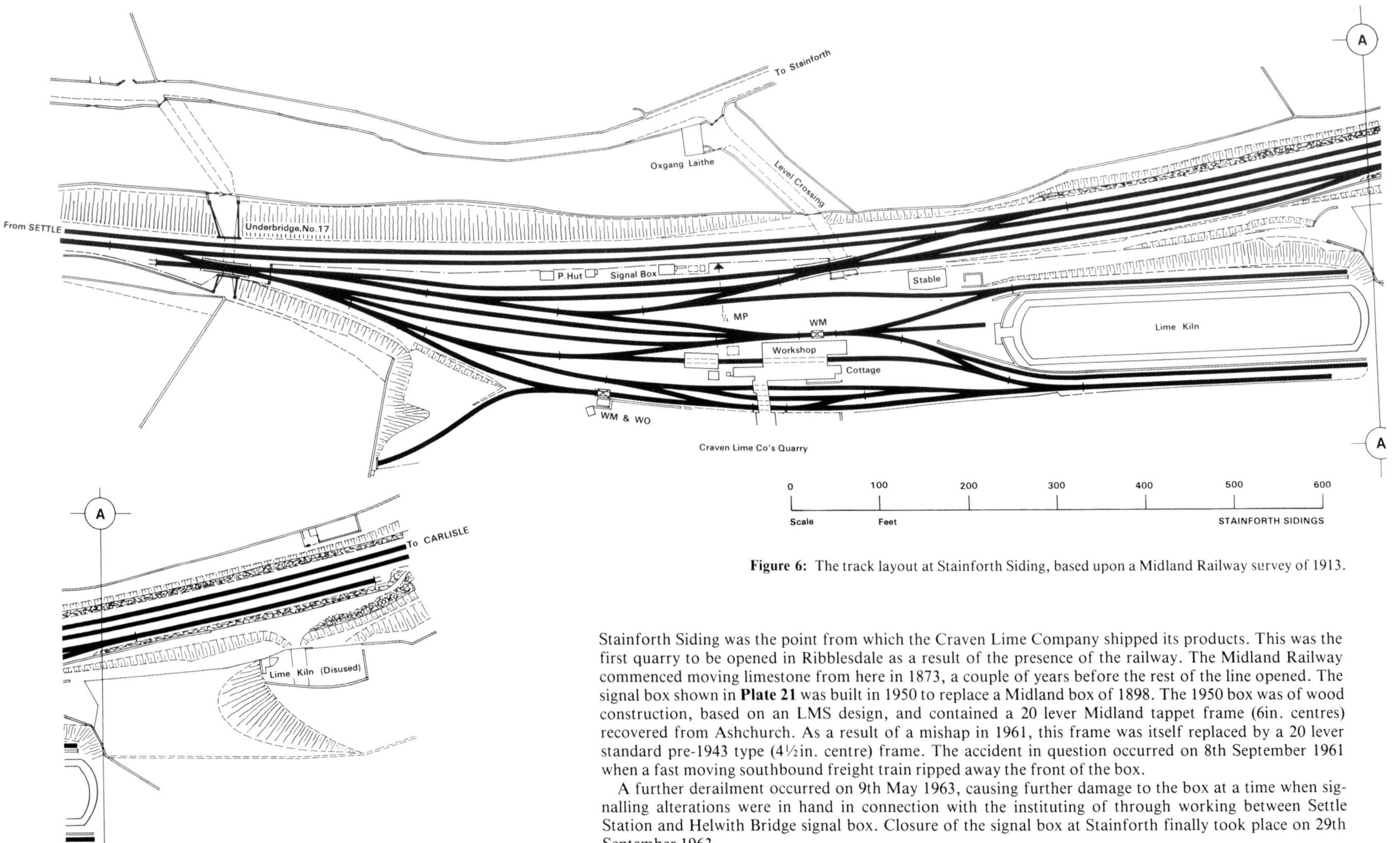

Figure 6: The track layout at Stainforth Siding, based upon a Midland Railway survey of 1913.

Stainforth Siding was the point from which the Craven Lime Company shipped its products. This was the first quarry to be opened in Ribblesdale as a result of the presence of the railway. The Midland Railway commenced moving limestone from here in 1873, a couple of years before the rest of the line opened. The signal box shown in **Plate 21** was built in 1950 to replace a Midland box of 1898. The 1950 box was of wood construction, based on an LMS design, and contained a 20 lever Midland tappet frame (6in. centres) recovered from Ashchurch. As a result of a mishap in 1961, this frame was itself replaced by a 20 lever standard pre-1943 type (4½in. centre) frame. The accident in question occurred on 8th September 1961 when a fast moving southbound freight train ripped away the front of the box.

A further derailment occurred on 9th May 1963, causing further damage to the box at a time when signalling alterations were in hand in connection with the instituting of through working between Settle Station and Helwith Bridge signal box. Closure of the signal box at Stainforth finally took place on 29th September 1963.

The 1898 signal box can be seen near the locomotive smoke in **Plate 22**. This was a standard Midland box 16ft. 6in. x 11ft. 6in. x 8ft. with a 16 lever tumbler frame.

Plate 22: Settle Limes, Craven Lime Works, at Stainforth on 30th May 1938, showing the effect of over sixty years of work in the quarry, the extensive plant, and the large lime kilns with the tall chimney which, incidentally, bears the date 1873, to the left of the picture. Settle lies 1½ miles to the right of the illustration.

Aerofilms

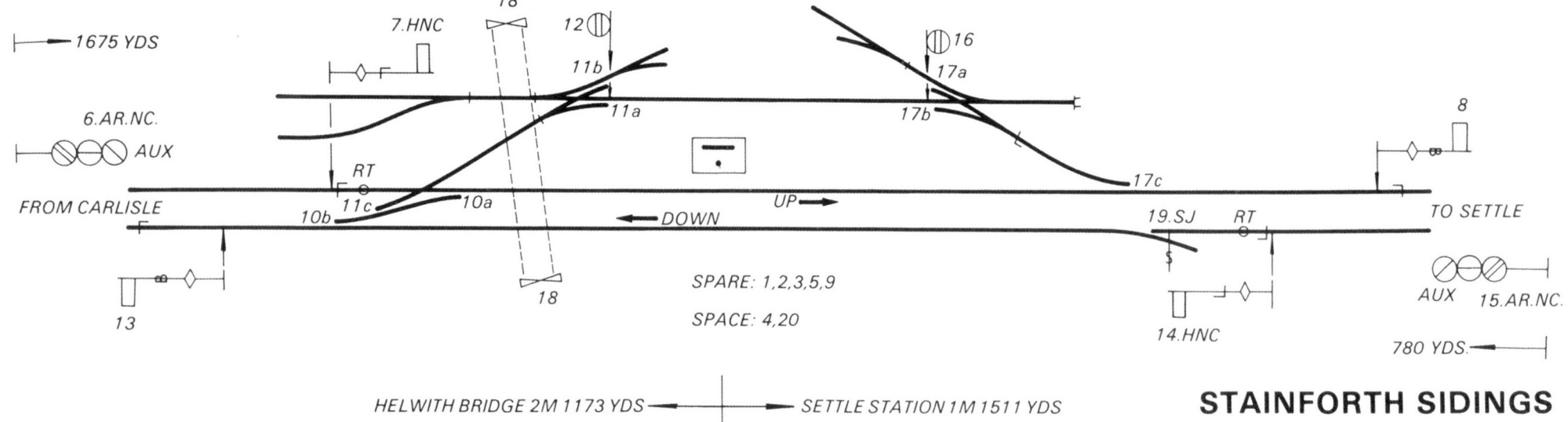

1675 YDS

7.HNC 18 12 11b 16 17a

6.AR.NC. AUX 11a 17b 8

FROM CARLISLE RT 10a 11c 10b UP DOWN 17c 19.SJ RT TO SETTLE

13 18 SPARE: 1,2,3,5,9 14.HNC AUX 15.AR.NC.

SPACE: 4,20 780 YDS.

HELWITH BRIDGE 2M 1173 YDS ← → SETTLE STATION 1M 1511 YDS

STAINFORTH SIDINGS

Figure 7: The signalling diagram for Stainforth, based upon information for 1963.

Plates 23 & 24: The cutting immediately north of Stainforth Siding leads into Stainforth Tunnel (238 miles 54 chains). This 120 yard long tunnel is often referred to as Taitlands, and has rock side walls and a brick arch faced at each end with stone. The shallow tunnel carries the Settle to Horton road. The southern approach **(Plate 23)** passes beneath a wrought-iron aqueduct, built in 1875. **Plate 24** shows the position of the tunnel name board at both ends of the short tunnel. The northerly board is being passed by a southbound unidentified 'Crab' 2-6-0 locomotive.

Plate 23: The south end of Stainforth Tunnel, 1984.

Plate 24: The north end of Stainforth Tunnel.

D. Ibbottson

Plate 25: On 7th April 1984, the northbound 'Cumbrian Mountain Express', hauled by 'West Country' class Pacific No. 34092 *City of Wells* passes over bridge No. 27 (239 miles 52 chains) often referred to as Sherrif Brow Viaduct, but is officially known as Ribble Bridge in the Midland Railway Engineer's Department. This bridge is detailed in **Figure 8**. Once again note the relieving arches in the wing walls. The 174ft. bridge was constructed in 1872 on the skew, with three arches of 30ft. span, and is 55ft. above water level. The dry stone wall in the foreground is a familiar feature of the line.

M. S. Welch

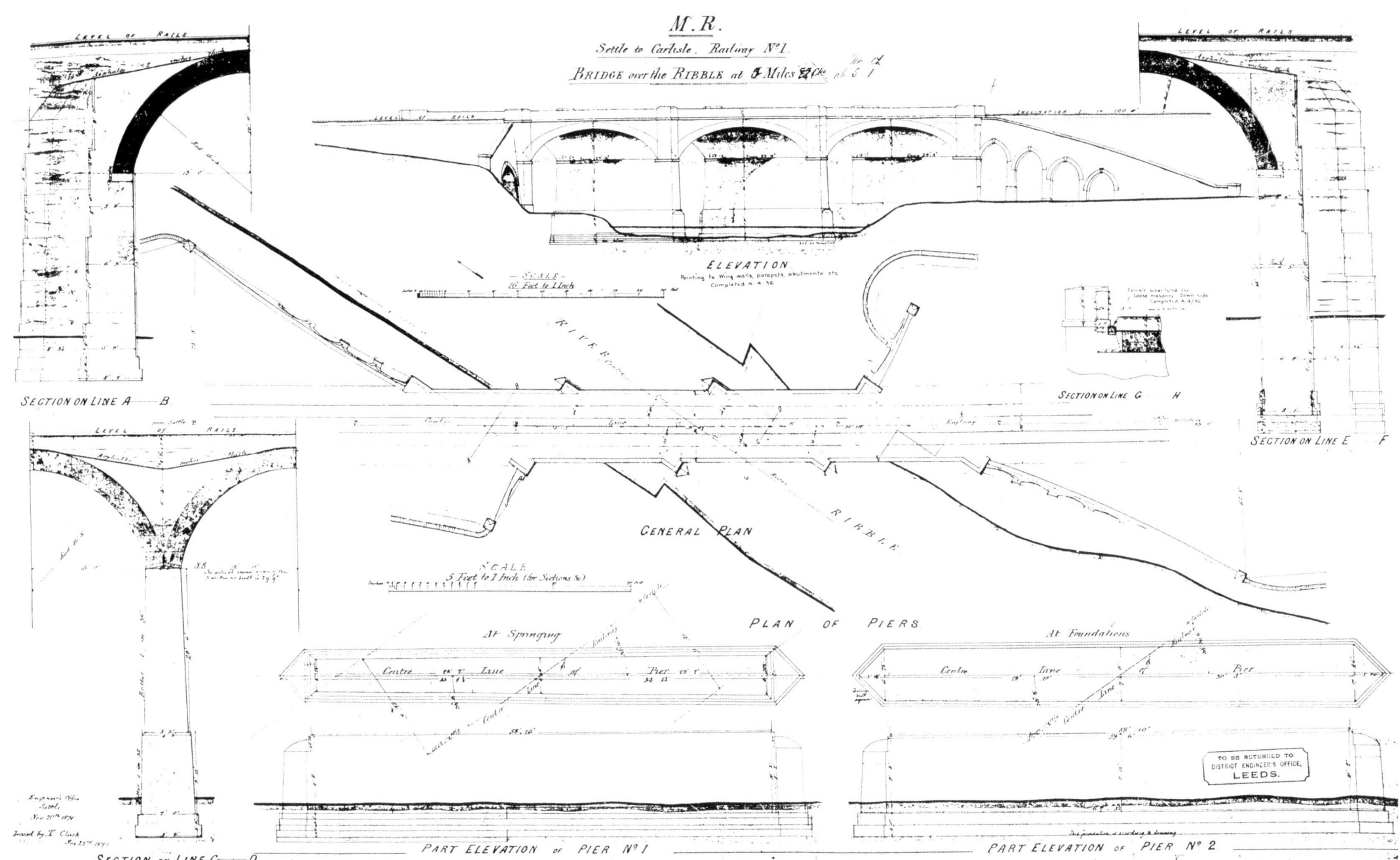

Figure 8: An official drawing of bridge No. 27.

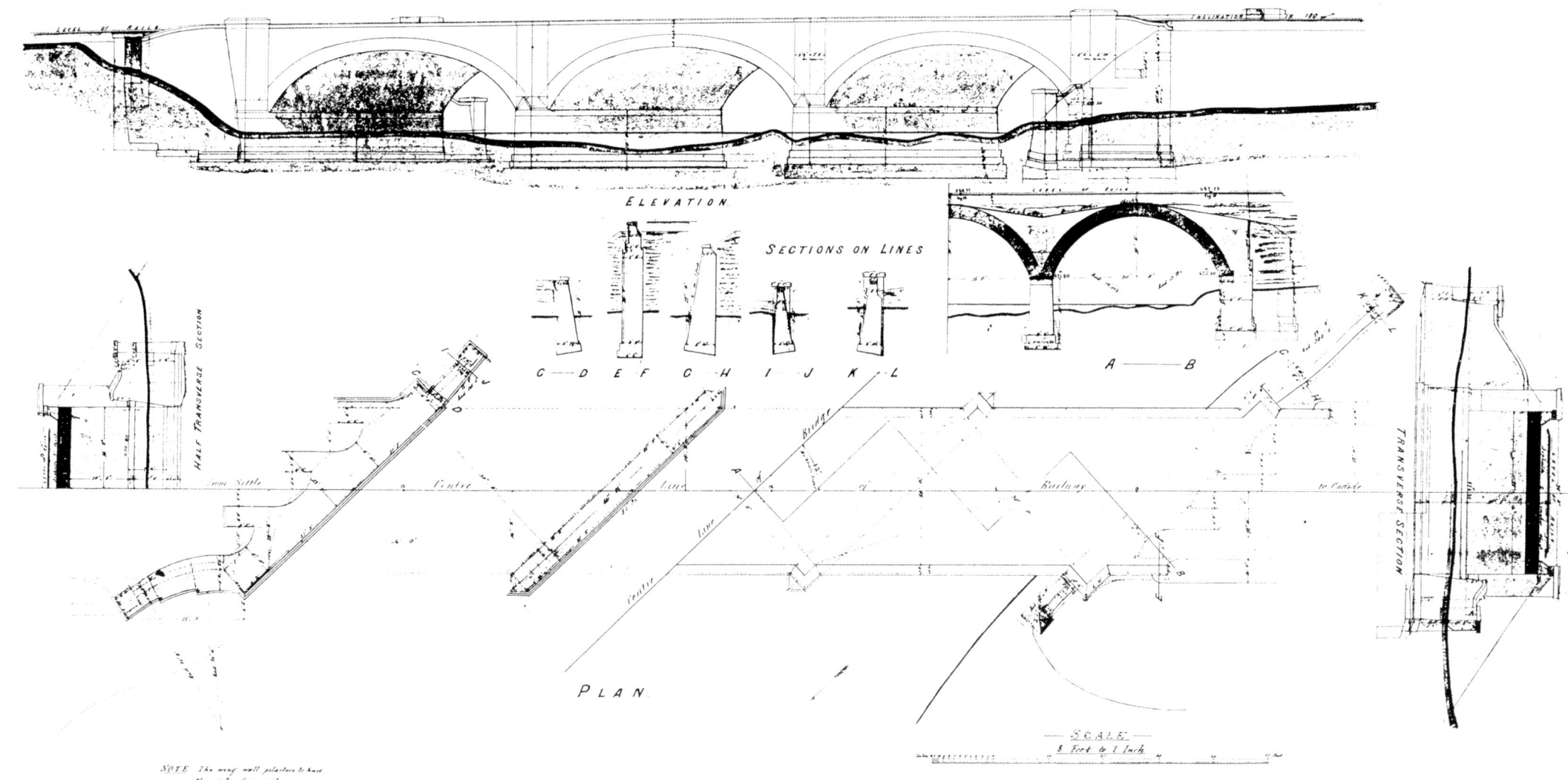

Figure 9: An official drawing of bridge No. 28. This, the second of the Ribble bridges, is at 239 miles 68 chains, is 165ft. long, but only 25ft. over the water; evidence of the sudden fall of the level of the River Ribble between the two bridges numbered 28 and 27. This viaduct is sometimes known as Little Viaduct.

HELWITH BRIDGE

Plate 26: Helwith Bridge on 19th August 1967, showing Class 8F locomotives Nos. 48077 and 48506, with a train of bogie wagons carrying concrete sleeper track from Dewsnap, near Guide Bridge, Manchester. The track was laid near Gretna the following day. The train is seen climbing past the siding of the Helwith Bridge Granite Company, whose conveyor can be seen crossing the river in the background. The siding is situated immediately to the right of the signal. The distant signal is for Helwith Bridge box and the home signal is controlled from the Granite Siding ground frame, brought into service in 1926. It opened as a covered timber structure (9ft. x 4ft.) containing a 3 lever tumbler frame of Midland design. The ground frame, and presumably the siding, were taken out of use on 7th September 1969.

M. S. Welch

Figure 10: The signalling diagram for Helwith Bridge, based upon information available for 1963. This diagram covers the signalling controlling the track associated with the Ribblesdale Lime Company Sidings, as well as the ground frame for the Helwith Bridge Granite Company Siding.

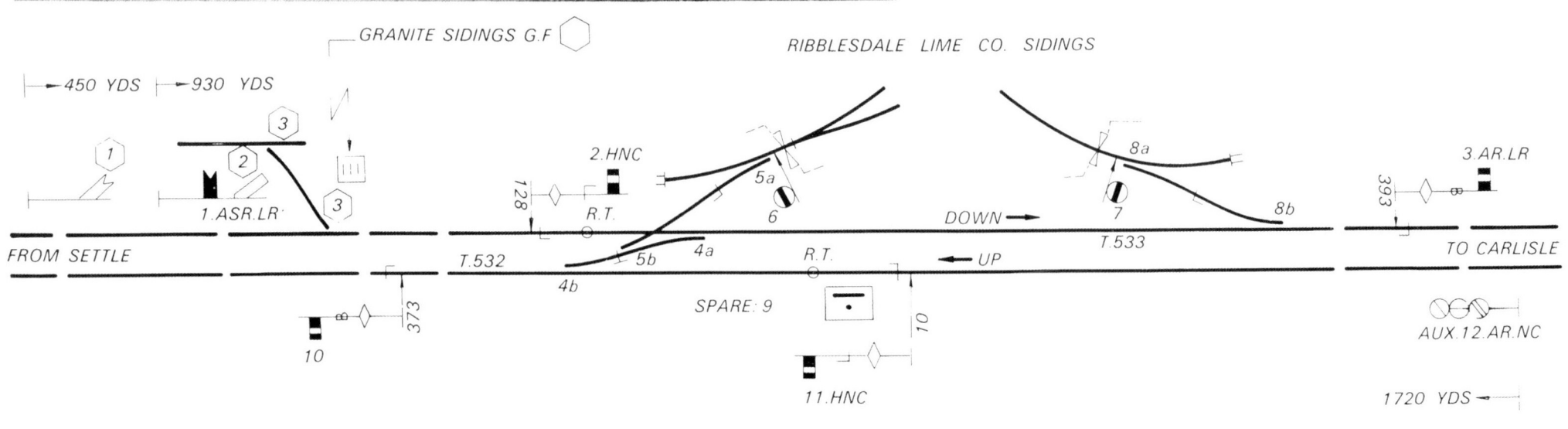

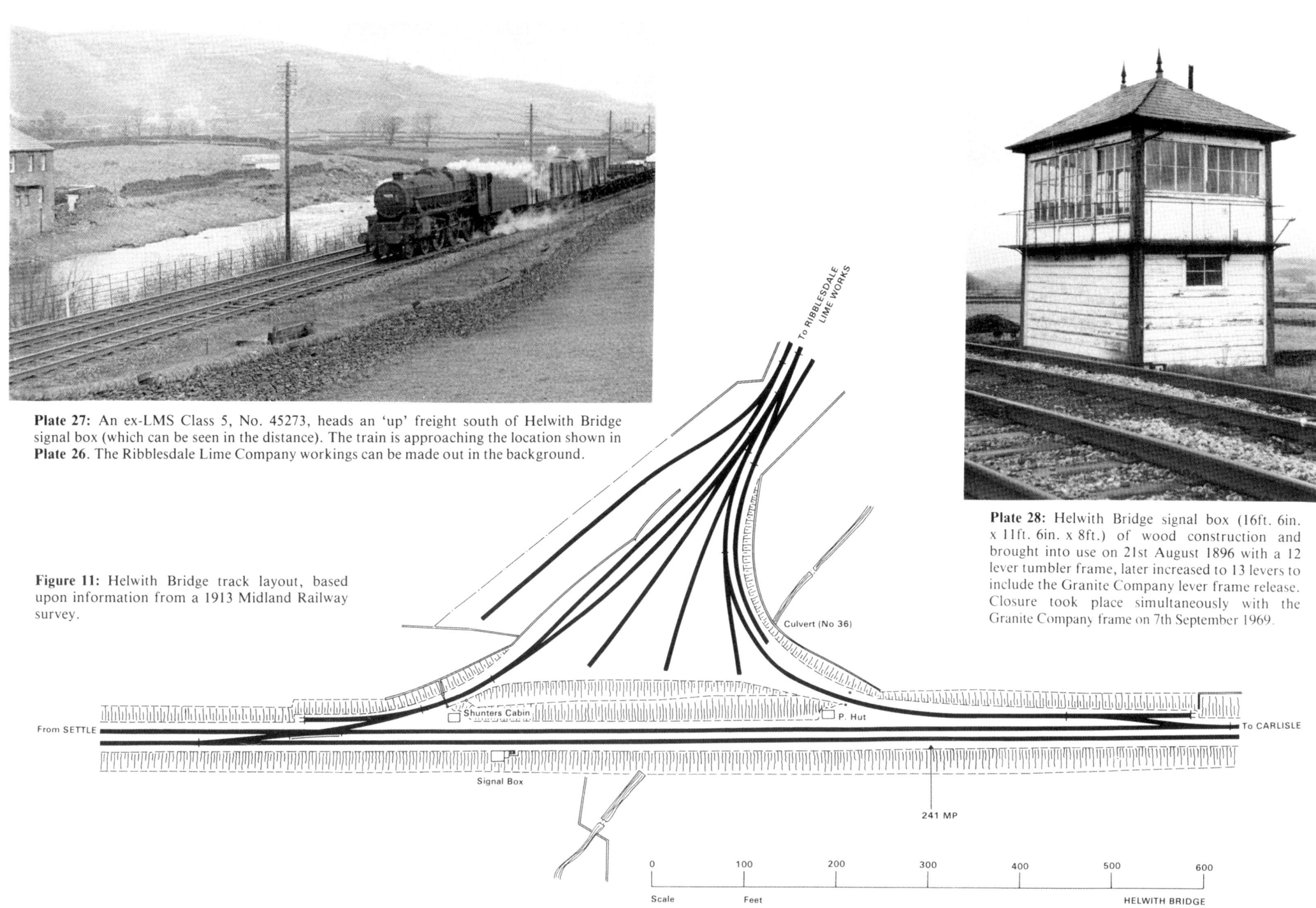

Plate 27: An ex-LMS Class 5, No. 45273, heads an 'up' freight south of Helwith Bridge signal box (which can be seen in the distance). The train is approaching the location shown in **Plate 26**. The Ribblesdale Lime Company workings can be made out in the background.

Figure 11: Helwith Bridge track layout, based upon information from a 1913 Midland Railway survey.

Plate 28: Helwith Bridge signal box (16ft. 6in. x 11ft. 6in. x 8ft.) of wood construction and brought into use on 21st August 1896 with a 12 lever tumbler frame, later increased to 13 levers to include the Granite Company lever frame release. Closure took place simultaneously with the Granite Company frame on 7th September 1969.

To RIBBLESDALE LIME WORKS

Culvert (No 36)

Shunters Cabin

P. Hut

From SETTLE

To CARLISLE

Signal Box

241 MP

0   100   200   300   400   500   600

Scale   Feet

HELWITH BRIDGE

HORTON-IN-RIBBLESDALE

Plate 29: Horton in Ribblesdale, 1967. The ornamental station sign created by Stationmaster Taylor who, in addition to the normal and abnormal duties associated with being a stationmaster, created beautiful station gardens, and was successful in winning the 'Best Kept Garden' competition for 17 years running, as well as winning each year the cleanliness and tidiness competition.

POP 700
ALTITUDE 850 FT
HORTON-IN-RIBBLESDALE
YORK-SHIRE
WEST RIDING
AUDI CONSILIUM

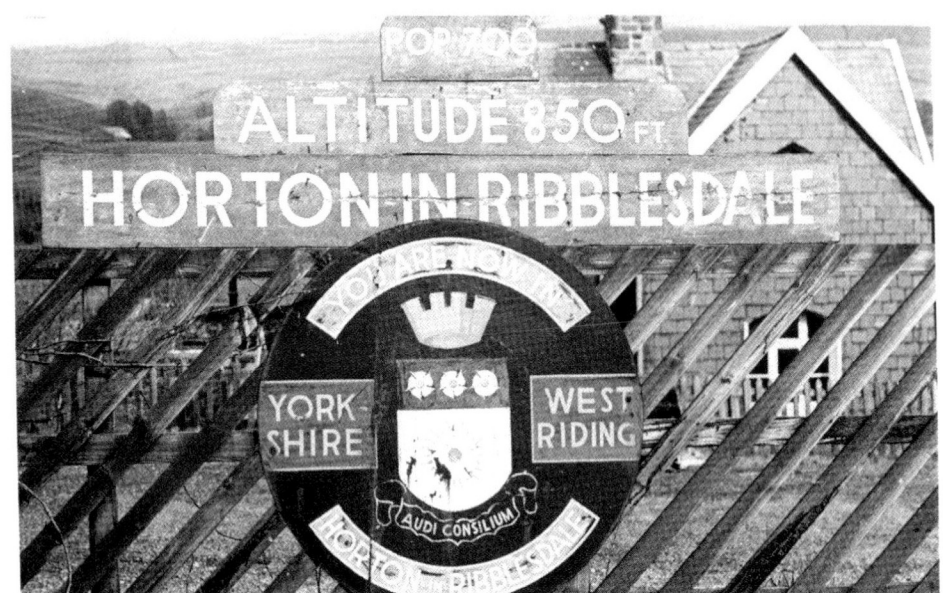

Figure 12: Horton in Ribblesdale track layout, based upon information from a 1913 Midland Railway survey and a 1926 LMS rating plan. Delaney's became part of Settle Limes Ltd., for whom additional siding accommodation was authorised in 1950 and completed by 1955. Work was concentrated at the works entrance with the provision of additional south departure and empties roads.

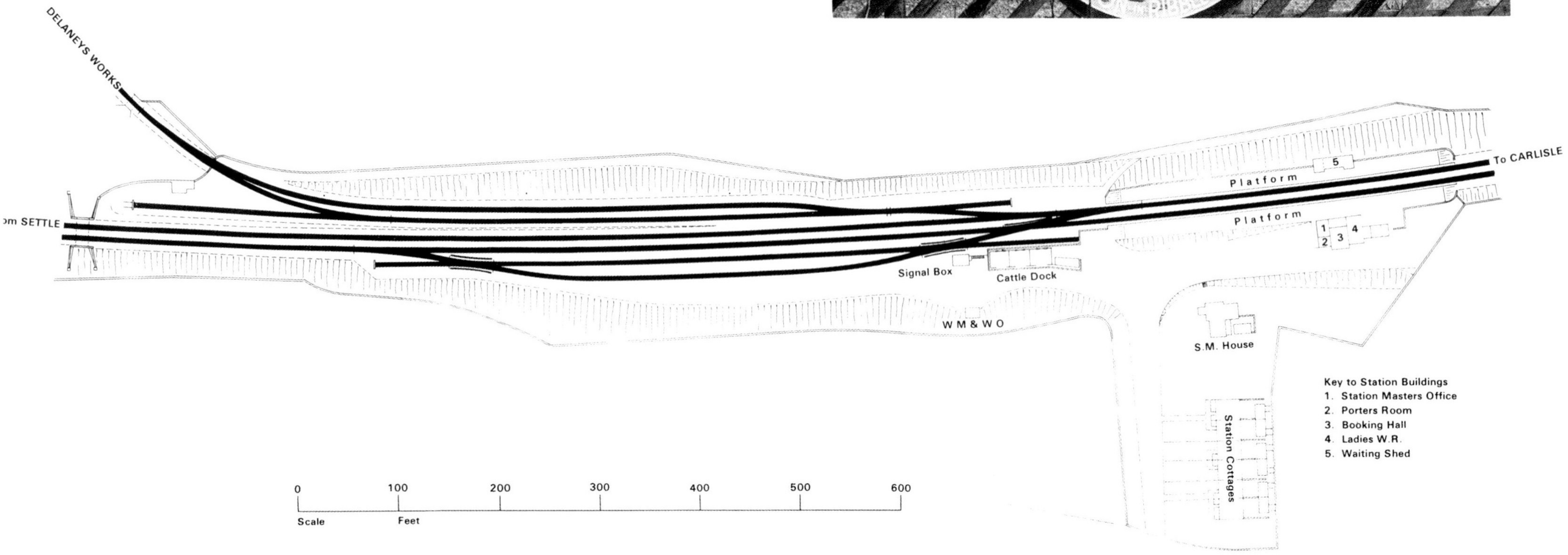

DELANEYS WORKS
om SETTLE
To CARLISLE
Platform
Platform
5
1
2
3
4
Signal Box
Cattle Dock
W M & W O
S.M. House
Station Cottages
Key to Station Buildings
1. Station Masters Office
2. Porters Room
3. Booking Hall
4. Ladies W.R.
5. Waiting Shed
0
100
200
300
400
500
600
Scale
Feet

Plate 30: Horton in Ribblesdale in May 1962, looking east from behind the 'down' platform; a view featuring the signal box and numerous other items of Midland origin. The cattle dock is of a well-known Midland pattern, but differed from that originally specified, the main variation being the addition of vertical palings between the main uprights (cf. *Midland Railway Architecture, Figure 13 and Plate 129*). Accommodation for three wagons was originally specified. Note the Midland warning sign, the weigh office, the post and rail fencing to the right of the signal box, and the diagonal fencing. The signal box, 16ft. 6in. x 11 ft. 6in. x 8ft., of wood construction, was brought into use on 9th August 1896 (W & W Committee Minute No. 14978, 5/6/1896) at a renewal cost of £210. The box closed on 1st May 1984. Horton in Ribblesdale closed to goods traffic on 2nd February 1965.

D. Jenkinson

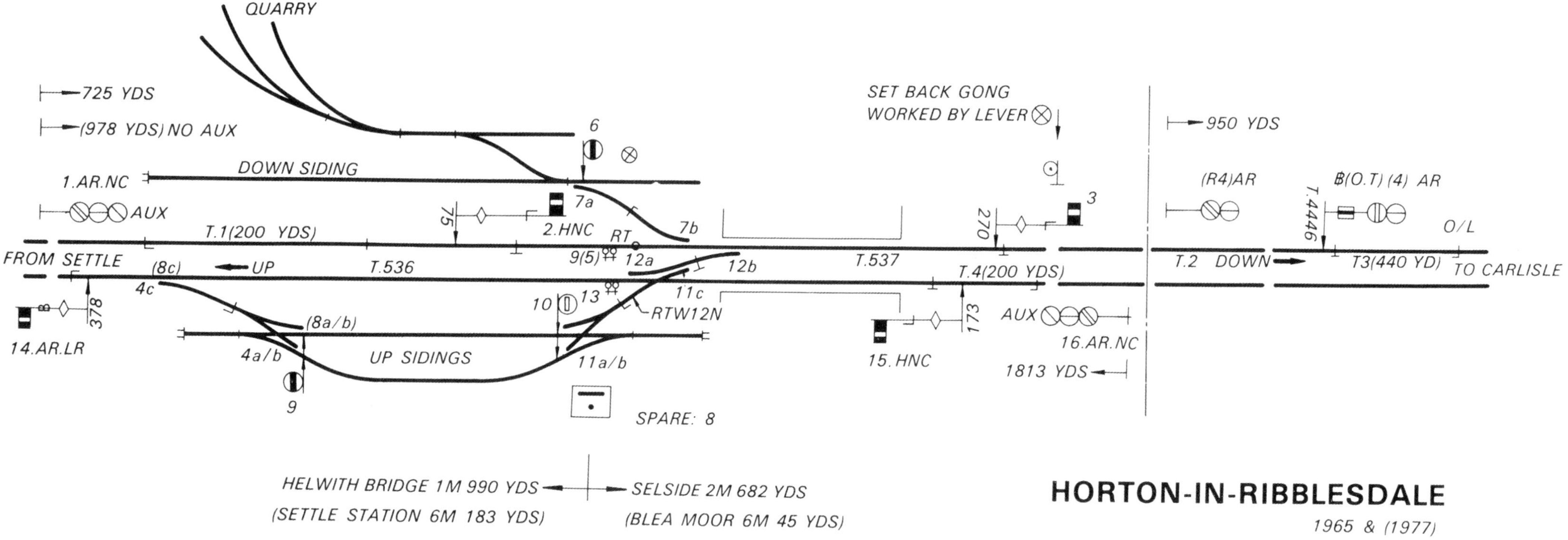

Figure 13: The signalling diagram for Horton in Ribblesdale, based upon information available for 1977. The arrangements include alterations in signalling due to the abolition of Selside signal box in 1975.

QUARRY

725 YDS

(978 YDS) NO AUX

DOWN SIDING

6

SET BACK GONG
WORKED BY LEVER

950 YDS

1.AR.NC

AUX

T.1(200 YDS)

7a

2.HNC   RT

7b

3

(R4)AR

B(O.T) (4) AR

O/L

FROM SETTLE

(8c)   ← UP

T.536

9(5)   12a

12b

T.537

T.4(200 YDS)

T.2   DOWN →   T3(440 YD)   TO CARLISLE

4c

10   13

11c

RTW12N

173

AUX

14.AR.LR

(8a/b)

4a/b

UP SIDINGS

11a/b

15. HNC

16.AR.NC

1813 YDS ←

9

SPARE: 8

HELWITH BRIDGE 1M 990 YDS → | ← SELSIDE 2M 682 YDS

(SETTLE STATION 6M 183 YDS)   (BLEA MOOR 6M 45 YDS)

HORTON-IN-RIBBLESDALE

1965 & (1977)

Plate 31: Horton in Ribblesdale in May 1962. This view, from the north, shows the small type of building in particularly well-maintained condition at a time when this station was receiving accolades for being well-kept. The architectural features of this type can be clearly seen; the change of roofline over the waiting area between the gables, the glass-fronted screen with timber tracery, the low-roofed extension to the left, the quatrefoil decoration in the gables, and the Gothic pointed arch to the window. It is unfortunate that the ravages of time have meant that all the ornate bargeboarding has had to be replaced. Note the position of another ornamental station sign.

D. Jenkinson

Plate 33: Horton in Ribblesdale on 28th March 1967. An ailing 9F, No. 92026, with a northbound freight was backed on to the 'up' main line to recuperate and allow time for the passage of the 'down' 'Thames Clyde Express'. Eventually, the freight was banked to Aisgill by a Class 5 locomotive which arrived to work a Delaney's train. The additional trackwork mentioned in **Figure 12** can be seen on the extreme right of the picture.

Plate 32: Horton in Ribblesdale on 27th April 1968, a No. 3 (small) type of building, photographed from the south. Note the position of the nameboard referred to in **Plate 29**. This station closed to passengers on 5th May 1970 after being an unstaffed halt for some years.

D. F. Tee

Plate 34: Horton in Ribblesdale in December 1967. Across the line from the main building stood a substantial stone shelter constructed of the same coursed stonework. Here a trefoil device is used on the gable, and again the bargeboarding has been renewed.

SELSIDE

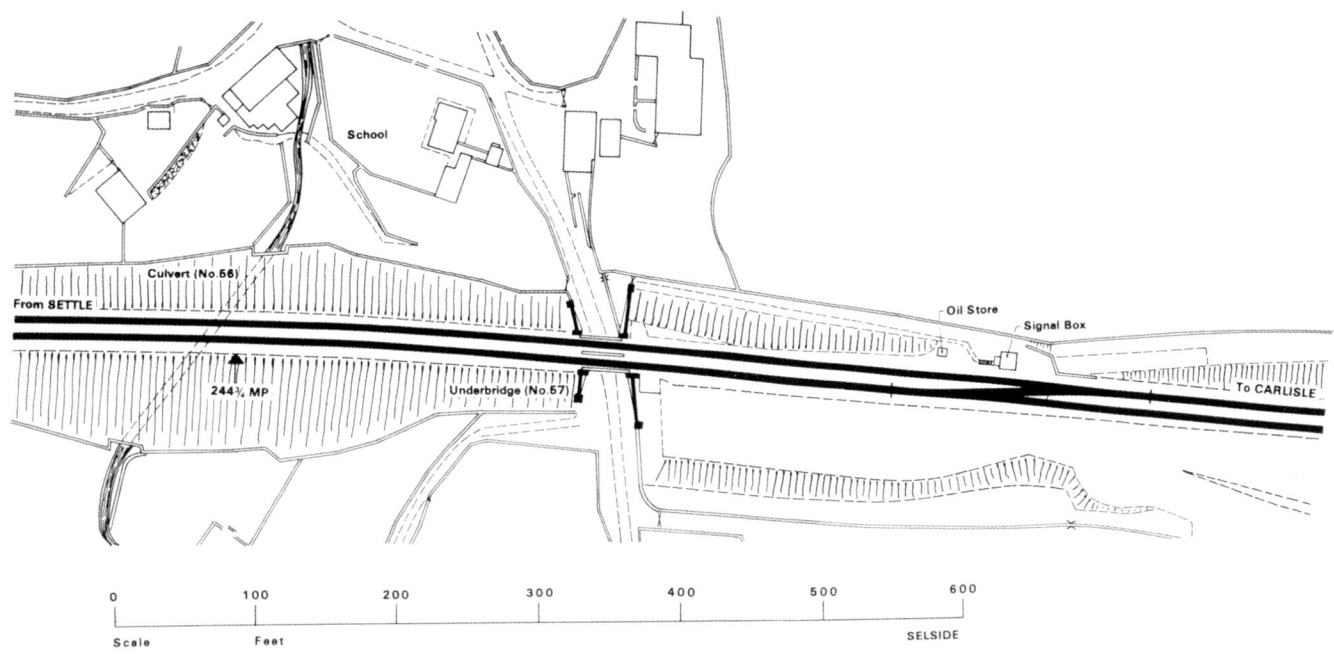

Figure 14: Selside track layout, based upon information from a 1913 Midland Railway survey.

Plate 35: A view of Selside, looking north, in 1973. Selside signal box was 10ft. x 11ft. 6in. x 8ft., of wood construction and brought into use on 16th June 1907 (W & W Committee Minute No. 22118, 2/11/1906 — renewal cost £220). The box was closed on 30th November 1975 and was ultimately removed for preservation. The crossover shown in **Figure 14** had most certainly been removed by 1932, but the exact date has not been confirmed; this would, however, explain the reason why the 18 lever tumbler frame had been reduced to 8. The upper quadrant home signals on tubular steel posts, replaced lower quadrant signals on timber posts in March 1946. The distant signals were similarly treated at a time when consideration was being given to closure of the box, in which case intermediate block colour light signals would have replaced the semaphores. Similar proposals for abolition had been considered in 1930 and 1932.

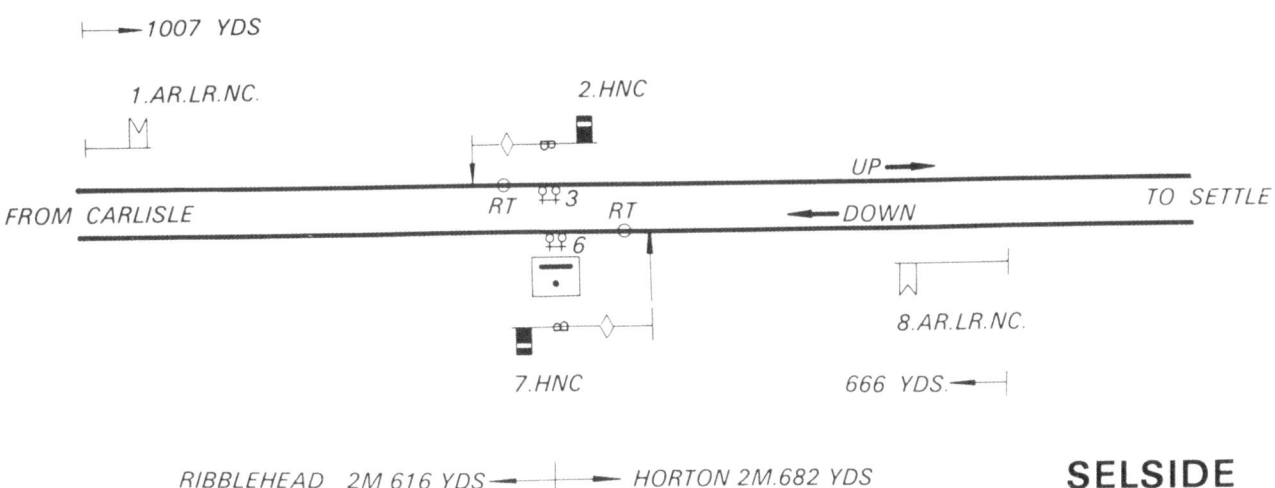

Figure 15: The signalling diagram for Selside, based on information available for 1975.

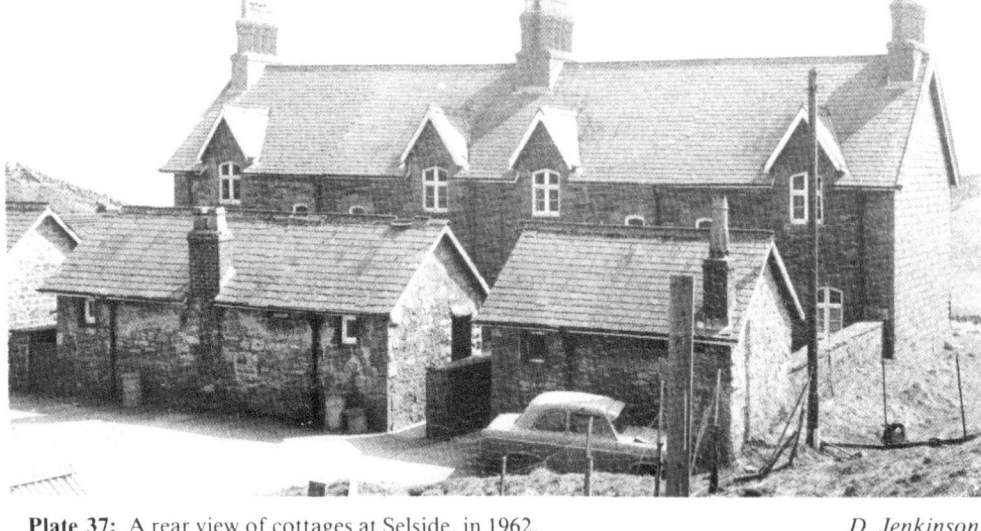

Plate 36: A front view of cottages at Selside, in 1962. *D. Jenkinson*

Plate 37: A rear view of cottages at Selside, in 1962. *D. Jenkinson*

Plates 36 & 37: A row of four cottages for railway-men built near Selside. This type of building was to be found in the vicinity of the line at many locations; indeed their presence can be seen marked on the track plans. Although detail differences occurred, these are typical, robustly-constructed and the front entrance was via a double-sided projecting porch. At the rear, each was provided with an extensive outhouse. The houses shown here all have the first floor windows surmounted by gables, this being the significant variant; the other type found, for example, at Garsdale, had a continuous eaves line unbroken by gables.

Plate 38: A Glasgow to Nottingham express, headed by Class 45 'Peak' No. 45053, passes Saltlake on 29th April 1977. In the distance can be seen a terrace of six cottages, similar to those above. Saltlake was the site of a shanty town built by the navvies constructing the line in this area; the name remained in use after the workers left. A quarry was opened in the area by the Craven Lime Company. They asked for a siding in 1876, and this was brought into use on 4th January 1877. This siding was a scheduled stop for the pick-up goods train at the time of the 1884 working timetable, although a signal box for the siding had closed in 1879.

M. S. Welch

RIBBLEHEAD

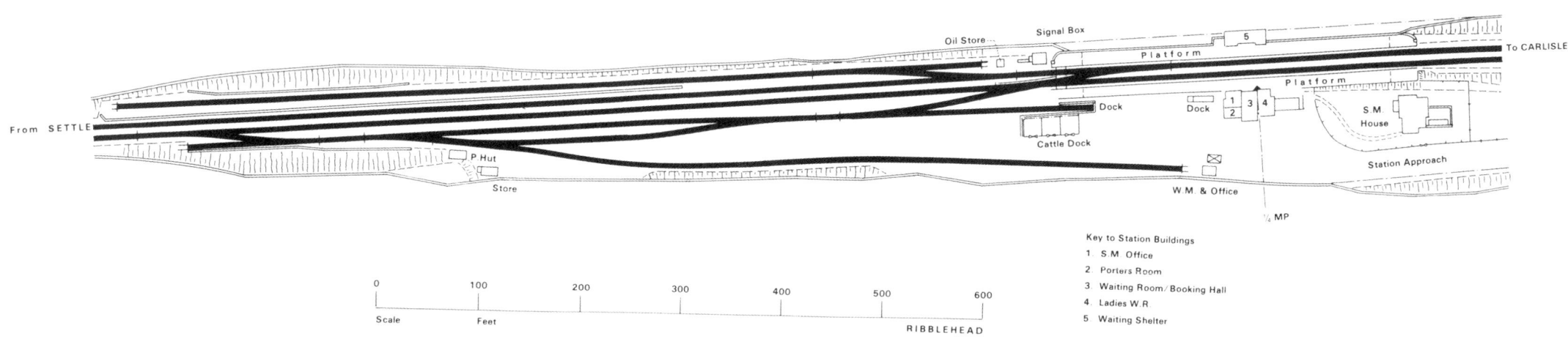

Plate 39: A view of Ribblehead Station looking south, in May 1960. This illustrates well the juxtaposition of the facilities at Ribblehead Station, again showing the smaller type of building, but in this case note how the end and projecting gables have been tiled to give added protection against the extreme weather conditions. It is not known whether this was originally specified or if it was a later modification; in any case the window head is different. The name for this station was at first uncertain; it was to be called Ingleton Road, then Batty Green, although the name Ribblehead was finally adopted, perhaps due to the intervention of the Revd Woodall of Settle, who wrote to the Company in June 1876. A station for this site was not suggested in the original report although, as one for Selside was not built, this may have been the location intended. The first mention was in 1875 when construction was well in hand. From 1880, religious services for the local community were conducted in the waiting-room by the vicar of Ingleton. Ribblehead Station closed to passengers on 4th May 1970, but goods services had ceased on 7th November 1966.

G. Biddle

Figure 16: Ribblehead track layout, based on information from 1874 and 1913 Midland Railway surveys.

Key to Station Buildings
1. S.M. Office
2. Porters Room
3. Waiting Room / Booking Hall
4. Ladies W.R
5. Waiting Shelter

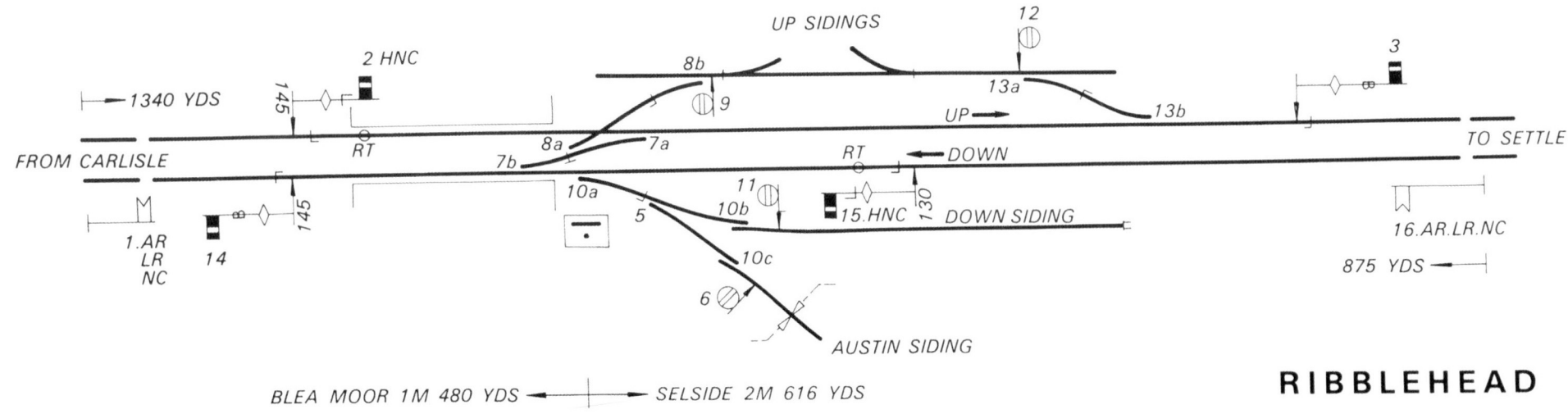

UP SIDINGS

FROM CARLISLE

TO SETTLE

RIBBLEHEAD

BLEA MOOR 1M 480 YDS ← → SELSIDE 2M 616 YDS

AUSTIN SIDING

Figure 17: The signalling diagram for Ribblehead, based upon information available for 1967.

Plate 40: Ribblehead, looking south, on 3rd September 1964. This signal box was 16ft. 6in. x 11ft. 6in x 8ft., of wood construction and brought into use on 10th July 1898 at a renewal cost of £260 (W & W Committee Minute No. 16362, 1/4/1898) and had a 16 lever MR tumbler frame. The box closed on 17th August 1969. An Ivatt Class 4MT, No. 43130, stands in the siding of H. Austin, a facility provided in 1945 and improved in 1950. A scheme for two additional sidings behind the 'down' platform was proposed in 1949, but not carried out.

P. Baughan

Plate 41: Ribblehead, looking north, on 3rd September 1964. Most of the track plans show the position of an 'oil store', and one is seen here as the ubiquitous MR-designed square corrugated-iron structure with the curved roof, standing alongside the signal box. On the right can be seen the cattle dock of the more common type, and not as seen at Horton. The tall post near the end of the station building carries an anemometer for use in connection with meteorological work carried out at this station.

P. Baughan

Plate 42: Ribblehead meteorological equipment, as seen on 3rd September 1964. In 1938, Ribblehead became a meteorological report point. The stationmaster and staff received special training to compile and send hourly reports on weather conditions. In this view, Stationmaster Sharpe demonstrates some of the equipment.

P. Baughan

Plate 43: Ribblehead, in the winter of 1962/63; a typical bleak winter's scene.

Figure 18: An end elevation of the smaller type of building at Ribblehead, showing the attachment of the pole to carry the anemometer.

ELEVATION

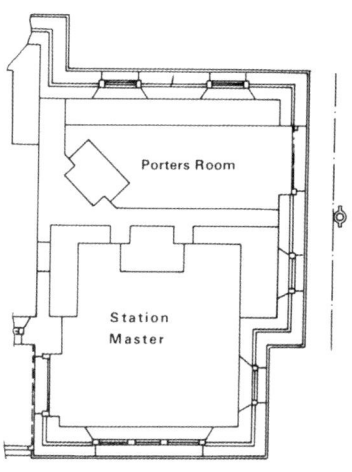

Porters Room

Station Master

GROUND PLAN

0   20

Scale Feet

Plate 44: Ribblehead, from the north. The exposed location of Batty Moss is crossed by possibly the most notable structure on the line, Ribblehead Viaduct (247 miles 60 chains) simply numbered by the Engineer's Department as bridge No. 66. On the extreme left, in the distance, can be seen Ribblehead Station. The double-sided distant signal was a long-standing feature at the northern approach to the viaduct. The bleak area to the left, bordering the Ingleton Road, was the site of a large township during the course of construction of the railway. It was known as Batty Wife Hole, and had a Sunday school, day school, mission house, library, post office, public house, shops and hospital.

D. F. Tee Collection

Plate 45: Ribblehead Viaduct, as seen on 15th April 1967. The extent of the 24 span structure (440yds.) can be seen as it sweeps across the landscape. Construction occupied a period of five years, although it was not decided until December 1872 whether to have 24 or 18 arches. This depended on the work-force available; either sufficient stonemasons to build the piers and turn the arches, or enough navvies to extend the embankments. With abutments, wings, piers and parapets of limestone, the brick arches of a nominal 45ft. span were sprung with stone voussoirs. The stone was quarried between Selside and Ribblehead.

D. F. Tee

Plate 46: Ribblehead Viaduct. This view from the valley floor shows the 104ft. high graceful but rugged outline of the piers, and illustrates well the construction. Note the strengthened or 'king' pier on the left. Each sixth pier was so treated, being 18ft. thick at the spring compared with the normal 6ft.

M. S. Welch

BLEA MOOR

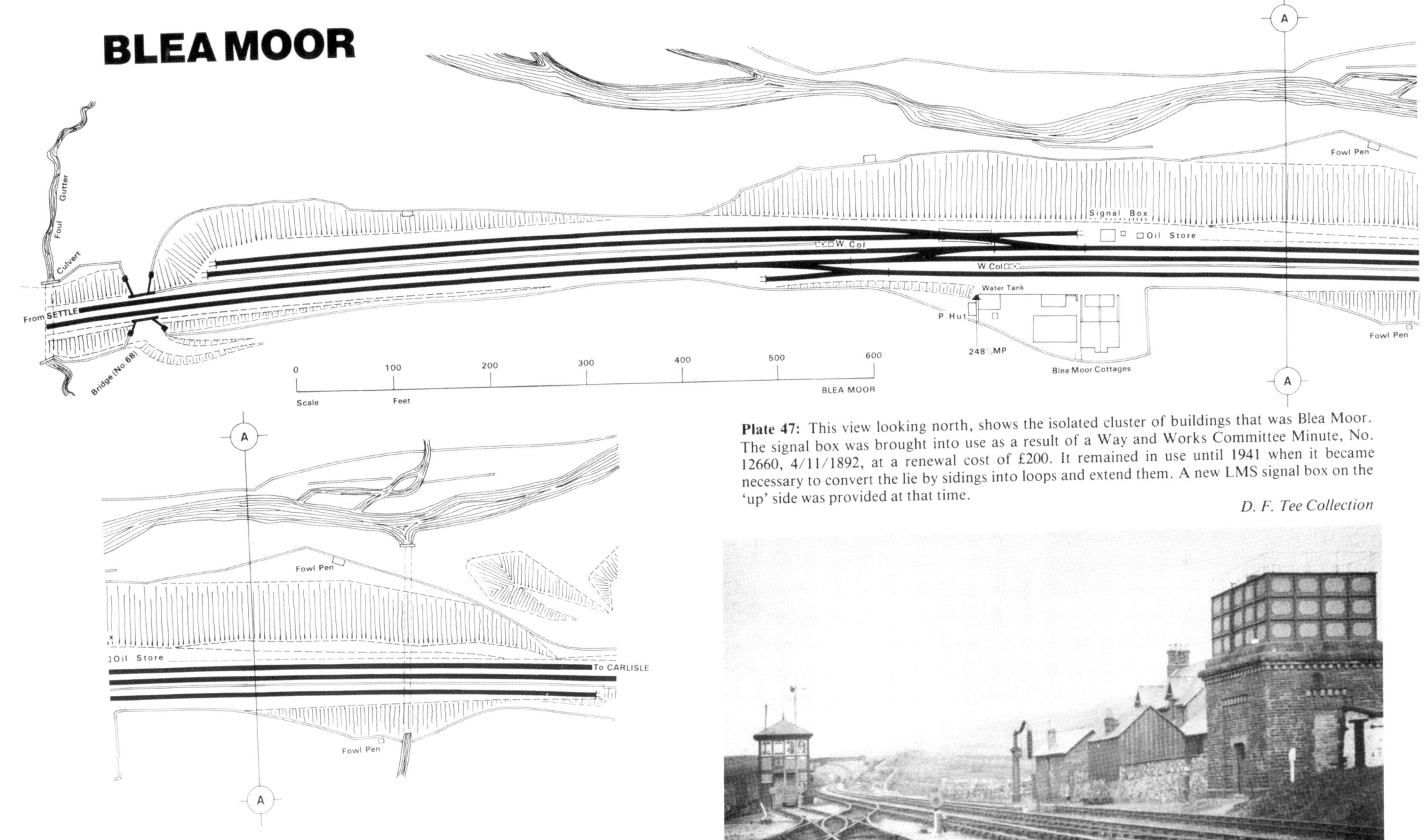

Scale — Feet

BLEA MOOR

Plate 47: This view looking north, shows the isolated cluster of buildings that was Blea Moor. The signal box was brought into use as a result of a Way and Works Committee Minute, No. 12660, 4/11/1892, at a renewal cost of £200. It remained in use until 1941 when it became necessary to convert the lie by sidings into loops and extend them. A new LMS signal box on the 'up' side was provided at that time.

D. F. Tee Collection

Figure 19: Blea Moor track layout, based upon information from a Midland Railway survey of 1913.

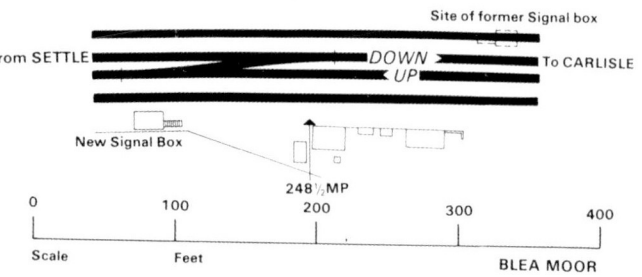

Plate 48: Blea Moor, looking north, on 1st May 1966. The 15.00 Glasgow to Euston express passes Blea Moor having been redirected from the Shap route due to track relaying. This picture shows the extended facilities completed in 1941, involving the creation of passing loops to replace the lie by sidings. The signal box on the 'down' side, seen in **Plate 47**, was replaced by a new brick and timber LMS box of 30 levers, brought into use on 20th September 1941. At the south end, land was purchased at each side of the track to widen the formation for new loops. This involved extending bridge No. 68, seen in the foreground, by the addition of concrete wing walls and parapets. The buffer stops of the outer lie by siding mark the limit of the original formation, and it was at this point that the original inner lie by ended. In the background, on the hillside, the spoil tips from the original workings mark the course of Blea Moor Tunnel.

M. S. Welch

Plate 49: The 1941 LMS pattern box at Blea Moor *(refer to LMS Architecture, Plates 573 to 580 for details of this type of box).*

Figure 20: The site plan showing the relative positions of the old and new signal boxes at Blea Moor, based upon information from a 1941 LMS drawing.

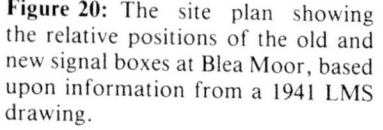

Site of former Signal box

From SETTLE — DOWN → To CARLISLE
UP

New Signal Box

248½MP

| 0 | 100 | 200 | 300 | 400 |

Scale Feet

BLEA MOOR

Plate 50: Blea Moor, looking south, on 19th August 1967. The train seen in **Plate 27** has made a water stop at Blea Moor. The original signal box **(Plate 47)** occupied a site required for the extension of the loops **(see Figure 19)**. We have not established when the pressed-steel water tank was provided at this northern end, but in all probability it was built in 1941 to serve the new loop. In the foreground, access to the 'up' side loop by a facing connection was created by extending the existing lie by.

M. S. Welch

Figure 21: The signalling diagram for Blea Moor, based upon information available for 1962.

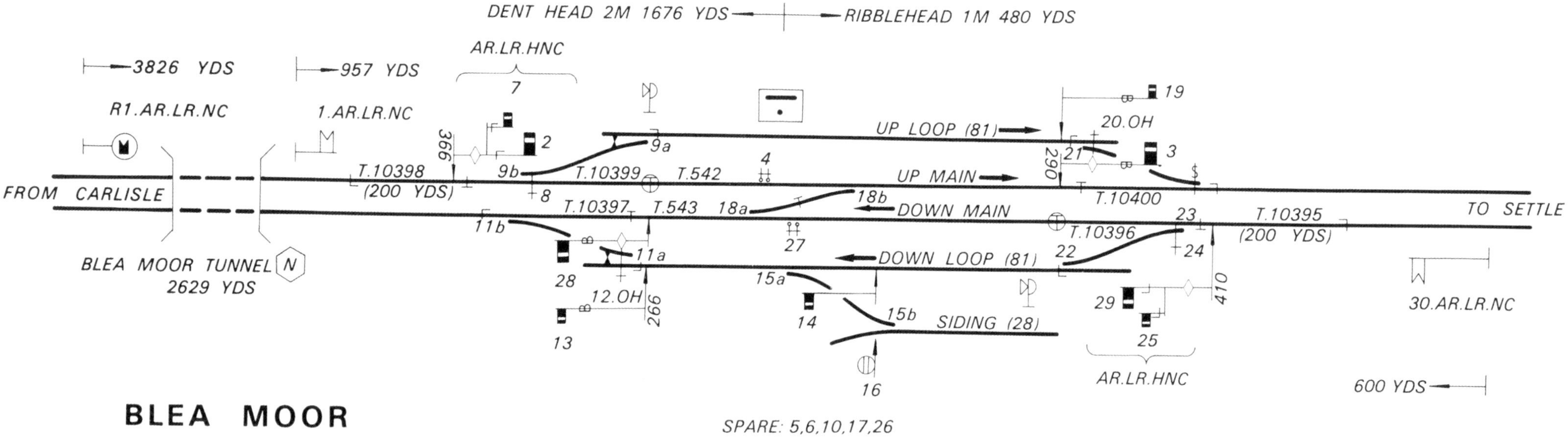

DENT HEAD 2M 1676 YDS ⟶ | ⟵ RIBBLEHEAD 1M 480 YDS

AR.LR.HNC

⟶ 3826 YDS   ⟶ 957 YDS   7   19

R1.AR.LR.NC   1.AR.LR.NC   UP LOOP (81) ⟶   20.OH

                                        366   2   9a   21   3
                                              9b   T.10399   T.542   4   UP MAIN ⟶   290
FROM CARLISLE   T.10398   8   T.10397   T.543   18a   18b   T.10400
                      (200 YDS)   DOWN MAIN ⟵   23   T.10395
                                   11b   T.10396   24   (200 YDS)   TO SETTLE

BLEA MOOR TUNNEL Ⓝ   11a   27   DOWN LOOP (81) ⟵   22
2629 YDS   28   29   410
                           12.OH   266   14   15a   15b   25   30.AR.LR.NC
                      13   SIDING (28)
                                          16   AR.LR.HNC   600 YDS ⟶

BLEA MOOR   SPARE: 5,6,10,17,26

Plate 52: Blea Moor in May 1963, showing the staff accommodation named 'Blea Moor Cottages'. A pair of Midland cottages has been supplemented by the addition of a more modern house. Although this has replaced an unidentified structure shown on the 1913 plan, it is of a design produced by the Architects' Section of the Midland Railway Engineer's Department at Derby. Houses to this design had appeared elsewhere by 1918, and were still being built by the LMS in 1933. The timber hut adjacent to the cottage outbuildings has the appearance of the LNWR-designed portable hut of Mr. F. W. Webb, which are known to have been transferred away from their home territory.

D. Jenkinson

Plate 51: Blea Moor, looking south, during Autumn 1972, showing the position of the 1941 signal box in relation to the original water tank. The corrugated-iron oil store is of Midland design and was moved to the location near the water tank as a result of the 1940/1 alterations.

Plate 53: The southern approach to the tunnel at Blea Moor (249 miles 25½ chains) was through this shallow rock cutting. The 2,629 yard long Blea Moor Tunnel reaches a depth of 500ft. below the moor. It took five years to construct, between 1870 and 1875. Work proceeded from sixteen faces using seven shafts sunk from the fell-side above. This was one of the most difficult feats of engineering on the line. Three of the construction shafts were retained for ventilation. The tunnel has rock-side walls with a brick arch.

D. F. Tee Collection

Plate 54: The northerly approach to Blea Moor Tunnel. On leaving the tunnel the upper reaches of Dentdale are entered over a shallow embankment. The signals seen here are the Dent Head distant (foreground) a Midland lower quadrant on a square post, and a banner repeater for the Blea Moor distant (near the tunnel). A feature of the tunnel mouth is the stepped channels down both sides of the portal, which enables beck and flood water to be contained as it runs down off the fells. On reaching ground level the water is diverted to drains located below track level.

Plate 55: Dent Head on 13th May 1965. The afternoon Carlisle to Bradford local train is captured by the photographer from above the northern portal of Blea Moor Tunnel. The route of the railway, as it curves along the hillside to avoid the 1,829ft. Woldfell, had to negotiate, on high viaducts, the deep cross-valleys running into Dentdale. One such structure, Dent Head Viaduct, can be seen on the left of the photograph.

M. S. Welch

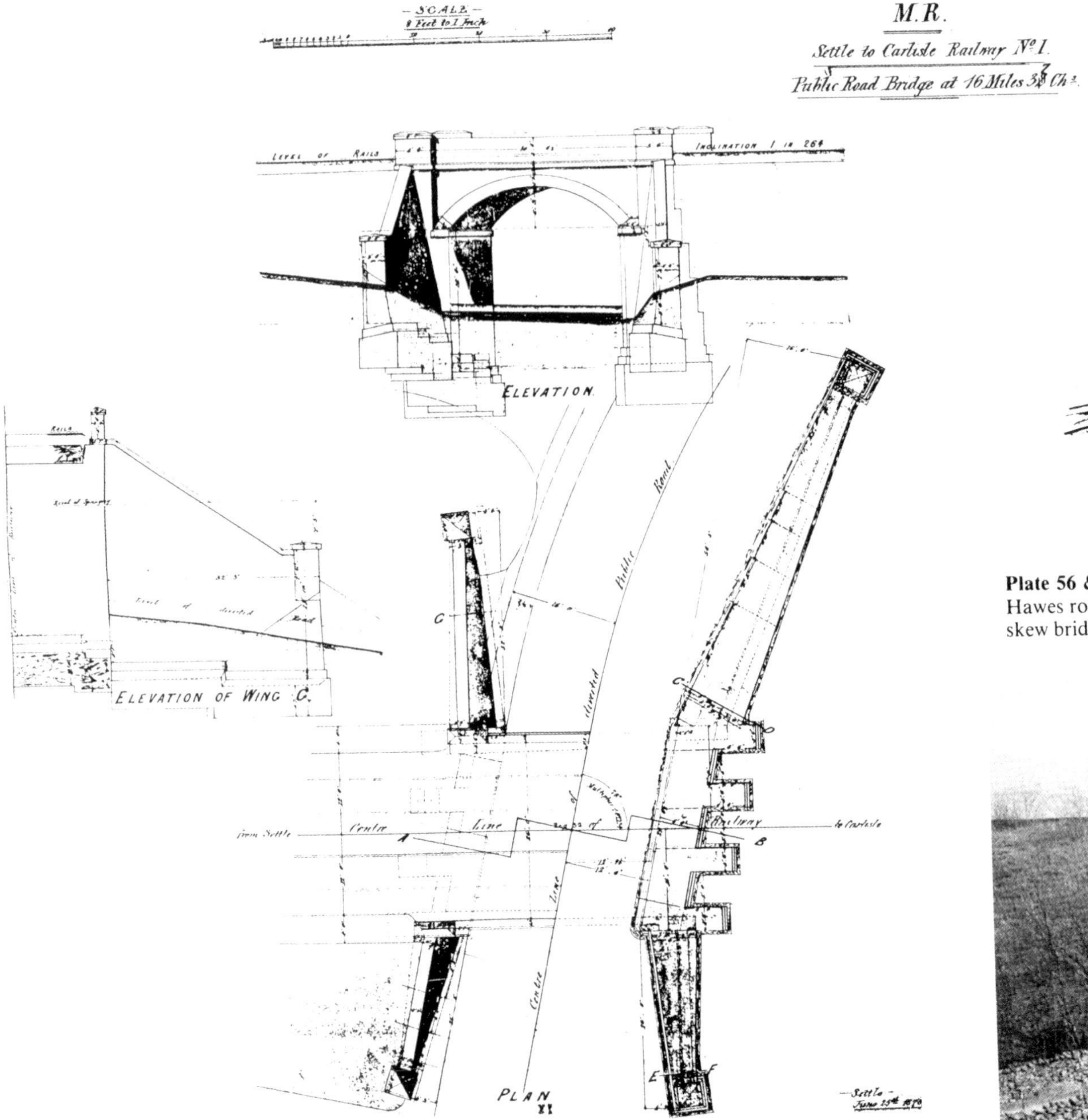

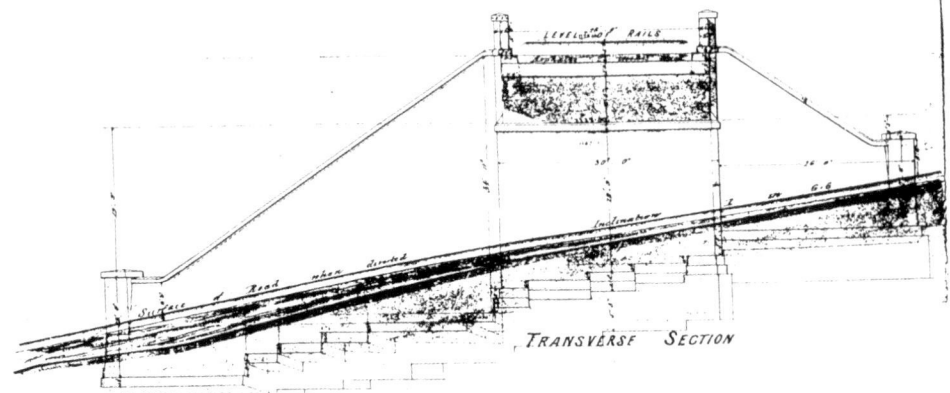

Plate 56 & Figure 22: These detail the bridge (No. 76) carrying the railway over the Dent to Hawes road at Greenbanks (251 miles 9 chains) shortly after leaving Blea Moor Tunnel. This skew bridge, constructed of stone in 1871, has a segmental arch with a span of 25ft. 6in.

D. Jenkinson, 1963

DENT HEAD

Plate 57: Dent Head Viaduct (251 miles 17 chains) marked the end of contract No. 1. It is 177yds. long and stands 100ft. above the valley. Construction is of blue limestone with brick arch rings and the ten openings are a nominal 45ft. *(details appear in LMS Architecture, Figure 52).* Construction occupied a period of five years from 1870. Note the strengthened centre pier.

D. Jenkinson, 1963

Figure 23: Dent Head track layout, based upon information from a Midland Railway survey of 1913.

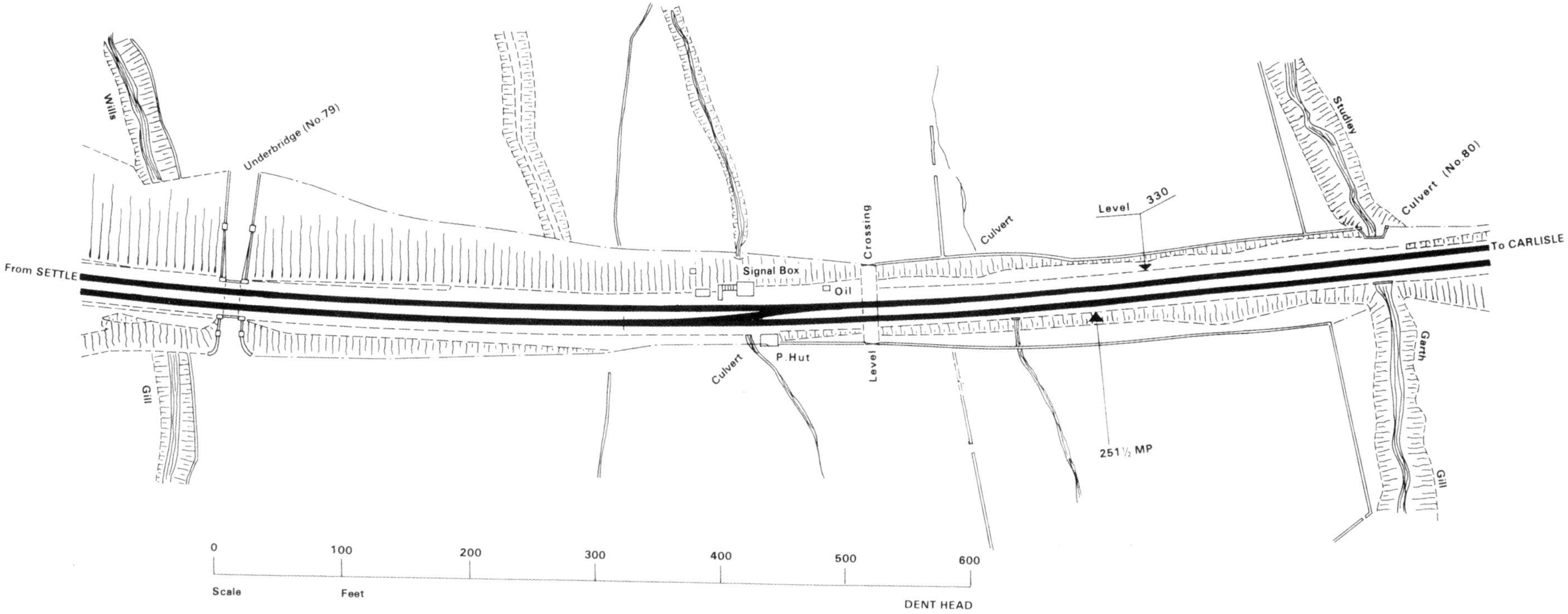

Wills

Underbridge (No. 79)

Studley

Culvert (No. 80)

Level 330

Crossing

Culvert

To CARLISLE

From SETTLE

Signal Box

Oil

Garth

Gill

Culvert

P. Hut

Level

Gill

251½ MP

| 0 | 100 | 200 | 300 | 400 | 500 | 600 |

Scale   Feet

DENT HEAD

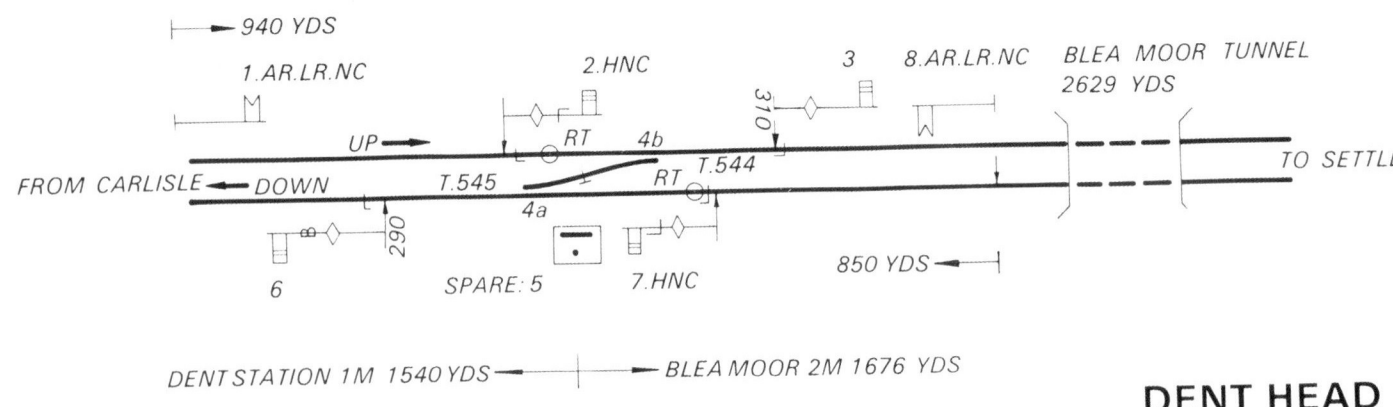

940 YDS

1.AR.LR.NC   2.HNC   3   8.AR.LR.NC   BLEA MOOR TUNNEL
2629 YDS

UP →   RT   4b   310

FROM CARLISLE ← DOWN   T.545   RT   T.544   TO SETTLE

290   4a

6   SPARE: 5   7.HNC   850 YDS ←

DENT STATION 1M 1540 YDS ———|——→ BLEA MOOR 2M 1676 YDS

DENT HEAD

Figure 24: The signalling diagram for Dent Head, based upon information available for 1965.

Plate 58 (left): Dent Head signal box, looking north, in 1963. The box shown here was brought into use on 19th November 1898, is of wood construction, and measures 21ft. 6in. × 11ft. 6in. × 8ft. carrying an 8 lever tumbler frame. It replaced an earlier structure but, although Company records suggest that a new cabin was raised in 1877, this cannot be substantiated. The signal box closed on 11th April 1965.

D. Jenkinson

Plate 59 (below): Dent Head, looking south, in 1963. A 'down' express passes the signal box after just negotiating Dent Head Viaduct.

D. Jenkinson

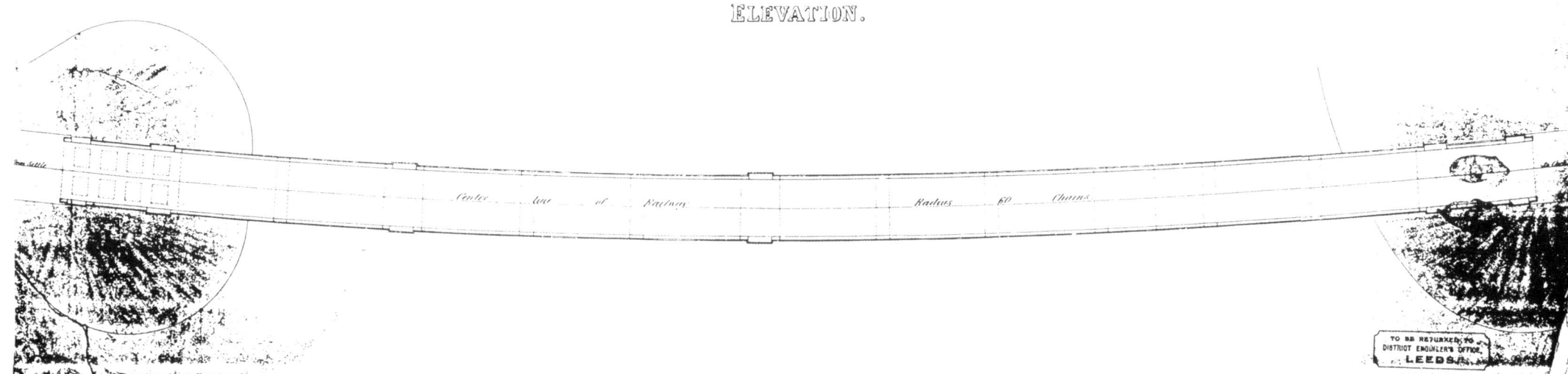

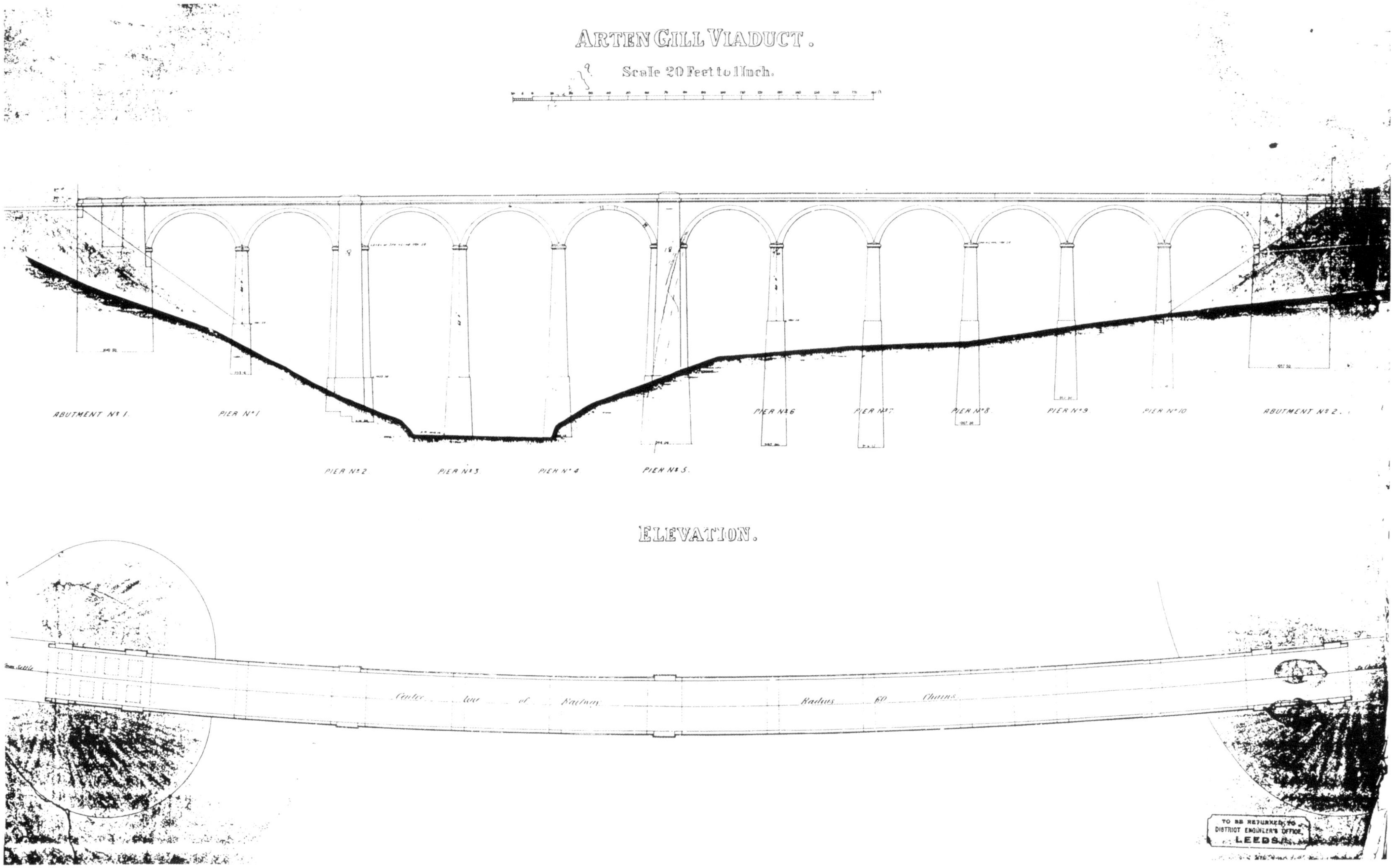

Figure 25: An official drawing of Arten Gill Viaduct.

Plate 60: This view of Arten Gill Viaduct shows the western face of this gently-curving structure, arguably the most graceful viaduct on the line, a point of view accentuated by this picture. Construction of the eleven arch structure was entirely of stone, quarried locally, and known as Dent marble, a dark grey limestone with white fossils. The 220 yard long viaduct was started on 3rd May 1871 and took four years to complete. The exposed nature of the watercourse at the foot of the 117ft. high elevation is evidenced by the sight of water being blown back upstream by

Plate 61: Kell Beck Culvert is thought to be the largest on the line with a 10ft. 6in. span. The culvert falls through 16ft. in small steps. The relieving arches over the main pointed arch help to strengthen the spandrel wall supporting the 50ft. embankment retaining wall above. The embankment here spans a small cross-valley.

Figure 25: An official drawing of the culvert (No. 90) for Kell Beck at 252 miles 60 chains.

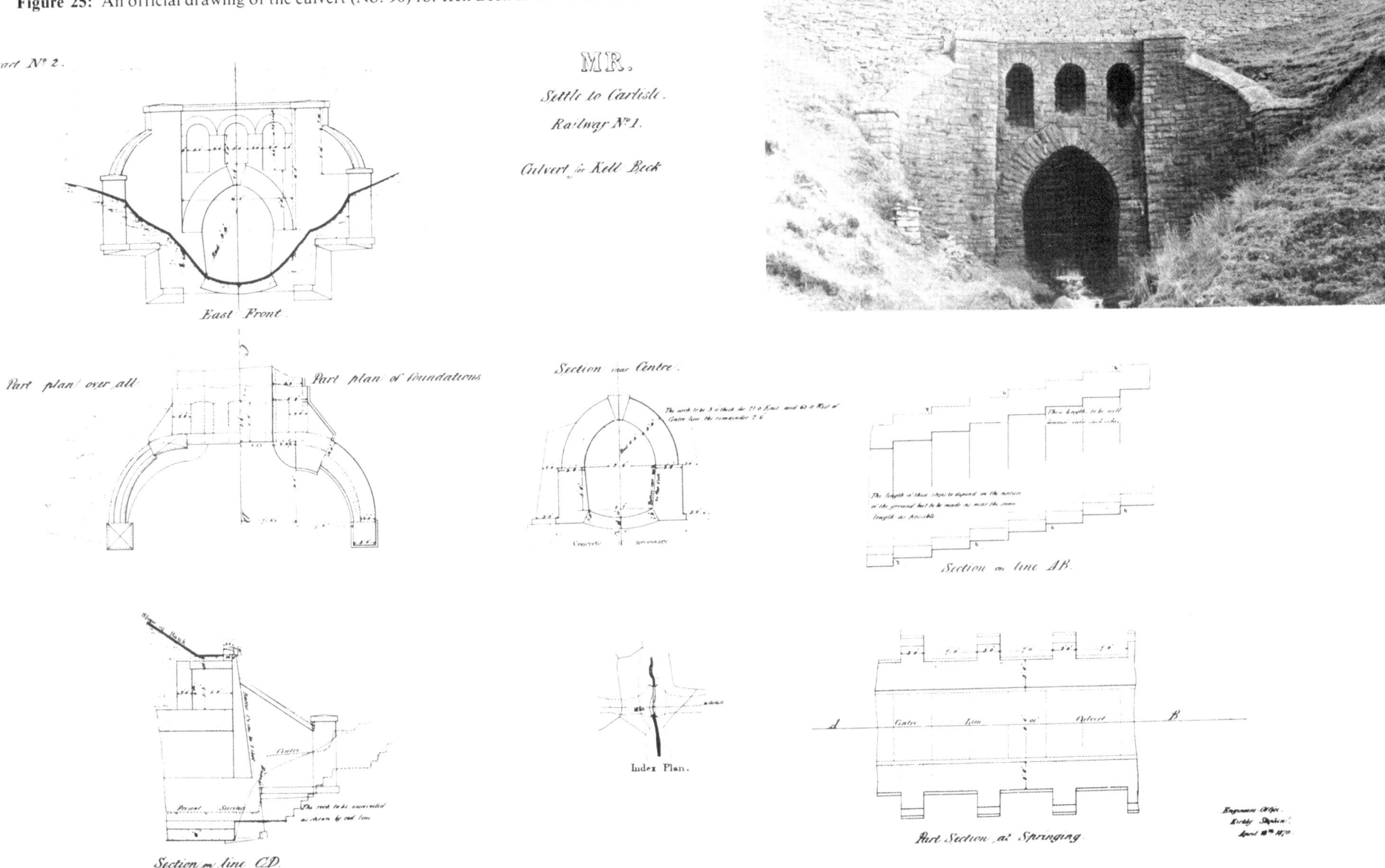

DENT

Plate 62: Dent Station, as seen on 1st May 1966. This spot is well-known to photographer and enthusiasts alike. The 10.55 Sundays Only Birmingham to Glasgow express, headed by a Brush Type 4, Class 47 diesel, passes Dent Station having been redirected from the West Coast Main Line to allow relaying work at Scout Green. The path of the railway skirting the dale can be traced by the appearance of Arten Gill Viaduct, above the waiting shelter, and Dent Head Viaduct above

drifts, particularly in the cutting north of the station. Note that the waiting shelter on the 'up' platform is built into the hillside, a retaining wall being provided at the back of the platform. The 'up' home signal on the bracket beyond the platform was installed in 1940 replacing a Midland lower quadrant signal situated on the north side of the overbridge, but on the 'down'

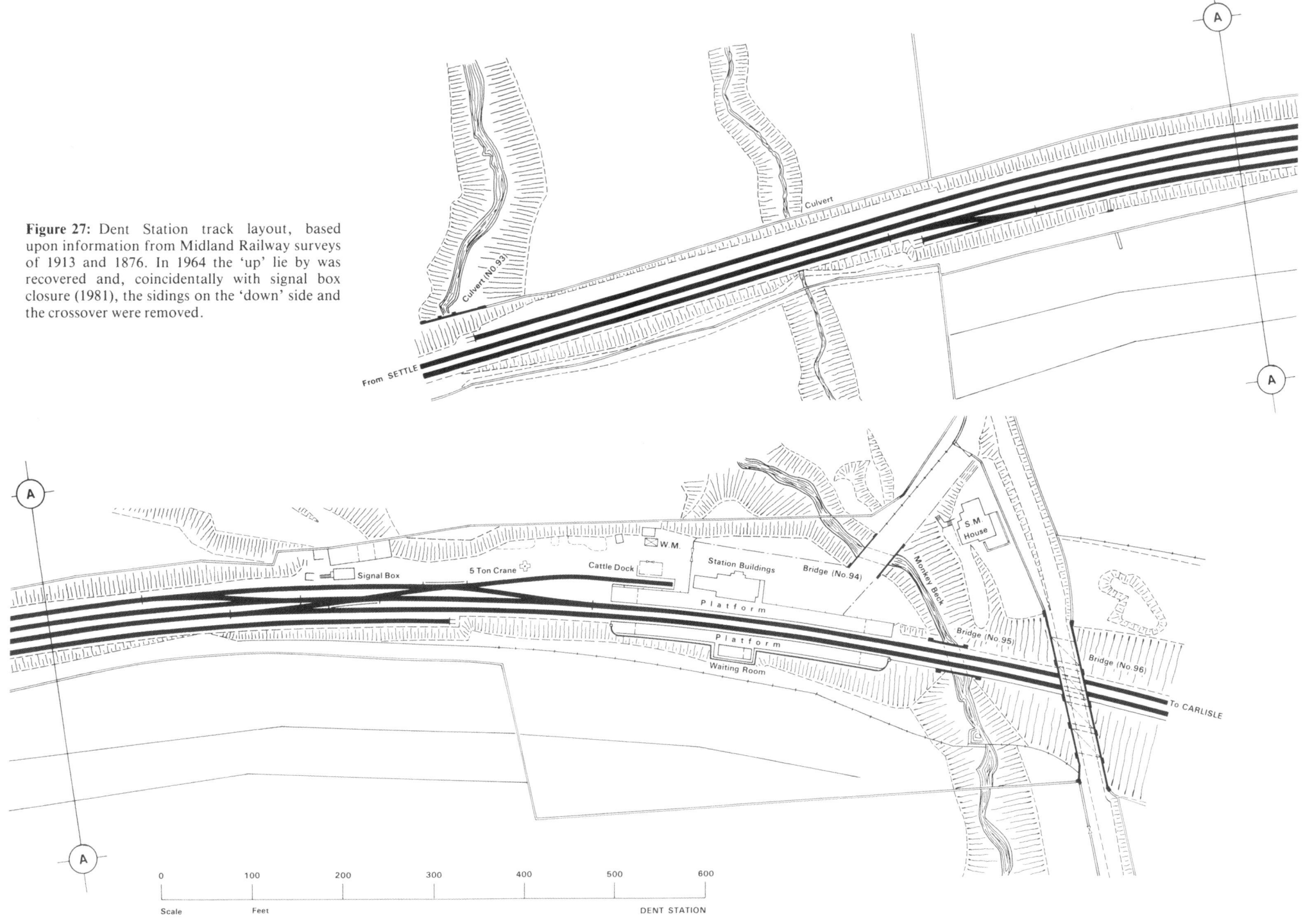

Figure 27: Dent Station track layout, based upon information from Midland Railway surveys of 1913 and 1876. In 1964 the 'up' lie by was recovered and, coincidentally with signal box closure (1981), the sidings on the 'down' side and the crossover were removed.

Culvert

Culvert (No.93)

From SETTLE

S.M. House

Signal Box

5 Ton Crane

Cattle Dock

W.M.

Station Buildings

Bridge (No.94)

Monkey Beck

Bridge (No.95)

Platform

Platform

Bridge (No.96)

Waiting Room

To CARLISLE

0   100   200   300   400   500   600

Scale   Feet   DENT STATION

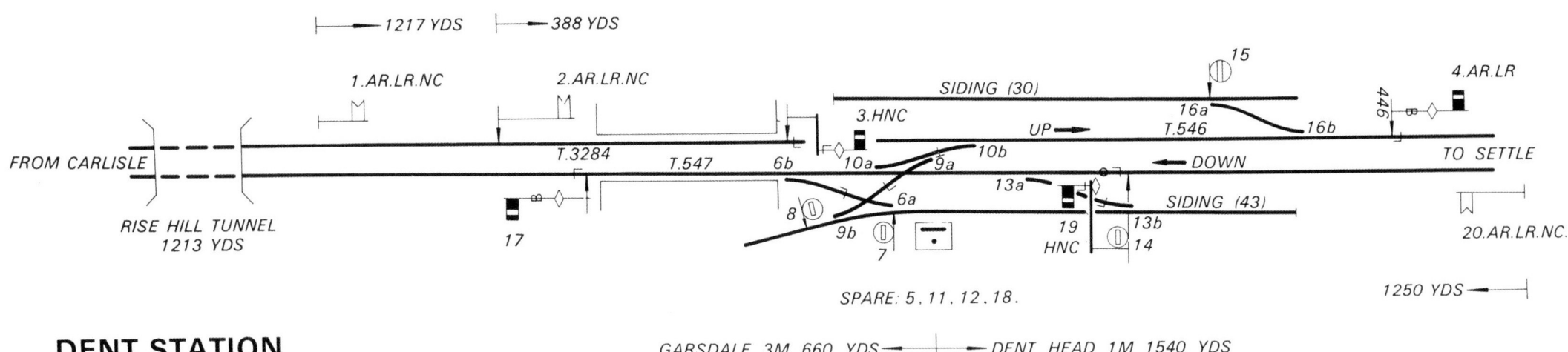

1217 YDS   388 YDS

1.AR.LR.NC   2.AR.LR.NC   SIDING (30)   15   4.AR.LR

3.HNC   16a   T.546   16b

FROM CARLISLE   T.3284   T.547   6b   10a   9a   10b   UP →   TO SETTLE

← DOWN

13a   SIDING (43)

RISE HILL TUNNEL   8   6a   19   13b   20.AR.LR.NC.
1213 YDS   9b   HNC   14
17   7

SPARE: 5.11.12.18.   1250 YDS →

DENT STATION

GARSDALE 3M 660 YDS ——|—— DENT HEAD 1M 1540 YDS

Figure 28: Dent Station signalling diagram, based upon information available for 1963.

Plate 64: This overall view of Dent Station, looking north, circa 1910, gives an impression of the spaciousness achieved at Settle & Carlisle locations. Although goods facilities were provided, these were minimal with crane, coal and cattle all being served from one siding. These facilities were withdrawn from 1st October 1964, but the existing track remained in use for engineering department purposes for some years. The stationmaster's house can be seen behind the station building, and this structure was double-glazed to combat the rigours of the winter winds, and in addition three sides of the house were covered with slates. The original Midland 'up' home signal, referred to in **Plate 62**, can be seen above the parapet of the over-bridge. A non-standard timber building to the left of the yard acts as a weigh office. A pair of employees' dwellings was proposed for a site behind the 'up' platform but was not built.

D. F. Tee Collection

Plate 63: Dent Station signal box in 1973. Brought into use on 9th August 1891, of wood construction with a 20 lever tumbler frame, the renewal cost was £220 (W & W Committee Minute No. 11590, 1/5/1891). The box closed on 28th January 1981.

ELEVATION NEXT PLATFORM

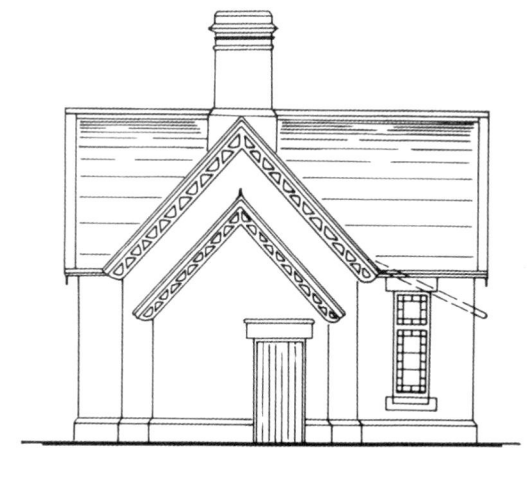

END ELEVATION ON B

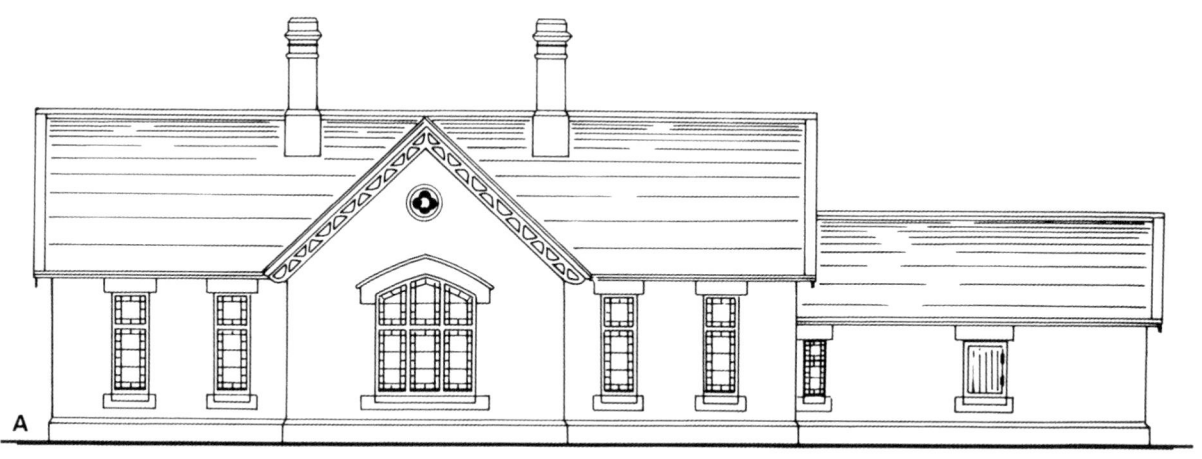

ELEVATION NEXT APPROACH ROAD

END ELEVATION ON A

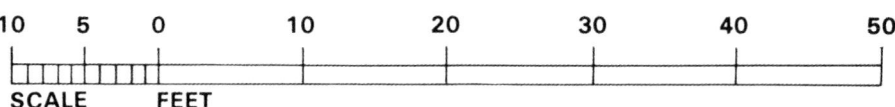

Figure 29: A drawing to show the elevations of the No. 3 (small) type of building for the Settle & Carlisle Railway.

Plate 65: Dent, 1970. After climbing a 1 in 4 hill, this would be the passengers' first view of the station. Of note are items of Midland 'furniture' such as the passenger V-trap, gates, post and rail-wrought fencing and diagonal platform fencing. The site of a station to serve Dentdale had been in doubt even after the line had opened to goods traffic. The 1872 proposals suggested a station at Dent Head, while later, Arten Gill was mentioned. However, the present site at Monkey Beck, now known as Cowgill, was decided upon in November 1875, the station eventually opening in 1877.

D. F. Tee

Plate 67: A view of the 'down' platform at Dent in 1962. The decorative barge boarding has been removed, and a 'non standard' feature in the shape of a hood is provided over each of the large front windows to afford extra protection.

D. Jenkinson

Plate 66: This view of Dent, in 1963, illustrates well the rear of the No. 3 (small) station building, and shows the central gabled extension with an arched window matching those on the front gables. Note the pierced cresting to the roof and the chimney stacks, only altered by the addition of short pots.

D. Jenkinson

Plate 68: A 1962 view of Dent, looking north from the end of the platform. The Coal Road overbridge (No. 96) is illustrated in **Figure 30**. The use of brick construction for the entire bridge was comparatively rare at the southern end of the line. The 'down' starter signal has a sighting 'board' in the form of a white panel painted on the bridge. In association with the resignalling referred to in *Plates 62 & 64*, a new 'up' distant signal was provided on the curve, and can be seen through the arch of the bridge; this signal was painted black and white for easier sighting.

D. Jenkinson

Figure 30: An official drawing of the bridge (No. 96), the 'Coal Road' at Dent Station.

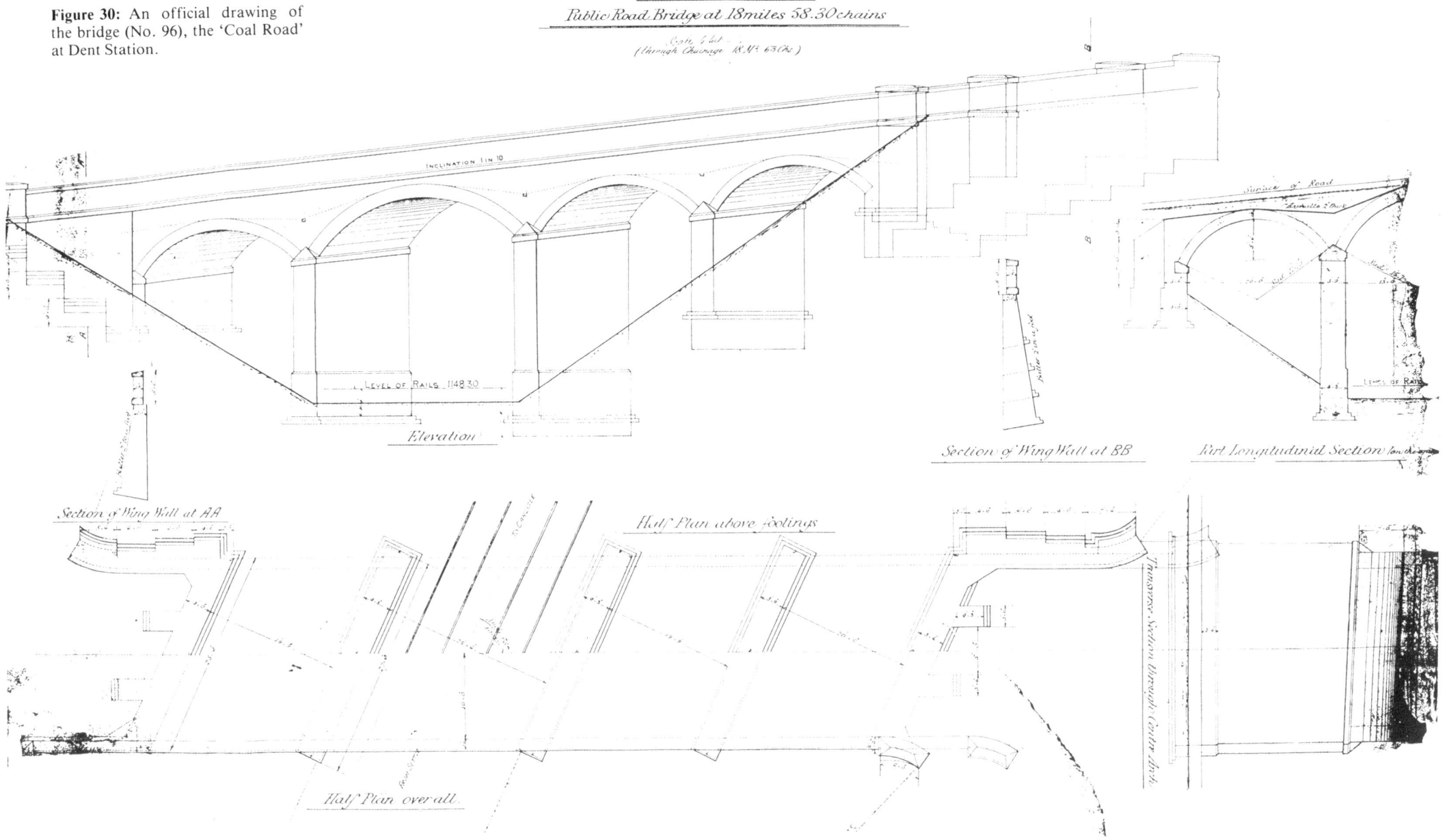

Settle to Carlisle.

Railway No. 21

Public Road Bridge at 18 miles 58.30 chains

(through Chainage 18 M. 63 chs.)

INCLINATION 1 IN 10

LEVEL OF RAILS 1148.30

Elevation

Section of Wing Wall at BB

Part Longitudinal Section

Section of Wing Wall at AA

Half Plan above footings

Half Plan over all

Plate 69: A view looking north, towards Rise Hill Tunnel, in October 1913. After leaving the cutting north of Dent Station, the line follows a valley on a shallow embankment. The occupation bridge in the foreground (No. 99 at 253 miles 70 chains) was in the course of reconstruction at the time this photograph was taken. The original stone arch of 1873 had to be rebuilt. To allow continuance of traffic, temporary weighbeams were inserted whilst work proceeded beneath. It is likely that the work was conducted by staff from Skipton District Engineer's Office. The weighbeams would be on loan from a girder yard such as those set up by the Midland Company at Leeds and Lenton, where suitable recoverable items of steel, wrought iron or cast iron were stored. Note the Dent 'up' distant signal sited on the 'down' side. This signal was relocated on the 'up' side during the 1940 signalling alterations previously referred to. The fogman's hut, opposite the signal is, for some unknown reason, facing the wrong direction; it was usual to lay them flat when not in use. On the hill above the tunnel mouth the irregular outline of a spoil heap can be seen, adajcent to a ventilating shaft.

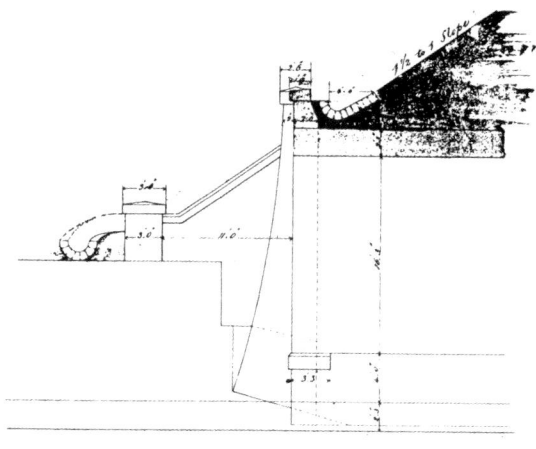

No 101.

Settle and Carlisle

Rise Hill Tunnel

Details of Face at 20 miles 8 chains 30 links
(through Chainage 20 M⁰ 11½ Chs.)

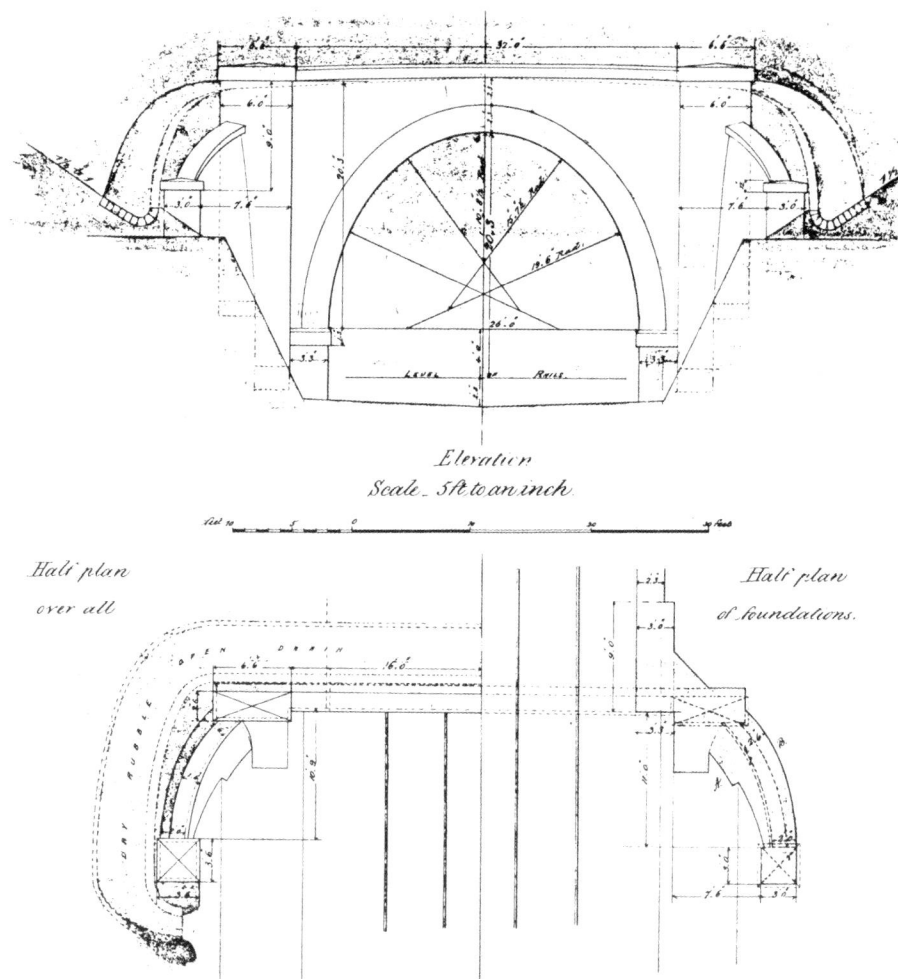

Elevation.
Scale 5 ft to an inch.

Half plan
over all

Half plan
of foundations.

Longitudinal Section.

Figure 31: An official drawing of the northern portal of Rise Hill Tunnel. This tunnel, numbered 101, commenced at 254 miles 11 chains, and ran for 1,213yds. through fells which stretched from Rise Hill to Mossdale Moor, separating Dentdale from Garsdale. The tunnel had stone side walls and arch at each end, and stone and brick side walls and a brick arch between. The two ventilation shafts (deepest 147ft.) were used during construction to form additional headings. At the time of building, the tunnel was known variously as Cowgill or Black Moss.

Plate 70: Reverting to bridge No. 99 **(see Plate 69)** this side view shows the heavy propping of the abutments during reconstruction. The arch centring has been installed in readiness for brickwork to form the new arch replacing the original stone arch, and stone facing was provided. Note the malleable iron fencing at each side of the road. This fencing was adopted as standard in 1909.

Plate 71: The northern portal of Rise Hill Tunnel on 1st October 1957, showing detail of the wing wall, using the rock formation as support.

BR/OPC

Plate 72: A view looking south, into the north end of Rise Hill Tunnel on 1st October 1957. Note the traditional position of the tunnel nameboard.

BR/OPC

Plate 73: A view from above Rise Hill Tunnel's northern portal on 1st October 1957, looking towards Garsdale. The bridge, featured in **Plate 74**, can be seen adjacent to the platelayer's hut.

BR/OPC

Plate 74: Occupation bridge No. 102 (254 miles 74 chains) in October 1984, officially known as Handleys, showing what was a typically constructed segmentally-arched underbridge. Many of these small bridges were, for some reason, constructed without a parapet wall, the protective element being provided by iron railings.

HAWES JUNCTION & GARSDALE

Plate 76: Garsdale water troughs on 28th July 1959, looking north from the top of the 43,000 gallon water tank serving the water troughs, which was installed in 1907. These are the highest troughs in Britain. The 1,670ft. troughs held between 5,000 and 6,000 gallons of water and, at one time, the tank was steam-heated to prevent winter freezing. The Garsdale distant signal was replaced in 1927.

BR/OPC

Plate 75: Garsdale water troughs on 28th July 1959, looking north through bridge No. 108 (255 miles 63 chains), Metcalfe's, at the commencement of the water troughs. This is another of the comparatively few bridges constructed entirely of brick.

BR/OPC

Plate 77: A view of Garsdale Station, looking north, circa 1960. The main line is to the left, and services to the Hawes branch used the platform to the right of the island. The bracketed lattice post 'up' branch starting signal appeared in September 1942 as a replacement for an ordinary timber post signal.

BR/OPC

Plate 78: Hawes Junction and Garsdale, before 1909, looking south from the station platform. The signal box, Hawes Junction South, had a comparatively short life, being erected in 1892 but being superseded in 1909. In the distance is the engine shed used by NER engines working services to Hawes. This shed was burnt down in 1917, rebuilt, and finally closed in 1939. In the centre of the picture is the large water tank referred to in the 1873 report. To the left, the extensive cattle docks are obviously well-maintained. Note the unusual gate in the right foreground decorated with ball finials; an elaborate version of a 'V' trap.

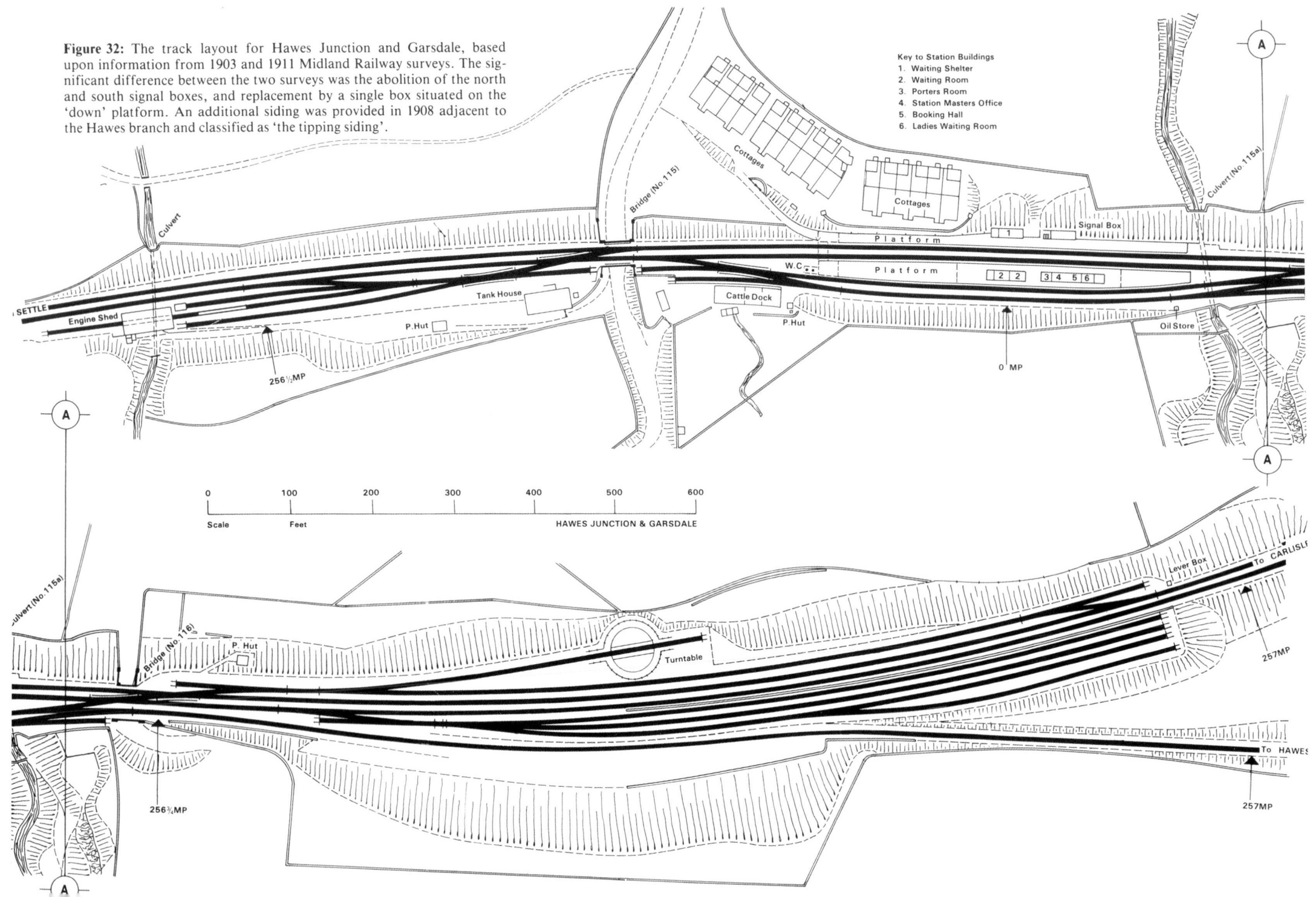

Figure 32: The track layout for Hawes Junction and Garsdale, based upon information from 1903 and 1911 Midland Railway surveys. The significant difference between the two surveys was the abolition of the north and south signal boxes, and replacement by a single box situated on the 'down' platform. An additional siding was provided in 1908 adjacent to the Hawes branch and classified as 'the tipping siding'.

Key to Station Buildings
1. Waiting Shelter
2. Waiting Room
3. Porters Room
4. Station Masters Office
5. Booking Hall
6. Ladies Waiting Room

HAWES JUNCTION & GARSDALE

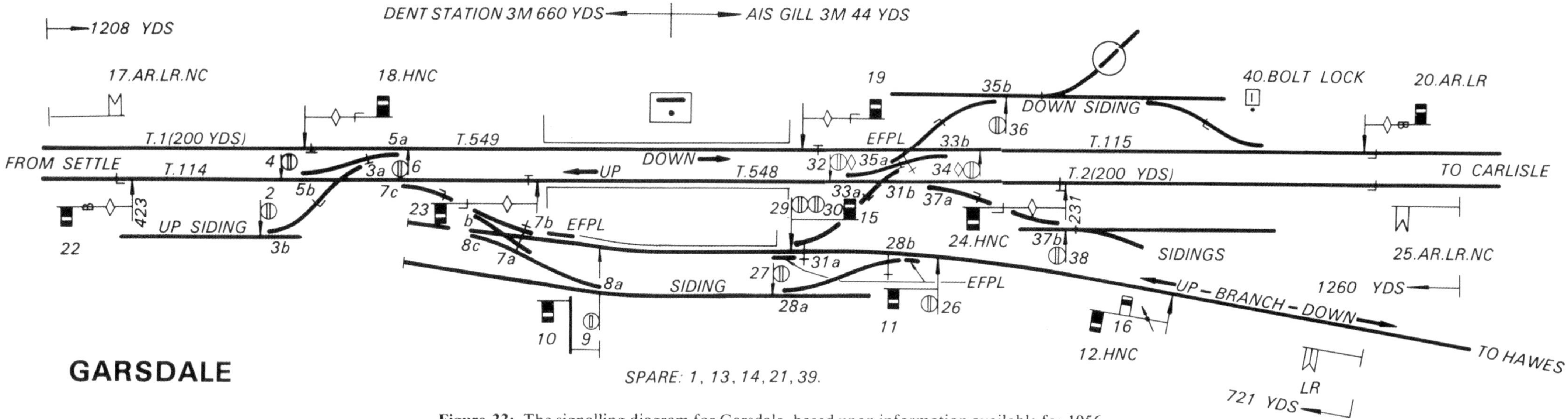

Figure 33 (signalling diagram)

├─→ 1208 YDS

DENT STATION 3M 660 YDS ──┤├── → AIS GILL 3M 44 YDS

17.AR.LR.NC   18.HNC   19   35b   DOWN SIDING   40.BOLT LOCK   20.AR.LR

T.1(200 YDS)   5a   T.549   DOWN →   EFPL   33b   36   T.115

FROM SETTLE   T.114   4   3a   6   ← UP   T.548   32   35a   34   T.2(200 YDS)   TO CARLISLE

2   5b   7c   33a   31b   37a   231

423   23   b   7b   EFPL   29   30   15   24.HNC   37b

22   UP SIDING   3b   8c   7a   28b   38   SIDINGS   25.AR.LR.NC

8a   SIDING   27   31a   EFPL   ← UP — BRANCH — DOWN →   1260 YDS →

10   9   28a   11   26   16   12.HNC

GARSDALE

SPARE: 1, 13, 14, 21, 39.

721 YDS ─┤ LR

Figure 33: The signalling diagram for Garsdale, based upon information available for 1956.

Plate 79: Garsdale signal box, pictured in 1963, was brought into use on 10th July 1910 when, as Hawes Junction, it superceded the North Junction and South Junction signal boxes (W & W Committee Minute No. 23950, 14/10/1909). It was larger than most of the other signal boxes on the line (30ft. x 10ft. 6in. x 8ft), contained a 40 lever tappet frame (6in. centres) and was situated on the 'down' platform. The box went out of primary use in 1983, but reopened for one day on 17th November 1983 to allow for diversionary working, following a mishap on the West Coast Main Line.

Plate 80: Hawes Junction and Garsdale Station, circa 1900. The 1872 report envisaged a small exchange station together with exchange sidings. The station opened in August 1876, facilities being housed in three stone buildings similar in style to waiting shelters used elsewhere. One of these, on the island platform, had a small ridge and furrow canopy added to give extra protection to the passengers. The signal in the foreground was the one replaced in 1942, as mentioned in **Plate 77**.

D. F. Tee Collection

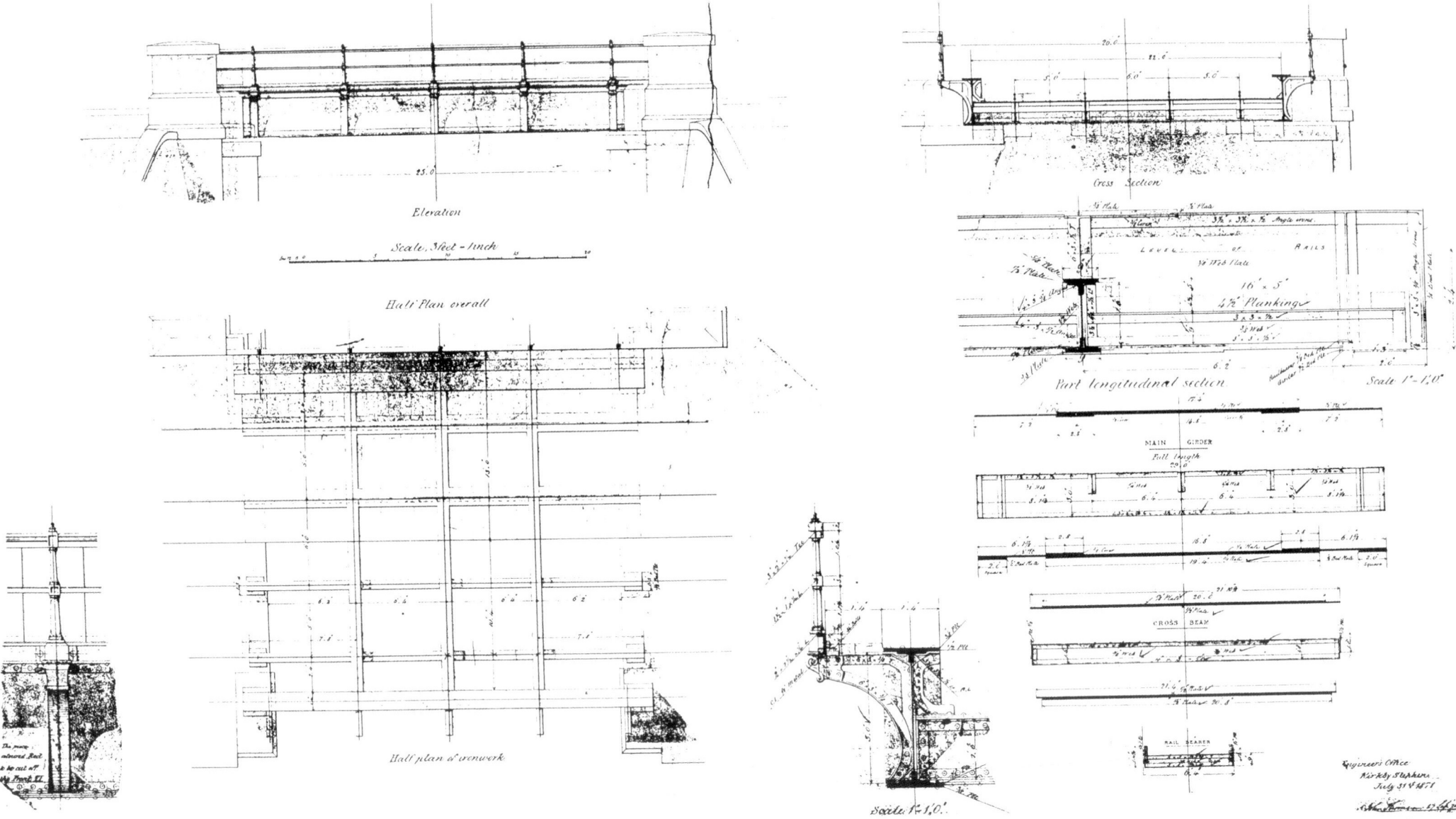

Figure 34: An official drawing of the original bridge (No. 115) which crossed the 'Coal Road' at Hawes Junction, and pictured to the left of **Plate 81**. The structure was of a type to be found elsewhere on the line (cf. Kirkby Stephen). The decorative parapet railings were originally hidden from view by wooden panelling. Due to the introduction of Compound engines in 1902, the Way and Works Committee gave authority to strengthen numerous underbridges and this was one of them. Although most bridges were altered during 1902/03, work at this bridge was not carried out until 1910 (W & W Committee Minute No. 24416) when reconstruction resulted in the removal of existing wrought-iron cross-girders and rail bearers, and the slewing and raising of the outer girders. This, and installation of new steelwork, was carried out by the Leeds firm of John Butler and Company at a cost of £503 15s. 6d. (£503. 77½). It is worth commenting that the contract had to be completed within three months of acceptance of the tender. £12 5s. 0d. (£12. 25) was deducted from the total cost of reconstruction by way of credit for recovered wrought-iron, i.e. 7 tons at 35s. (£1.75) per ton.

Plate 82: Hawes Junction and Garsdale, circa 1905. Hawes Junction North signal box can be seen beyond the platform. This was renewed in 1891 and abolished following the opening of the 1910 Hawes Junction box, located immediately to the right of the 'down' platform waiting-room. The small awnings, seen on the island platform building in **Plate 80**, have been extended to surround both buildings.

Plate 83: A view of Garsdale, looking north. A well-known feature at Garsdale was the engine turntable with its protective stockade of old sleepers. The lie by between the turntable and the 'down' main held 43 wagons, and at one time was controlled by a small ground frame situated near the end of Moorcock Viaduct. It is believed that the frame was brought into use in 1917. The siding to the right of the wagon is the 1908 addition. The Hawes branch disappears to the right.

BR/OPC

HAWES JOINT

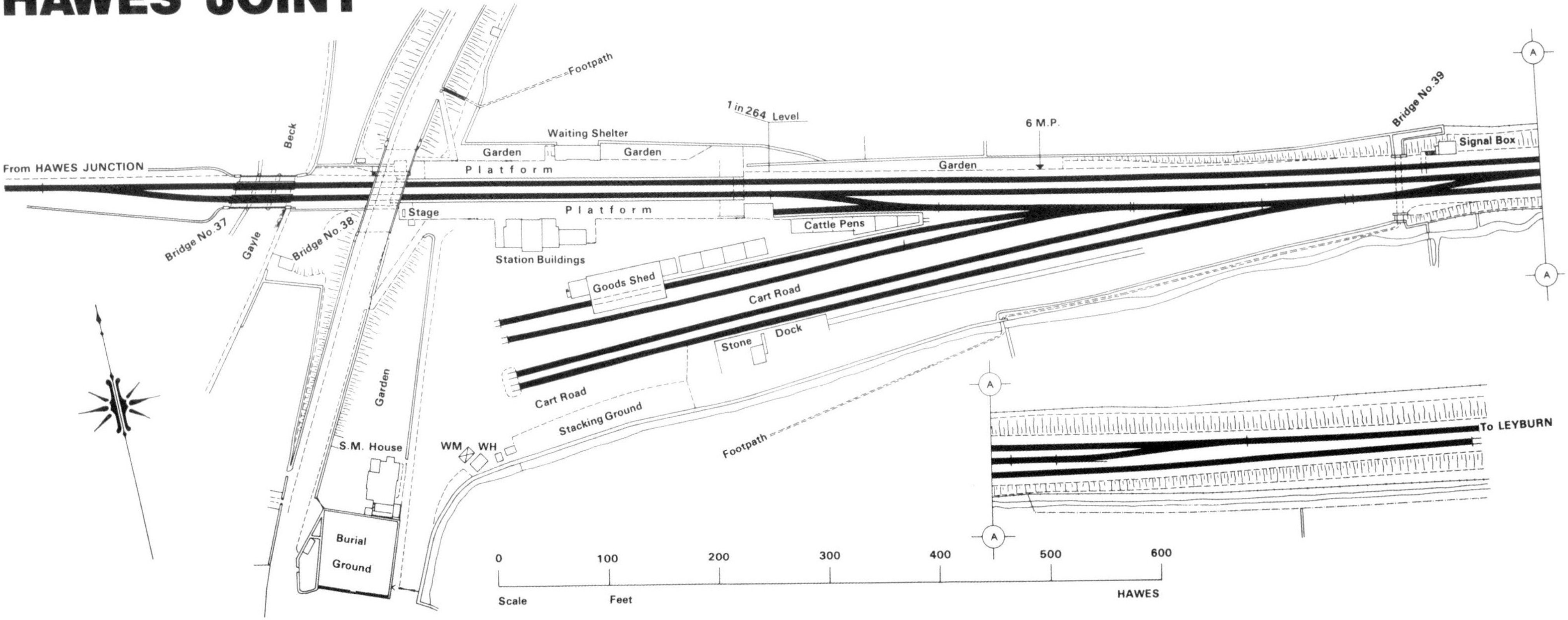

[Track layout diagram with labels:]

From HAWES JUNCTION

Beck · Footpath · Waiting Shelter · Garden · Garden · Platform · 1 in 264 Level · 6 M.P. · Garden · Bridge No.39 · Signal Box

Gayle · Bridge No. 37 · Bridge No. 38 · Stage · Platform · Cattle Pens · Station Buildings · Goods Shed · Cart Road · Stone · Dock · Cart Road · Stacking Ground

Garden · S.M. House · WM · WH · Footpath · To LEYBURN

Burial Ground

Scale · Feet · 0 · 100 · 200 · 300 · 400 · 500 · 600 · HAWES

Figure 35: The track layout of Hawes Joint Station, based upon information from 1913 and 1915 Midland Railway surveys. Work on the branch from Hawes Junction to Hawes Station was delayed until most of the main line had been completed, and so the Midland section of the branch did not open until 1878. From the beginning, Hawes had two signal boxes, Hawes East with 12 levers (1 spare), and Hawes West or Station with 8 levers (2 spare). Both were brought into use on 20th June 1878 for connection with the North Eastern's Wensleydale branch. This situation lasted until 1900, when a new box at Hawes East was brought into use containing a 20 lever Midland tumbler frame (W & W Committee Minute No. 18026, 6/7/1900). In 1907 the name of East box was changed to Hawes Station, and Hawes West was superseded by a lever frame at the end of the station platform. All signalling equipment was maintained by the North Eastern Railway (later LNER).

Plate 84: Hawes Station, in 1984. After several years of inactivity, Hawes Station was refurbished and opened as a tourist information centre. The yard became an extensive car-park. To the right is the goods shed; it was proposed in 1872 that Hawes should have a shed for four wagons, and a cattle dock for eight wagons. The station main building to the left is of the No. 3 (small) type. Here is the only example where a small building was paired with a goods shed.

Plate 85: Mossdale Head Tunnel (258 miles 66 chains) was the only tunnel on the Midland branch to Hawes. It was built entirely of stone for 245yds. and took two years to construct (1873 to 1875).

D. Ibbotson

Plate 86: Appersett Viaduct (261 miles 26 chains) was one of the two viaducts on the branch. The five openings varied in span between 42ft. 6in. and 45ft. The entire structure was in stone. Widdale Beck passed 56ft. beneath the centre arch on its way to the River Ure. A similar four-arch structure stood over Mossdale Gill (259 miles 17 chains).

D. Jenkinson

Plate 87: The Midland & NER Joint Station at Hawes, looking towards Hawes Junction. It is interesting to note that the three-arch public overbridge at the west end of the platforms carried an NER bridge numberplate (No. 38), suggesting that the NER were responsible for maintenance. The Hawes West lever frame was on the platform adjacent to the left-hand pier of the bridge.

N. Wilkinson Collection

Plate 88: A view of Hawes Joint Station, looking east. In the distance can be seen the Hawes Station signal box (previously East box) and the line to Leyburn. Note the position of the cattle dock; this was later extended along the platform fence. Passenger services to Northallerton terminated on 26th April 1954 but goods were carried until 1964. The branch to Garsdale closed completely on 16th March 1959.

Plate 89: Moorcock Viaduct (257 miles 5 chains). Dandry Mire was the site of Moorcock Viaduct, which was created following problems encountered trying to produce the originally planned embankment. For months, earth was tipped, but sank into the moss. Finally, in 1871, the seat of the embankment was drained and a trench was cut into the peat to find solid bottom for the foundation of a viaduct. The resulting 227 yard long curved structure, contained twelve openings varying from 44ft. 3in. to 45ft. The fourth and eighth piers of this all-stone structure were strengthened.

D. F. Tee Collection

Plate 90: Moorcock Road Bridge on 21st October 1984 (257 miles 19 chains) showing the west face. This impressive 39ft. 6in. skew arch carried the railway over the Hawes to Sedbergh road. Once again we see an example of the arch-relieved wing walls in this all-stone structure built in 1872.

Plate 91: Moorcock Road Company houses, pictured in 1970, a row of six cottages built to house Company employees. Note the added protection of the slates covering the gable end and the front of the first cottage.

D. F. Tee

Plate 92: Ex-LMS 'Black Five' No. 5407 and 'Jubilee' No. 5690 *Leander* with the 'Cumbrian Mountain Pullman' have just crossed the Moorcock Viaduct, and are pictured on their way north to Carlisle on 29th May 1982.

M. S. Welch

Plate 93: Moorcock Tunnel (No. 119) south end, on 15th October 1959 (257 miles 41 chains). The comparatively short tunnel, 98yds., constructed on a slight curve, with stone side walls, wings and arch, was cut through boulder clay. Again, note the namebord.

BR/OPC

Plate 94: The north end of Moorcock Tunnel on 21st October 1984. Having left this end of the tunnel the line climbs steadily over Lunds Viaduct (No. 121) – (257 miles 56 chains) – also featured in **Plate 95**.

Plate 95: Lunds, looking north, on 1st May 1966. Again we feature a train diverted from the West Coast Main Line, this time the 11.00 Glasgow to Euston express headed by Brush type 4, No. D1616, as it crosses Lunds Viaduct. This all-stone viaduct is 103yds. long and stands 63ft. above the valley. Each of the five arches has a span of 45ft.

M. S. Welch

Plate 96: Grisedale Crossing (No. 122A) on 21st October 1984 (257 miles 69 chains). Unique on the line is this plate-girder footbridge of 1936. This replaced a timber structure which was originally provided in 1886.

Plate 97 (left): Shotlock Hill Tunnel, photographed in 1938. The need for a tunnel at this location can be questioned on examining the shallowness of the hillside through which the tunnel passes. This 106 yard long tunnel was cut through boulder clay and took two years to construct. Stone was used throughout.

N. Wilkinson

Plate 98 (right): The south end of Shotlock Hill Tunnel on 21st October 1984. Somewhat typical of Midland Railway practice was the method of surface water drainage from above the tunnel, well illustrated here.

Plate 99: A Class 40, No. 40008, heads a northbound freight and leaves the north end of Shotlock Hill Tunnel on 15th June 1978.

M. S. Welch

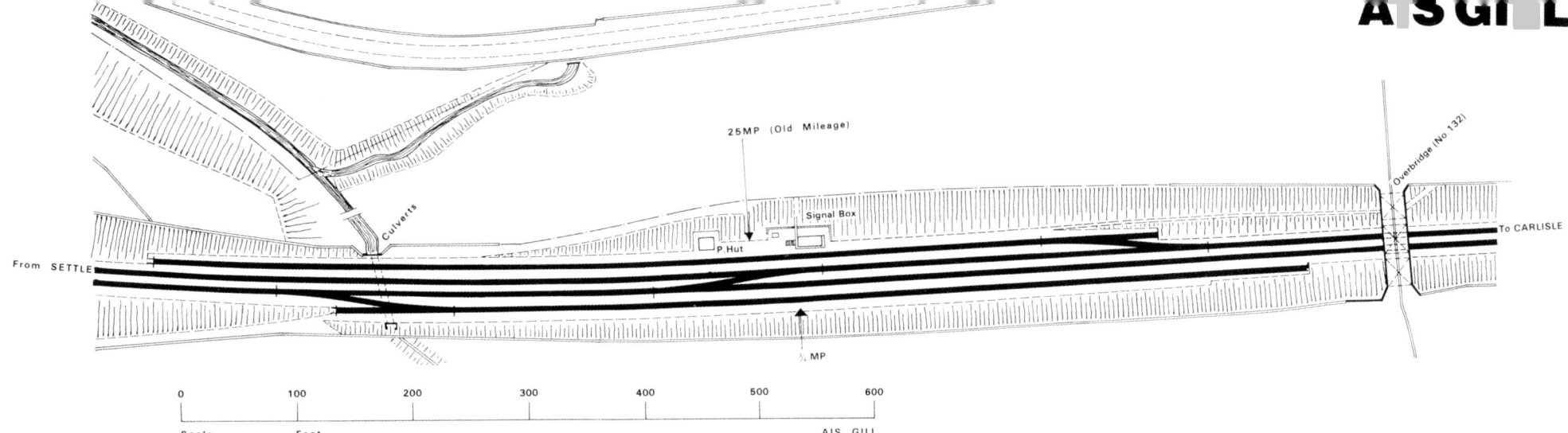

25MP (Old Mileage)

Overbridge (No 132)

Culverts

Signal Box

P. Hut

To CARLISLE

From SETTLE

½ MP

| 0 | 100 | 200 | 300 | 400 | 500 | 600 |

Scale   Feet

AIS GILL

Figure 36: The track layout at Ais Gill, based upon information from a Midland Railway survey of 1913 and an LMS survey of 1938.

Plate 100: The summit of the line at 1,169ft., Ais Gill, is reached at 259 miles 57 chains where lie by sidings were provided for the refuge of slower trains. On 29th July 1965, Class 5 4-6-0, No. 45228, heads a southbound freight over Ais Gill Summit and passes the 'down' 'Waverley'.

M. S. Welch

Figure 37: The signalling diagram for Ais Gill, based upon information available for 1963.

Plate 102 (above): Ais Gill, in May 1961. A Kingmoor engine, No. 48536, heads a northbound freight, the 10.05 Brindle Heath to Kingmoor. The nameboard to the left proclaims 'Ais Gill Summit 1,169ft. above sea level', but the Midland Railway map at the front of the book indicates 1,166ft.

J. M. Hammond

Plate 101 (left): Ais Gill, in 1963. No. 44671 on a southbound freight passes Ais Gill signal box and works hard to breast the summit. The signal box was brought into use on 26th April 1890 replacing an earlier structure at a cost of £250 (W & W Committee Minute No. 17517, 3/11/1889). It was of wood construction, 16ft 6in. x 11ft. 6in. x 8ft., contained a 16 lever tumbler frame, closed on 28th January 1981 and subsequently was removed for preservation. Note the walkway from the back of the box to the embankment.

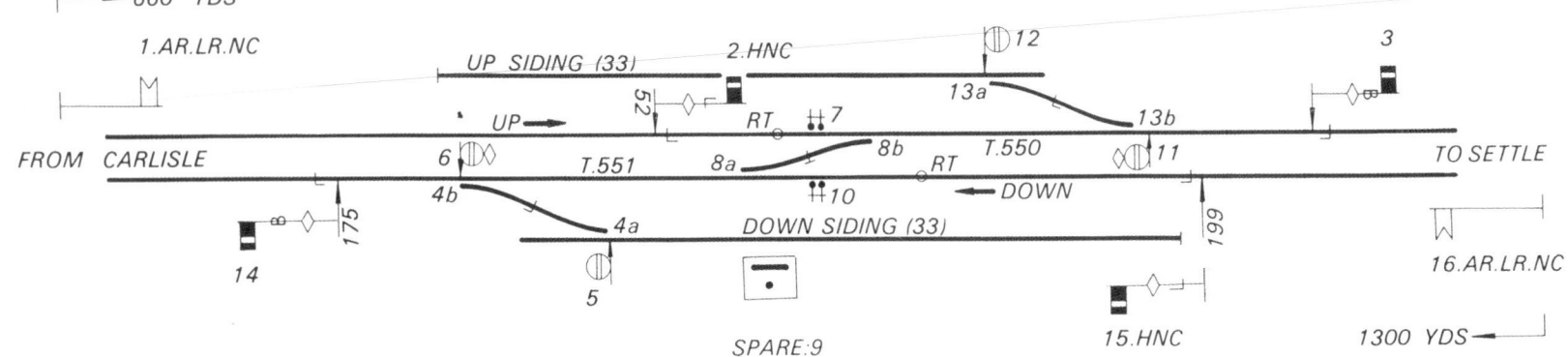

AIS GILL

Plate 103: The Company cottages near Ais Gill, pictured on 21st October 1984. These are built with a continuous roofline instead of the small dormers to the upstairs rooms.

Plate 104: The east face of the Ais Gill Viaduct (No. 137) — 260 miles 53 chains — viewed from the road below on 21st October 1984. The train standing on the viaduct is the London Midland Regional Civil Engineer's Viaduct Inspection Unit, and is hauled by Class 25 diesel No. 25060.

Plate 105: Ais Gill Viaduct pictured in 1963. A southbound freight, with Class 5, No. 44900, in charge, climbs towards the summit of the line over the 87 yard long four-arch structure. Each of the four stone-built spans is 45ft., and it stands 75ft. above the valley floor.

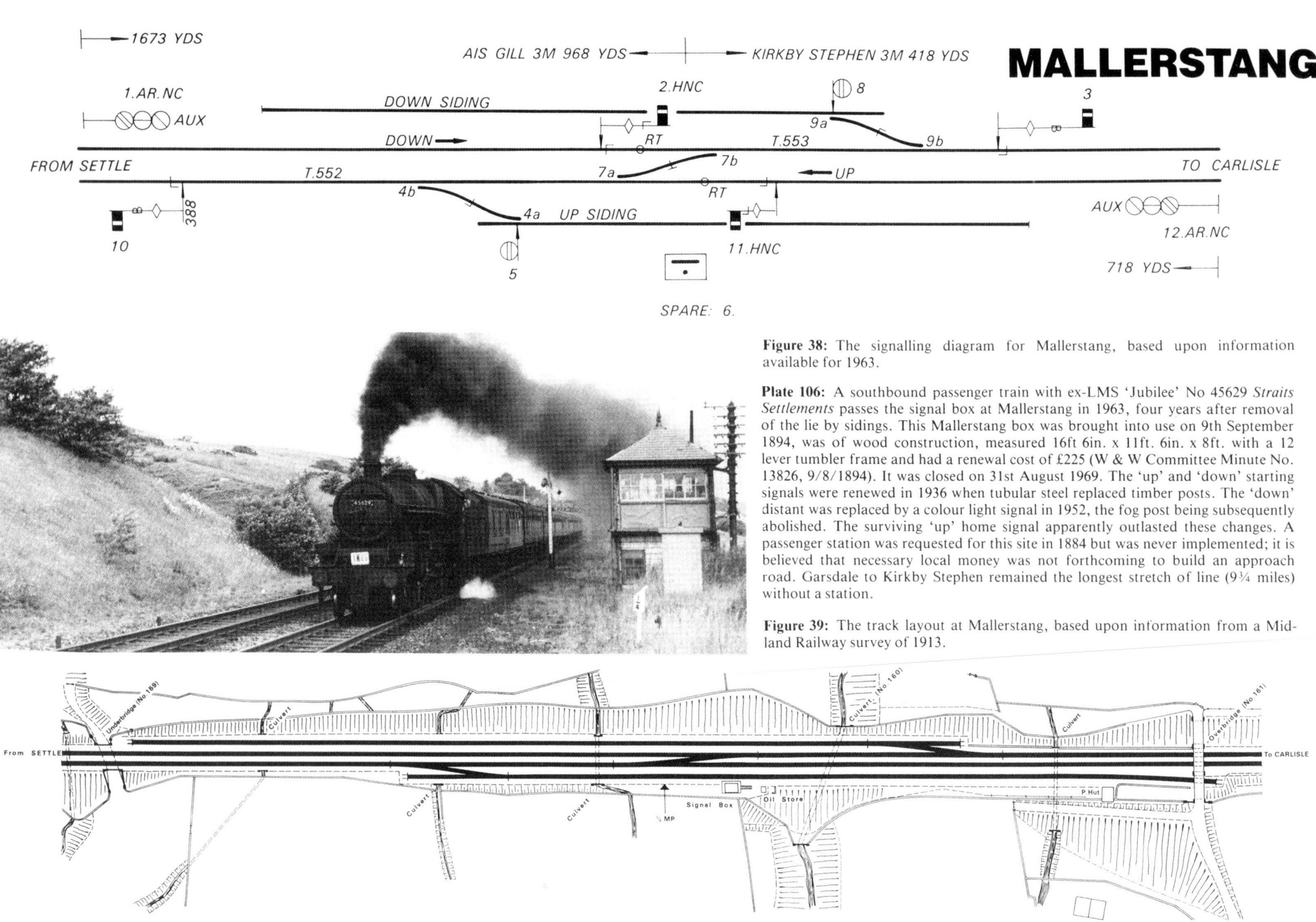

MALLERSTANG

1673 YDS

AIS GILL 3M 968 YDS ← → KIRKBY STEPHEN 3M 418 YDS

1.AR.NC

DOWN SIDING

2.HNC

8

3

AUX

DOWN →

RT

T.553

9a

9b

FROM SETTLE

T.552

7a

7b

← UP

TO CARLISLE

RT

388

4b

4a   UP SIDING

AUX

12.AR.NC

10

11.HNC

718 YDS →

5

SPARE: 6.

Figure 38: The signalling diagram for Mallerstang, based upon information available for 1963.

Plate 106: A southbound passenger train with ex-LMS 'Jubilee' No 45629 *Straits Settlements* passes the signal box at Mallerstang in 1963, four years after removal of the lie by sidings. This Mallerstang box was brought into use on 9th September 1894, was of wood construction, measured 16ft 6in. x 11ft. 6in. x 8ft. with a 12 lever tumbler frame and had a renewal cost of £225 (W & W Committee Minute No. 13826, 9/8/1894). It was closed on 31st August 1969. The 'up' and 'down' starting signals were renewed in 1936 when tubular steel replaced timber posts. The 'down' distant was replaced by a colour light signal in 1952, the fog post being subsequently abolished. The surviving 'up' home signal apparently outlasted these changes. A passenger station was requested for this site in 1884 but was never implemented; it is believed that necessary local money was not forthcoming to build an approach road. Garsdale to Kirkby Stephen remained the longest stretch of line (9¾ miles) without a station.

Figure 39: The track layout at Mallerstang, based upon information from a Midland Railway survey of 1913.

Plate 108 (above): An earlier view of the south entrance to Birkett Tunnel; again notice the position of the tunnel nameboard. This 424 yard long tunnel was constructed with a brick arch ring throughout.

D. Ibbotson

Plate 107: The south end of Birkett Tunnel (No. 168) — 264 miles 32 chains — pictured on 26th August 1978. A double-headed freight train with diesel locomotives Nos. 40087 and 20135 leaves the tunnel. The tunnel portal is inscribed 'MR' above each pilaster and '1875' above the keystone.

M. S. Welch

Plate 109 (left): This view shows the north end of Birkett Tunnel, on 21st October 1984. The tunnel was driven through a geological phenomena in which shale, mountain limestone, magnesium limestone, slate, grit, iron, coal and lead ore were encountered.

Plate 110 (right): Near the north end of Birkett Tunnel is bridge No. 169 (264 miles 46 chains) called Fothergill Syphon by the Engineering Department, or Fothergill Sike by the Estate Agent; a 7ft. span bridge with relieving arches in the spandrel wall.

Plate 111: Kirkby Stephen Station, circa 1905, is the second station we have seen with the large type of building, a view epitomising the Midand Railway at its best. Note the angled nameboard; all the stations on the line had these until the outbreak of World War II. An unusual sight is the two rows of what appear to be gas lamps; these are actually illuminated by oil. This station has undergone a number of name changes. In 1900 'and Ravenstonedale' was added, although it reverted to Kirkby Stephen in January 1935 only to have the suffix 'West' added in June 1953 when the ex-LNER station became 'East'. However, normality returned in May 1968 when the simple title was reinstated until passenger services were withdrawn in May 1970. It had been an unstaffed halt for some three years.

Lens of Sutton

KIRKBY STEPHEN

Figure 40: The track layout for Kirkby Stephen, based upon information from Midland Railway surveys of 1911 and 1912.

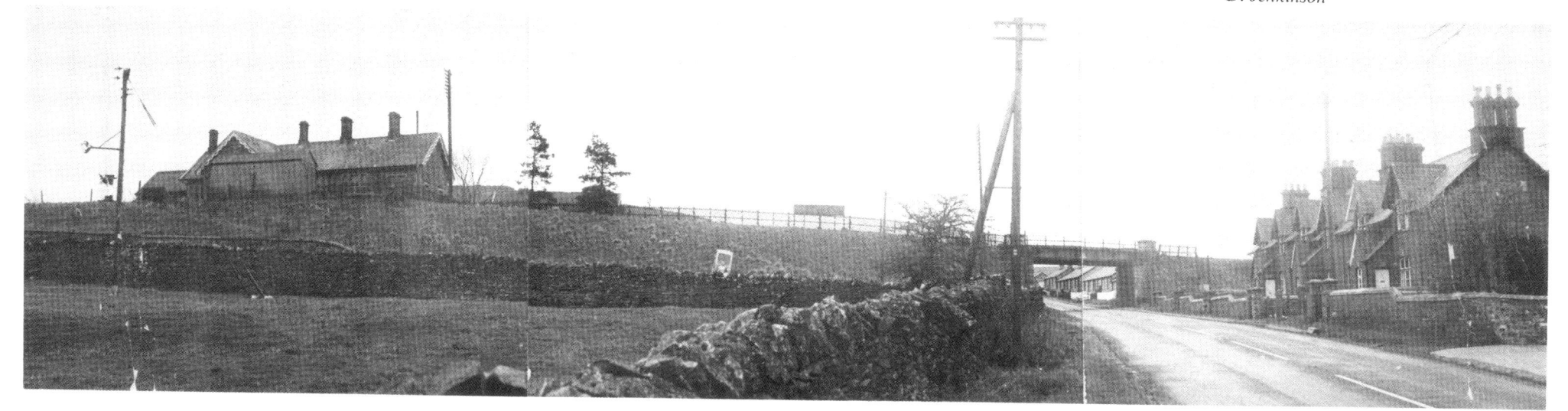

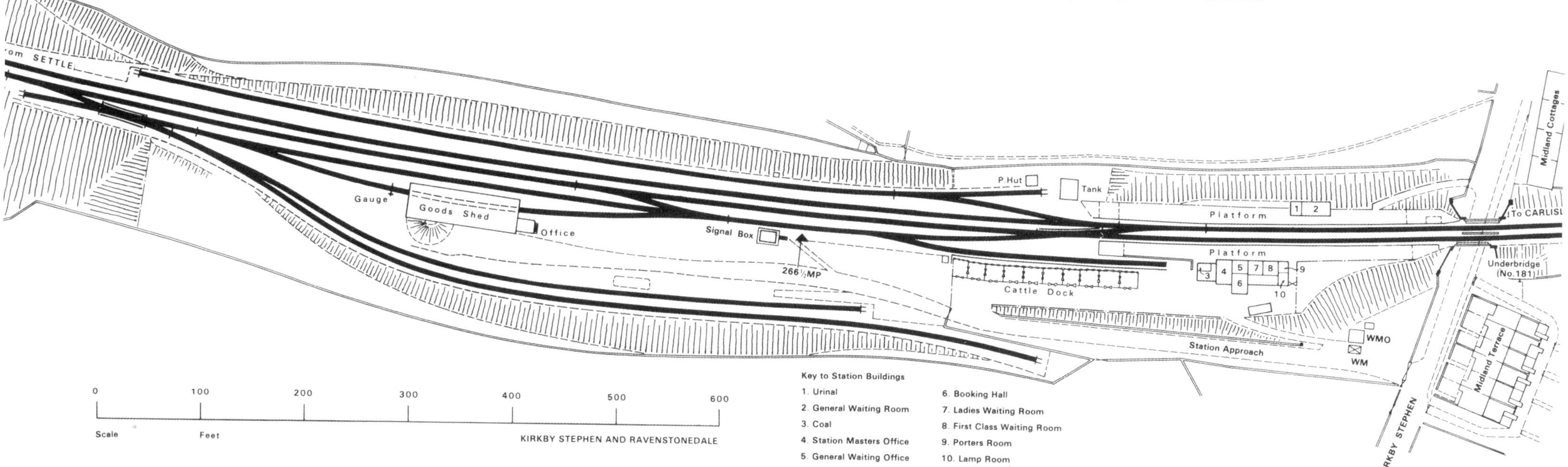
From SETTLE
Gauge
Goods Shed
Office
Signal Box
266½MP
P.Hut
Tank
Platform
Platform
Cattle Dock
Station Approach
WMO
WM
To CARLISLE
Underbridge (No.181)
Midland Cottages
Midland Terrace
From KIRKBY STEPHEN
0
100
200
300
400
500
600
Scale
Feet
KIRKBY STEPHEN AND RAVENSTONEDALE
Key to Station Buildings
1. Urinal
2. General Waiting Room
3. Coal
4. Station Masters Office
5. General Waiting Office
6. Booking Hall
7. Ladies Waiting Room
8. First Class Waiting Room
9. Porters Room
10. Lamp Room

Plate 112: A panoramic view of the eastern side of Kirkby Stephen station in 1970. The station approach is behind the wall which runs from right to left. The row of houses to the right is called Midland Terrace, whilst those to be seen beyond the bridge are Midland Cottages. The stationmaster occupied a house just off the picture, on the right.

D. Jenkinson

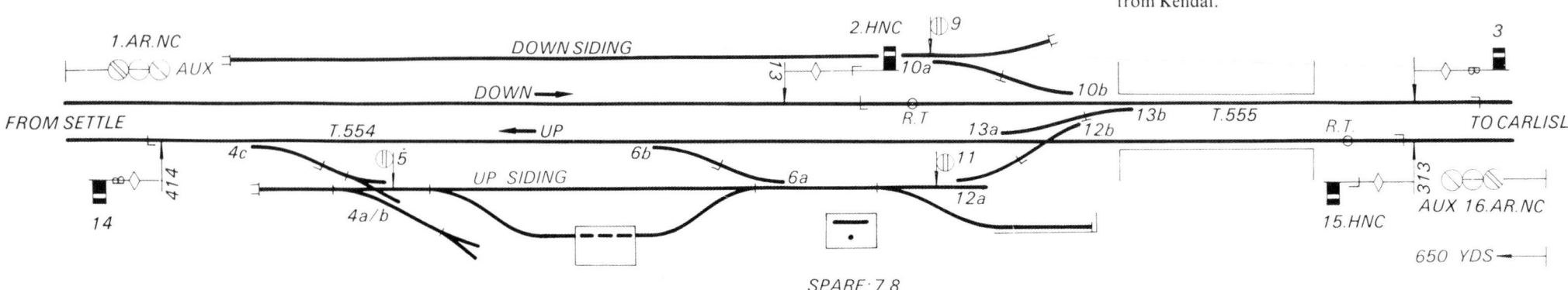

Plate 113: A Class 47 diesel, No. 47478, heads a Glasgow to Nottingham express through Kirkby Stephen on 26th August 1981.

M. S. Welch

Figure 41: The signalling diagram for Kirkby Stephen, based upon information available for 1963.

Plate 114: Kirkby Stephen West signal box in 1972, brought into use on 6th May 1894. Of wood construction, it measured 15ft. x 11ft. 6in. x 8ft., had a 16 lever tumbler frame, and a renewal cost of £223 (W & W Committee Minute No. 13589, 6/4/1894). This box was formally known as Kirkby Stephen (Midland) as far as the Signalling Department was concerned, as Kirkby Stephen West was also a signal box at the west end of Kirkby Stephen (East) Station on the ex-NER line. It was erroneously referred to as 'West' because of the station siting in relation to the village; thus the confusion. This structure was closed on 27th October 1974 and replaced by a BR standard type signal box containing a 20 lever standard 1943 pattern frame, which had been recovered from Kendal.

KIRKBY STEPHEN

MALLERSTANG 3M 418 YDS ←—|—→ CROSBY GARRETT 3M 770 YDS

Plate 115: A view, looking south, of Kirkby Stephen on 10th June 1967, from the end of the 'down' platform. The configuration of the signal box and goods shed can be seen. A five wagon shed was proposed in the 1872 report together with a cattle dock for ten wagons; much movement of livestock was obviously anticipated. Goods facilities ceased on 28th September 1964. The comparison between MR and BR notices is of interest.

D. F. Tee

Plate 116: Again, looking south, another view of Kirkby Stephen, on 10th June 1967. Although the station was still open to the public, part of the building had been taken over by the Engineers' Department, who had caused a small porch to be erected (under the smaller gable) protecting the entrance to what was originally a 1st class waiting-room. Kirkby Stephen was the only station on the line to boast the luxury of a 1st class waiting-room.

D. F. Tee

Plate 117: Looking south, towards Kirkby Stephen, on 30th July 1966, as a Class 9F, No. 92075, climbs towards the summit with an 'up' anhydrite train from Long Meg. Note the weigh office on the road approach to the station and, to the right, a number of single-storey cottages for workers.

M. S. Welch

Plate 118: Kirkby Stephen, looking north from the 'down' platform, in May 1962. Bridge No. 181 (266 miles 50 chains) which carried the railway over Kirkby Stephen Road was similar to the one detailed at Garsdale **(Figure 34)** and was strengthened in 1903 with the addition of a steel centre girder. Note the timber panelling still intact over the parapet railings. In the foreground is a Midland swan-necked water column.

D. Jenkinson

Plate 119: The east face of Smardale Viaduct (No. 193) in October 1984 (268 miles 54 chains). This graceful viaduct crossed Scandal (or Smardale) Beck and, at 130ft., was the tallest viaduct on the line. Its 237yds. was constructed entirely of grey limestone. There are twelve openings, each of 45ft. span, and the fourth and tenth piers are strengthened king piers. This viaduct marked the end of Contract No. 2. After 5 years of construction, Mrs Agnes Crossley, wife of the Engineer, laid the last stone, on 8th June 1875.

Plate 120: Over Smardale Viaduct, a Stanier Class 8F 2-8-0, No. 48612, heads south with an anhydrite train, the 09.20 Long Meg to Widnes, on 16th March 1961. The ruling grade of 1 in 100 commences at the north end of the viaduct, marking a steepening of the Eden Valley contours that continues to the summit at Ais Gill. The permanent way cabin, identified throughout the book as platelayers' huts (P. Hut) is of a style repeated frequently along the route.

J. M. Hammond

Plate 121: The southern most opening of Smardale Viaduct crossed the single track line from Kirkby Stephen (East) to Tebay, a section of the North Eastern Railway. An Ivatt Class 4 2-6-0 locomotive, No. 43099, makes its way through the encroaching trees in August 1961 with a summer Saturdays only Newcastle to Blackpool service, via Stainmoor. This service had commenced in 1932 and, by this time, represented the only passenger working on the branch, local services having been withdrawn towards the end of 1952.

J. M. Hammond

CROSBY GARRETT

Plate 122: The 181 yard long Crosby Garrett Tunnel (No. 195, 269 miles 3 chains) cut through the grit-stone, limestone and flint of Crosby Garrett fell, was constructed with stone side walls and faces with a brick arch. Ex-LMS 'Jubilee' class 5XP, No. 45568, *Western Australia*, with the 'up' 'Waverley' in August 1961, has the benefit of a short section of level track before attacking the main ascent to the summit at Ais Gill, some 19 miles to the south.

J. M. Hammond

Plate 123: Crosby Garrett village, as seen from the east (from an old postcard) dominated by the six-arch viaduct.

Plate 124: Pictured in October 1984, is the west face of Crosby Garrett Viaduct (No. 197, 269 miles 36 chains). Built of local limestone in 1871, the 110 yard long viaduct passes 55ft. above the village, and the 43ft. skew spans have brick arch rings.

Plate 125: This view from the north, of Crosby Garrett, taking in all the facilities provided at this location, illustrates well the Midland Railway and the Settle & Carlisle Line; even the wagons are lettered with pre-group company initials. However, the photograph was taken some years after the formation of the LMS Company. On the left is the goods shed for three wagons, a cattle dock for six wagons, then the station building sited near the platform end. For most of their length the platforms stood at the foot of the cutting, spanned by the three arch bridge. Incidentally, it was at the end of this bridge, on the hillside to the right, that it was at first planned to build the stationmaster's house. The signal box brought into use on 16th April 1899, was of wood construction, measured 16ft. 6in. x 11ft. 6in. x 8ft., and had a 20 lever tumbler frame, and a renewal cost of £250 (W & W Committee Minute No. 16760, 4/11/1898). Initial closure of the signal box took place on 12th April 1965, but it remained available for use until 1967. Note the weather vane on the telegraph post and the Midland signal box nameboard.

Weston Collection

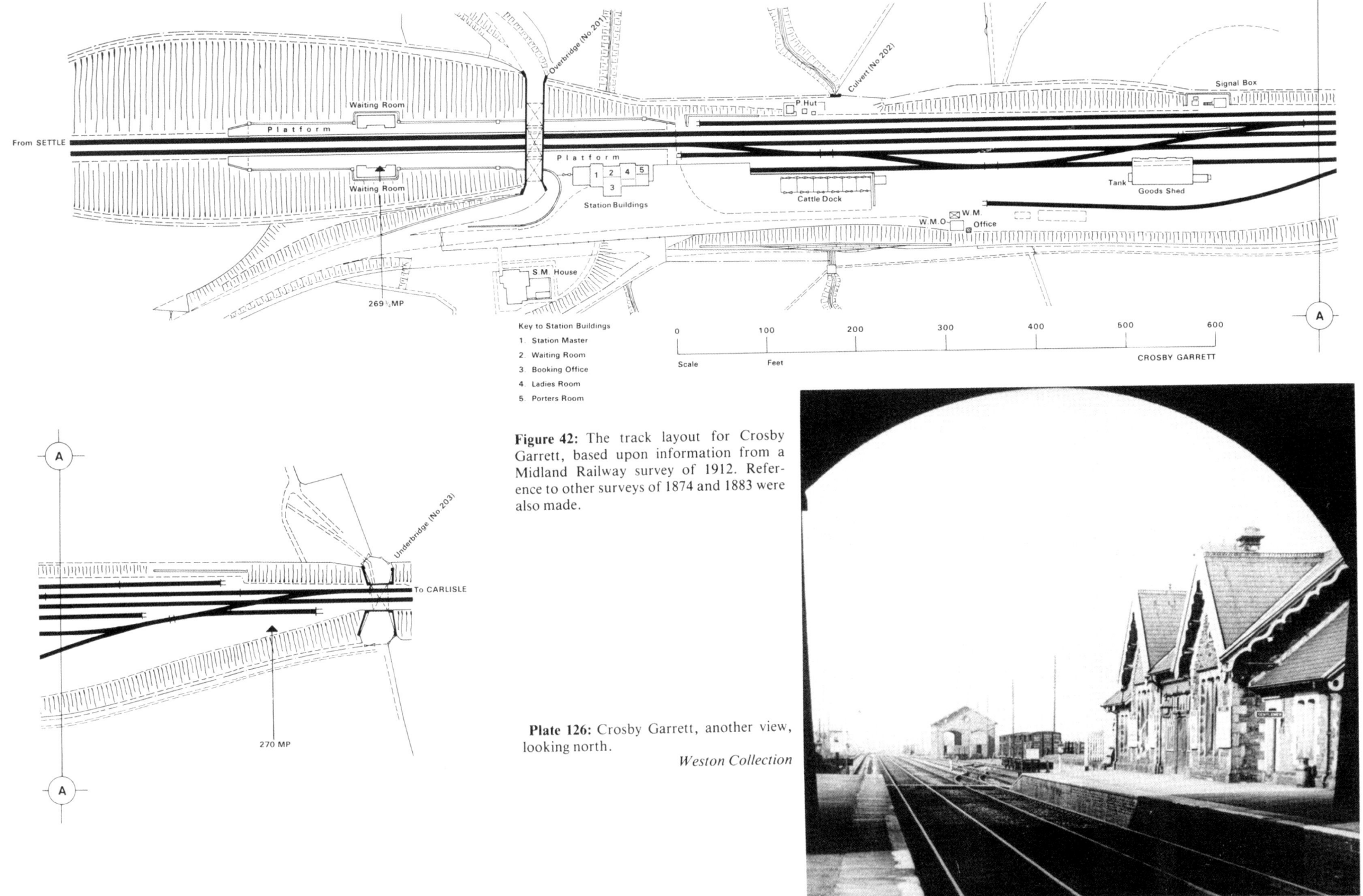

Figure 42: The track layout for Crosby Garrett, based upon information from a Midland Railway survey of 1912. Reference to other surveys of 1874 and 1883 were also made.

Plate 126: Crosby Garrett, another view, looking north.

Weston Collection

Key to Station Buildings

1. Station Master
2. Waiting Room
3. Booking Office
4. Ladies Room
5. Porters Room

CROSBY GARRETT

Plate 127: Crosby Garrett, at about the turn of the century. The stationmaster's house was built in a revised position to that mentioned in **Plate 125.** The main station building is of the No. 2 (medium) style, set near the platform end because of the siting of the passenger station along the 55 foot deep cutting. Unusually, a waiting shelter, set into the retaining wall, was provided on the same platform as the main building. The main line permanent way has by now been conventionally laid with outside keys, but sidings, etc. have retained their inside-keyed feature. The small four-wheeled permanent way trolley to the left, is of a type still to be found in use, with only minor modifications. The station nameboard, erected at an angle, looks to be of the painted or enamelled variety; this was later replaced by a much taller conventional nameboard with cast letters.

Plate 128: A view of Crosby Garrett in 1964. All traffic had ceased to use Crosby Garrett some eight years before this picture was taken and, by May 1964, the platforms had been graded and the waiting shelter on the 'up' side had been removed. For some reason, the 'down' side shelter had a reprieve. The bridge in the background was reconstructed in 1923, using recovered wrought-iron lattice girders to replace timber lattice girders. Behind this bridge the line can be seen crossing Crosby Garrett Viaduct and leading to the tunnel some 50 chains to the south.

D. Jenkinson

Figure 43: The signalling diagram for Crosby Garrett, based on information available for 1963.

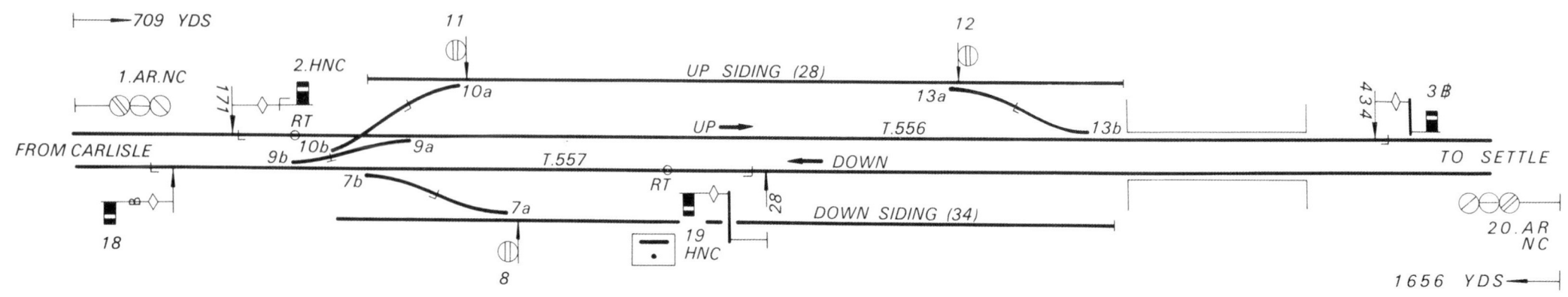

SPARE: 4,5,6,14,15,16,17

GRISEBURN BALLAST SIDINGS 1M 1738 YDS ◄── ──► *KIRKBY STEPHEN 3M 770 YDS*

CROSBY GARRETT

Plate 129: A view of Griseburn Viaduct (No. 214) — 271 miles 56 chains — showing the west face, in 1962. This seven-arch limestone structure marks the halfway point of the line. It was built between 1873 and 1875 to span the valley of Potts Beck, known by the Midland Railway cartographers as Helm Beck and by the Estate Agents as Waterhouses Beck. Stone is used for abutments, wings, piers and parapets, although that used to face the brick arches and the parapets is of red sandstone, giving a pleasant decorative effect. The viaduct is 142 yards long and 74ft. high.

D. Jenkinson

Figure 44: The signalling diagram for Griseburn Ballast Sidings, based upon information available for 1963.

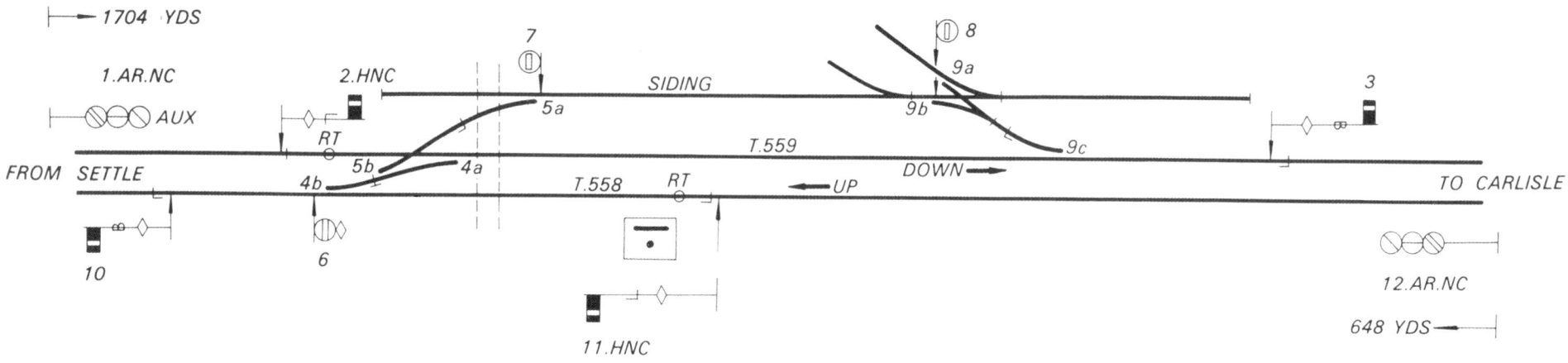

1704 YDS

1.AR.NC

2.HNC

7

8

9a

SIGNAL

9b

3

AUX

5a

RT

T.559

9c

FROM SETTLE

5b

4a

DOWN →

4b

T.558

RT

← UP

TO CARLISLE

10

6

11.HNC

12.AR.NC

648 YDS →

CROSBY GARRATT 1M 1738 YDS ——— | ——— ORMSIDE 2M 1628 YDS

GRISEBURN BALLAST SIDINGS

GRISEBURN BALLAST SIDINGS

Plate 130: Griseburn Ballast Sidings, looking south, in 1973. The signal box brought into use on 10th December 1905, was of wood construction, and measured 16ft. 6in. x 11ft. 6in. x 8ft. It had a 12 lever frame and a renewal cost of £250 (Way & Works Committee Minute No. 21440, 3/11/1905). Connections to the sidings were recovered in 1971, and the box closed on 28th January 1981.

Plate 131: Griseburn Ballast Sidings, looking north, in 1973. From the late 1880s until World War I, stone was quarried here for use as ballast on the railway. The sidings were provided as a stabling point for wagons of ballast, ready for use whenever necessary We are unable to confirm at what date the sidings ceased to be used for this purpose after the quarry was no longer in production, but the signal box remained in use as a block post.

Figure 45: The Griseburn Ballast Sidings track layout, based upon information from a Midland Railway survey of 1912.

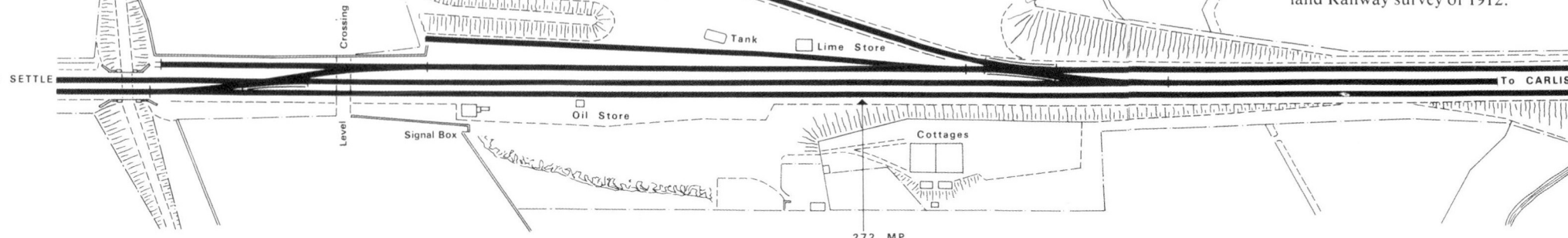

Quarry

Blacksmith Shop (Disused)

Tank   Lime Store

From SETTLE   To CARLISLE

Crossing

Level

Oil Store

Signal Box

Cottages

272 MP

0   100   200   300   400   500   600

ORMSIDE

Plate 132: Helm Tunnel (No. 223) — 273 miles 25 chains — 571yds. in length, was cut through red marl between the years 1870 and 1873. Stone side walls, invert and faces, and a brick arch were provided. The northern portal is illustrated here. Note the position of the nameboard, with 4in. cast letters on a 2ft. 9in. x 1ft. 9in. cast-iron plate, and mounted on recovered and machined sleepers with a finished size 11in. x 5in. In this instance the top of the plate stood 6ft. above ground level.

D. Ibbotson

Figure 46: The Ormside track layout, based upon information from a Midland Railway survey for 1912.

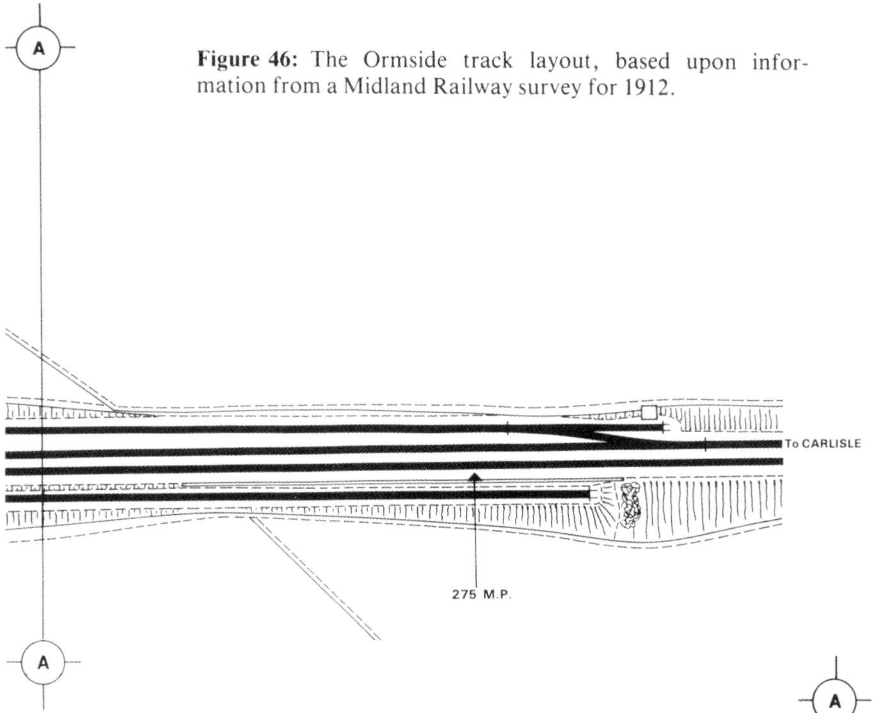

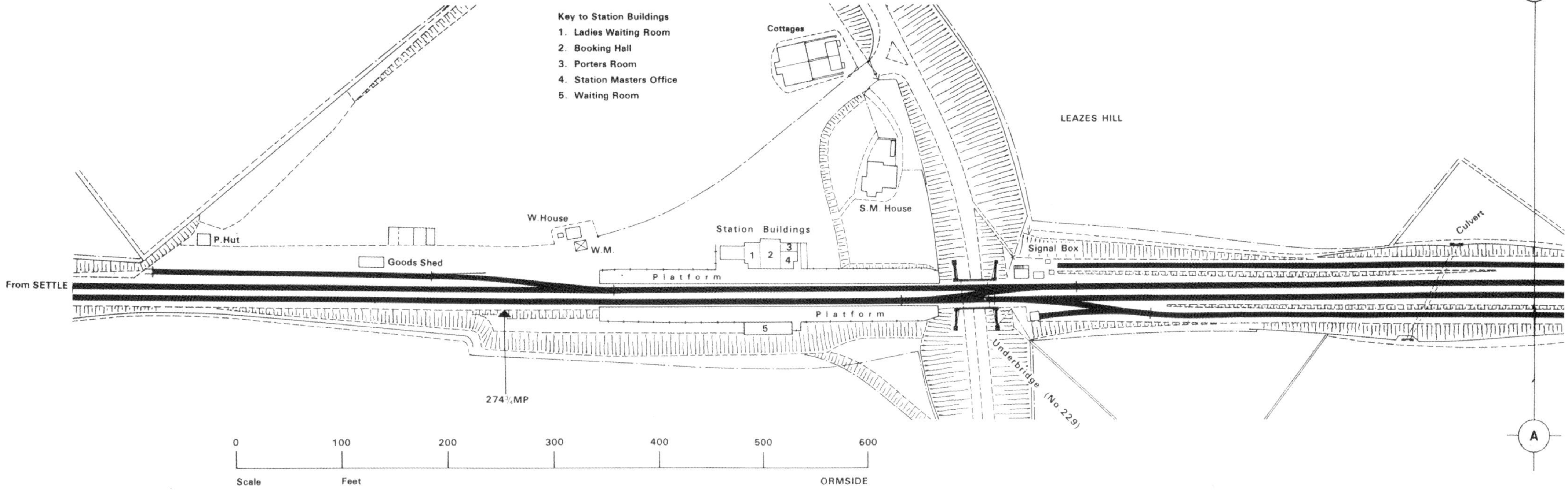

To CARLISLE

275 M.P.

Key to Station Buildings
1. Ladies Waiting Room
2. Booking Hall
3. Porters Room
4. Station Masters Office
5. Waiting Room

Cottages

LEAZES HILL

S.M. House

W.House

P.Hut

Goods Shed

W.M.

Station Buildings

Signal Box

Culvert

Platform

From SETTLE

Platform

Underbridge (No 229)

274¾ MP

| 0 | 100 | 200 | 300 | 400 | 500 | 600 |

Scale Feet

ORMSIDE

Plate 134: The station, stationmaster's house and workers' cottages at Ormside form a small community some distance from the village of Great Ormside. Goods facilities, which were minimal, were not decided upon until December 1876. All traffic to this station ceased in June 1952.

Lens of Sutton

Plate 133: A view of Ormside Station, looking north. Original proposals suggested a station at Asby, the next parish south of Ormside. This would have resulted in a passenger station being sited in the vicinity of Griseburn some three miles away. Later representation from local landowners resulted in the site being moved to this location. Again we have a No. 3 (small) building, looking very attractive with the contrasting light and dark stonework. We have been unable to obtain information to produce a signalling diagram, but the signal box brought into use in 1907, was of wood construction, measured 16ft. 6in. x 11ft. 6in. x 8ft., with a 16 lever tumbler frame and had a renewal cost of £250 (W & W Committee Minute No. 22118, 2/11/1906). The box closed on 8th March 1960, from which time, although signal arms were removed, the pointwork remained secured in the normal position. Official records imply that, from 1886, a frame of 10 levers was worked from the station.

D. F. Tee Collection

Plate 135: Ormside Viaduct (No. 231) — 275 miles 24 chains. At this point, the railway crosses the River Eden for the first time, and one pier of the viaduct stands in the river. The ten-arch, 200 yard long viaduct, with the third and the seventh piers reinforced, stands 90ft. above the river. The viaduct is made up of stone abutments, piers and parapets with brick arches, with 45ft. spans.

APPLEBY

Plate 136: Half a mile south of Appleby Station was the Appleby plant of the Express Dairy Company, and milk was shipped in tankers from this plant to Cricklewood for the benefit of the people of London. Connections were made with the railway during 1930/1 and extended in 1935. A ground frame (Appleby West ground frame) consisting of five levers, was released from Appleby West signal box, and closed on 11th January 1970. The 'up' 'Thames Clyde Express', hauled by 'Peak' class diesel locomotive No. D29, passes the dairy siding on 29th July 1965.

M. S. Welch

Figure 47: The signalling diagram for Appleby West, based upon information available for 1965.

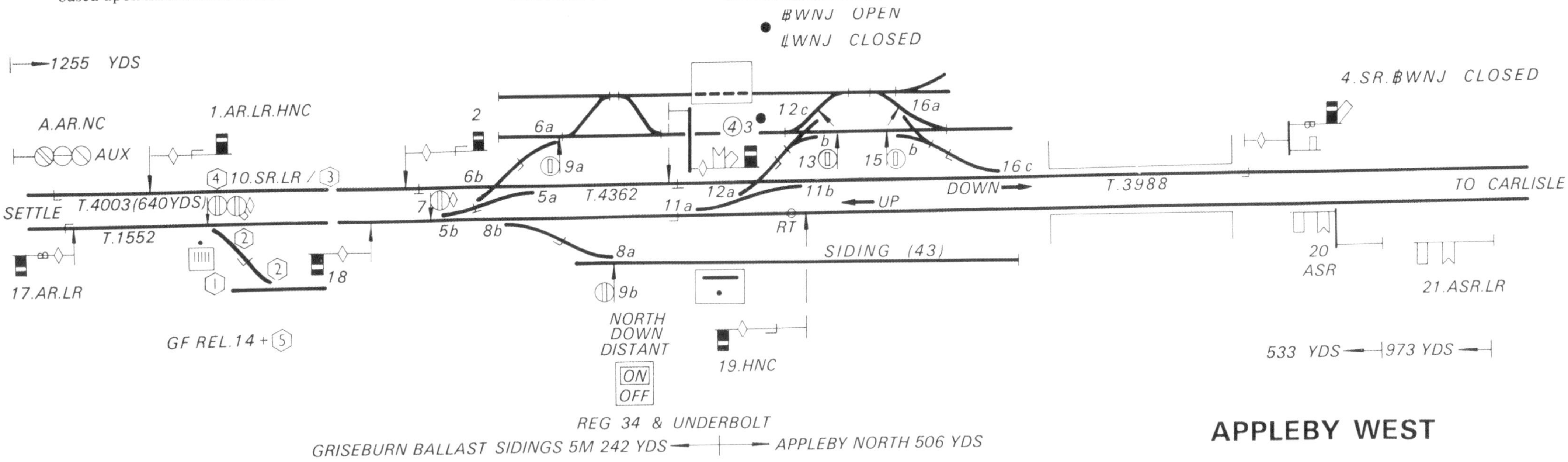

APPLEBY WEST

Figure 48a: This details the track layout at Appleby in three parts, **Figures 48a, 48b & 48c**, and is based upon information from an LMS survey of 1946, with other information from Midland Railway surveys for 1911 and 1912.

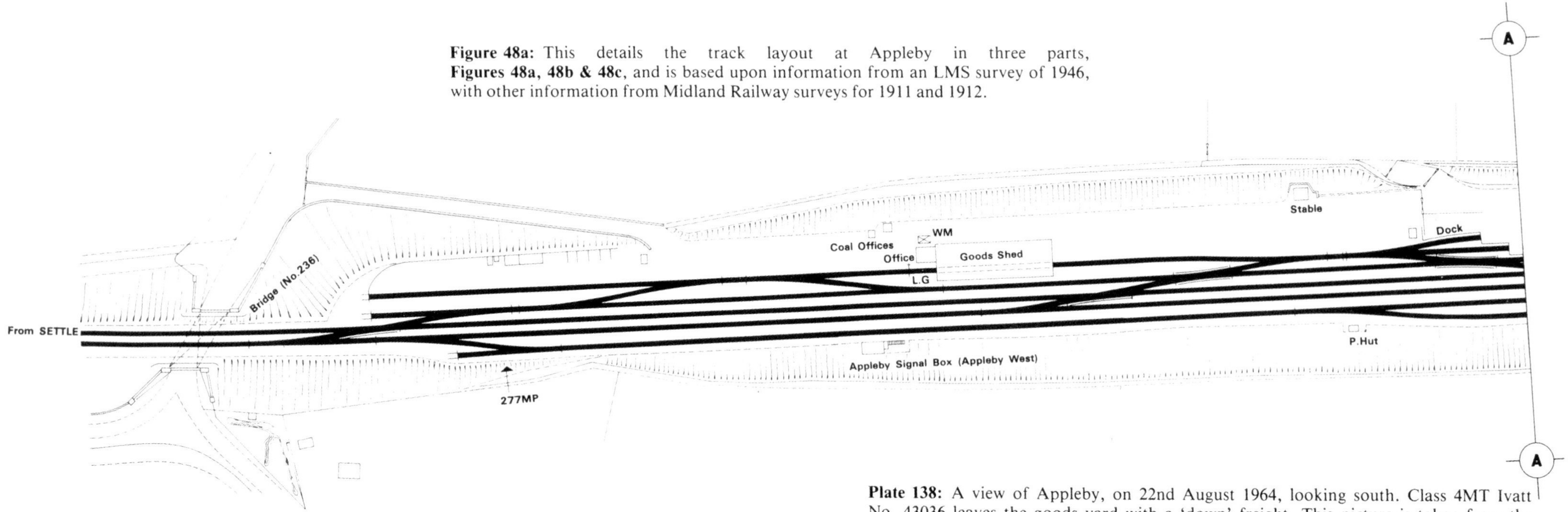

Plate 137: Appleby West signal box in 1973. Brought into use in 1890, it was of wood construction, measured 22ft. x 11ft. 6in. x 12ft., and contained a 21 lever Midland tumbler frame (later 22 levers for the creamery ground frame release). The box closed on 14th October 1973. Originally called 'Appleby' signal box, the name changed to 'Appleby Station' for a period between 1937 and 1945, when it became 'Appleby West'.

P. Baughan

Plate 138: A view of Appleby, on 22nd August 1964, looking south. Class 4MT Ivatt No. 43036 leaves the goods yard with a 'down' freight. This picture is taken from the footbridge and clearly shows the southern approaches to the station. In the distance can be seen the outline of the Express Dairy Company Creamery. On the left, hidden by trees, is the water tank. The goods shed for five wagons can be seen beyond the train, and across the line from this is Appleby West signal box. In the goods yard extensive facilities were provided for the movement of livestock with a 10 wagon cattle dock. A small stable was provided to the rear of the goods yard.

P. Baughan

Plate 139: Appleby Station, looking north, in May 1961. The large No. 1 type building is constructed of brick with stone dressing. This station is the only one on the line which is provided with a passenger footbridge (No. 236A) — *see A Pictorial Record of LMS Architecture, Figure 60 and Plates 522 & 523.* Cast-iron columns support steel-latticed girders and stepways, with timber floor and steps. The main girder is not the original, as it was renewed in 1902 following a mishap barely a year after erection.

G. Biddle Collection)

Plate 140: The rear of the main building at Appleby Station. The name 'Appleby' was changed to 'Appleby West' in 1952 to avoid confusion with the ex-NER station 'Appleby East'. After the NER station closed in 1962, the name of this Midland station reverted, in May 1968, to the original.

BR/OPC

Figure 48b: Appleby Station.

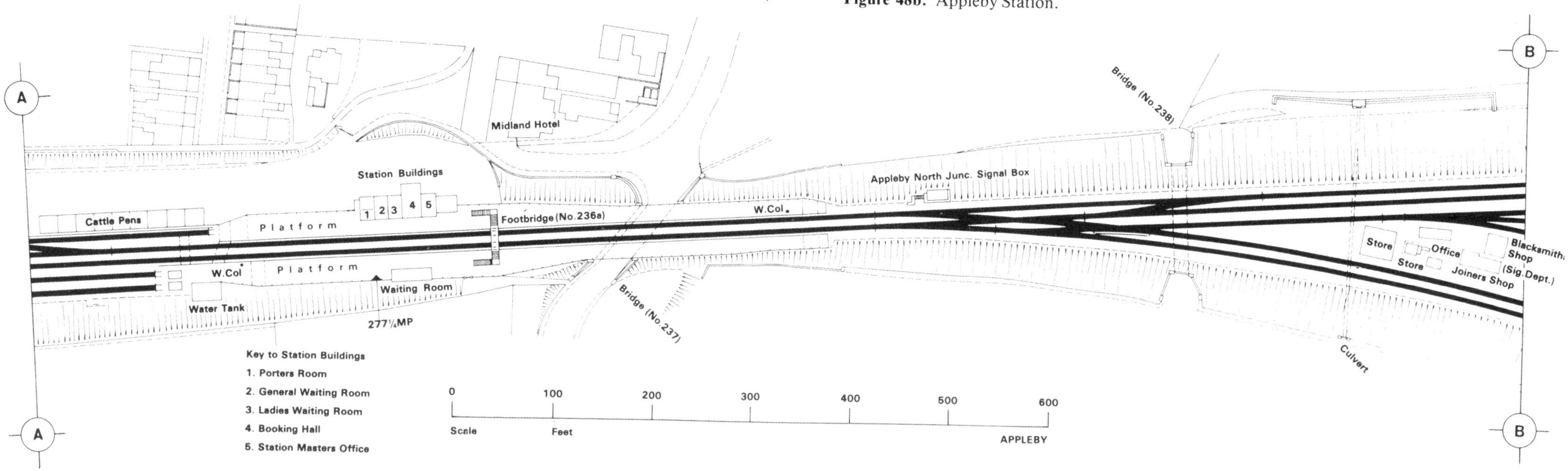

Midland Hotel

Station Buildings

1 2 3 4 5

Cattle Pens

P l a t f o r m

Footbridge (No.236a)

Appleby North Junc. Signal Box

W.Col.

Bridge (No. 238)

W.Col.

P l a t f o r m

Waiting Room

Water Tank

277¼MP

Bridge (No. 237)

Store

Office

Store

Joiners Shop

Blacksmiths Shop (Sig. Dept.)

Culvert

Key to Station Buildings

1. Porters Room
2. General Waiting Room
3. Ladies Waiting Room
4. Booking Hall
5. Station Masters Office

| 0 | 100 | 200 | 300 | 400 | 500 | 600 |

Scale   Feet

APPLEBY

Figure 48c: Appleby Engineer's Yard and Midland Junction (NER).

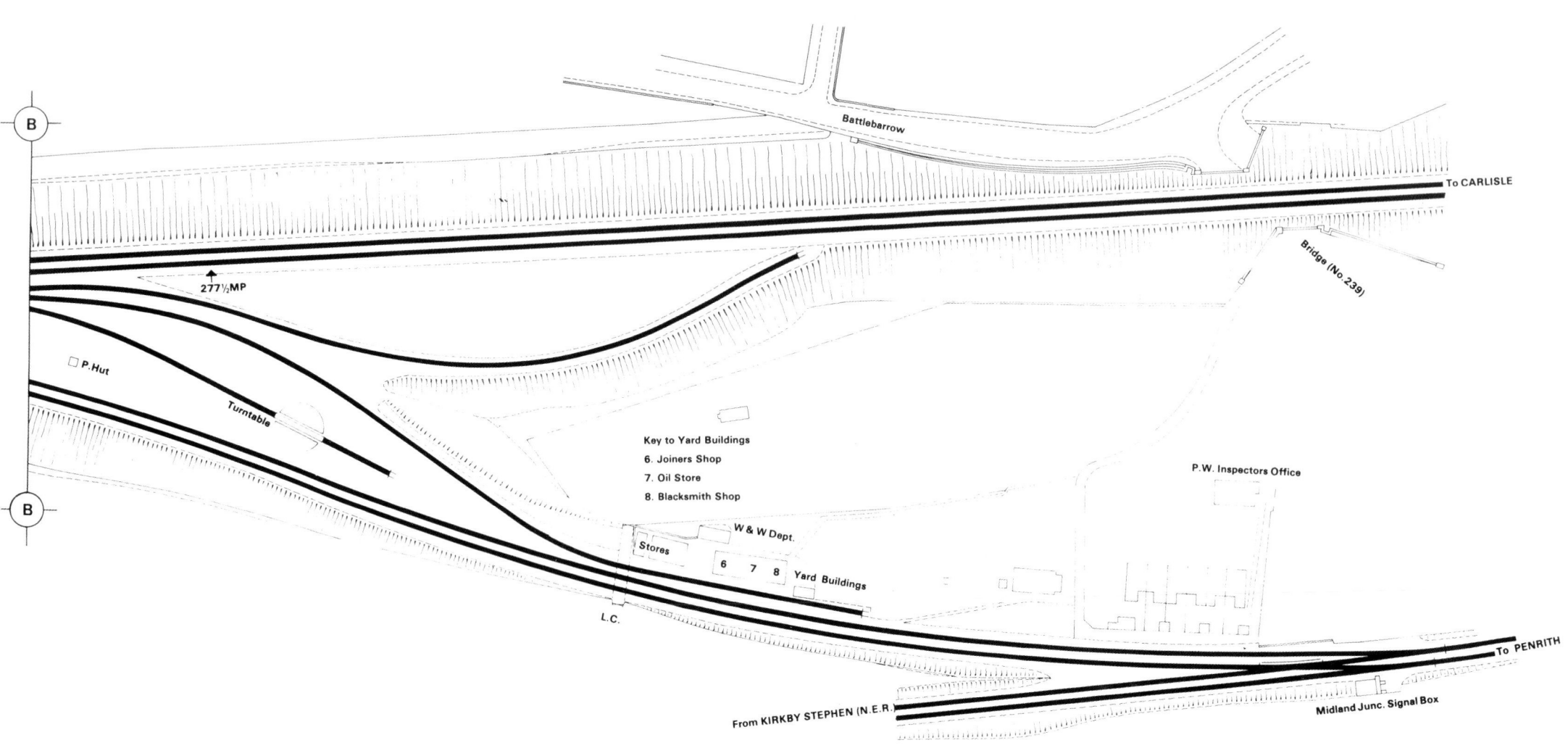

To CARLISLE

Battlebarrow

Bridge (No. 239)

B

277½MP

P. Hut

Turntable

Key to Yard Buildings
6. Joiners Shop
7. Oil Store
8. Blacksmith Shop

P.W. Inspectors Office

B

W & W Dept.

Stores

6 7 8 Yard Buildings

L.C.

To PENRITH

From KIRKBY STEPHEN (N.E.R.)

Midland Junc. Signal Box

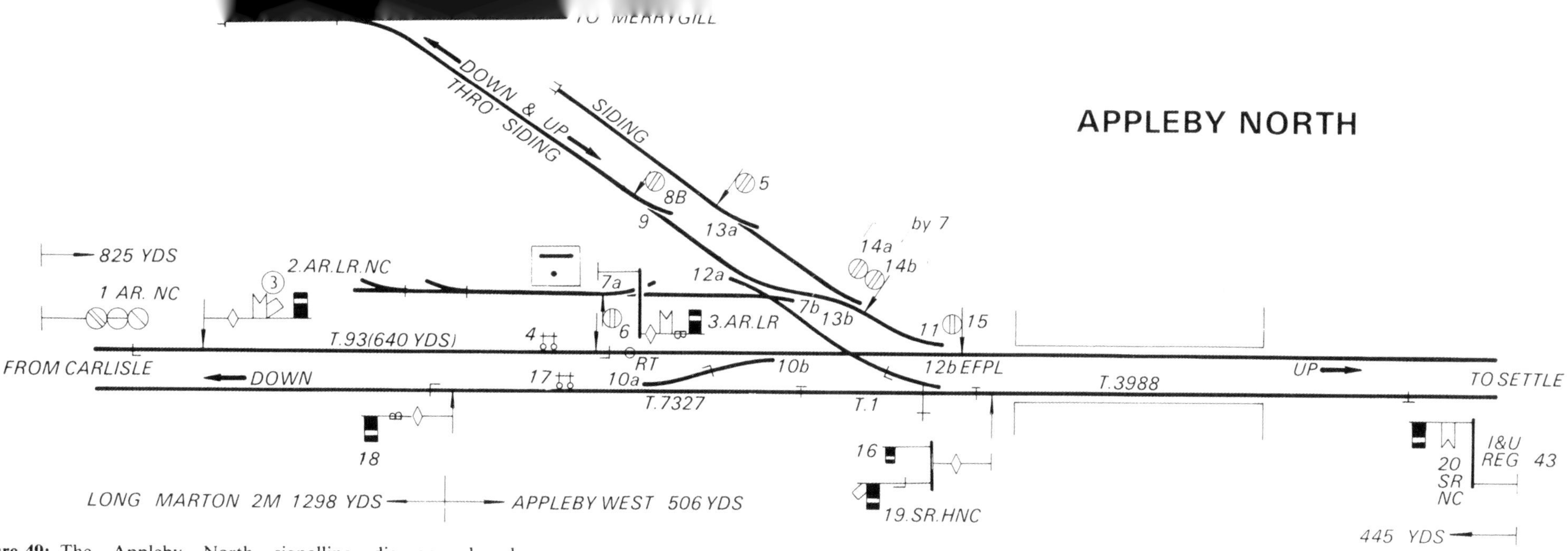

APPLEBY NORTH

Figure 49: The Appleby North signalling diagram, based upon information available for 1965.

TO MERRYGILL

DOWN & UP SIDING
THRO' SIDING

8B 5
9 13a
by 7
14a 14b

825 YDS
2.AR.LR.NC
3
1 AR. NC
7a 12a
7b 13b
11 15
4 6
3.AR.LR
T.93(640 YDS)
RT
FROM CARLISLE DOWN 10b 12b EFPL UP TO SETTLE
17 10a T.3988
T.7327 T.1
18 16
I&U REG 43
20 SR NC
LONG MARTON 2M 1298 YDS APPLEBY WEST 506 YDS 19.SR.HNC
445 YDS

Plate 141: A view from Appleby Station, looking north, in 1939. Appleby North Junction and signal box can be seen beyond the platforms. This Midland box was brought into use in 1890 and was of wood construction. Records indicate that this signal box was destroyed by fire on 4th June 1951. A new box and frame was provided on a site diagonally opposite, in the fork of the junction (**see Figure 49 & Plate 142**).

N. Wilkinson

Plate 142: A similar view of Appleby, looking north, on 27th August 1966, but showing the new signal box built in 1951. It was of wood construction, measured 22ft. 1in. x 11ft. 6in. x 10ft., was of LMS design, and contained a standard pre-1943 lever frame with 20 levers at 4½in. centres. The frame was then extended to 21 levers, and later to 25 levers (22/7/73) in connection with the closure of Appleby West signal box. Note the changed signals.

D. F. Tee

LONG MARTON

Plate 143: Long Marton Viaduct (No. 252) 279 miles 69 chains — is 108 yards long and 60ft. high, and has stone abutments, piers and parapets, brick arches and stone voussoirs. The five spans vary from 43ft. to 45ft. It was built between 1871 and 1874 from red sandstone quarried at Dufton Gill, two miles away. It crosses Troutbeck, which also lends its name to an alternative title for the viaduct.

Plate 144: This attractive row of six workers' houses at Long Marton, photographed in October 1984, was provided in rural surroundings on the outskirts of the village of Long Marton.

Plate 145: Bridge No. 254 (280 miles 11 chains) at Long Marton, photographed on 12th October 1965, was strengthened in 1904 by the addition of a steel centre girder, similar to No. 115 (Garsdale) and No. 181 (Kirkby Stephen). Detail of the decorative parapet railing can be seen, as the wooden panelling has been removed.

D. Jenkinson

Plate 146: Long Marton, from the southern end of the 'down' platform on 27th August 1966. This is our first encounter with a No. 2 (medium) style of building. More details of this type will be seen later. Materials used for construction at this location were brick with red sandstone, used for quoins, plinth and window surrounds. The station is obviously well-kept and has well-tended gardens but, by January of the following year, it became an unstaffed halt until final closure on 4th May 1970. Since closure, the building has been used as the 'Long Marton Centre'.

D. F. Tee

Plate 147: Approaching Long Marton from the south, a small development of 1941 for the Laporte Chemical Company of Luton is passed, and is photographed on 3rd September 1963. Barytes, produced by the Silverband Mine, was carried by aerial rope-way from a crushing plant at the mine to the bunker and hopper located by a new siding to the right of the goods shed **(cf. Figure 51)**. By the time the photograph was taken the siding had been removed, but we do not know how long it remained in operation. The goods shed is for three wagons, as originally planned. Note the typical Settle & Carlisle location of the loading gauge near the entrance to the good shed; on this occasion an LMS pattern reinforced-concrete posted structure has replaced the Midland variety. Also note the weigh office and the hipped roof plate-layers' hut.

P. Baughan

Figure 50: The track layout for Long Marton, based upon information from Midland Railway surveys for 1911 and 1912.

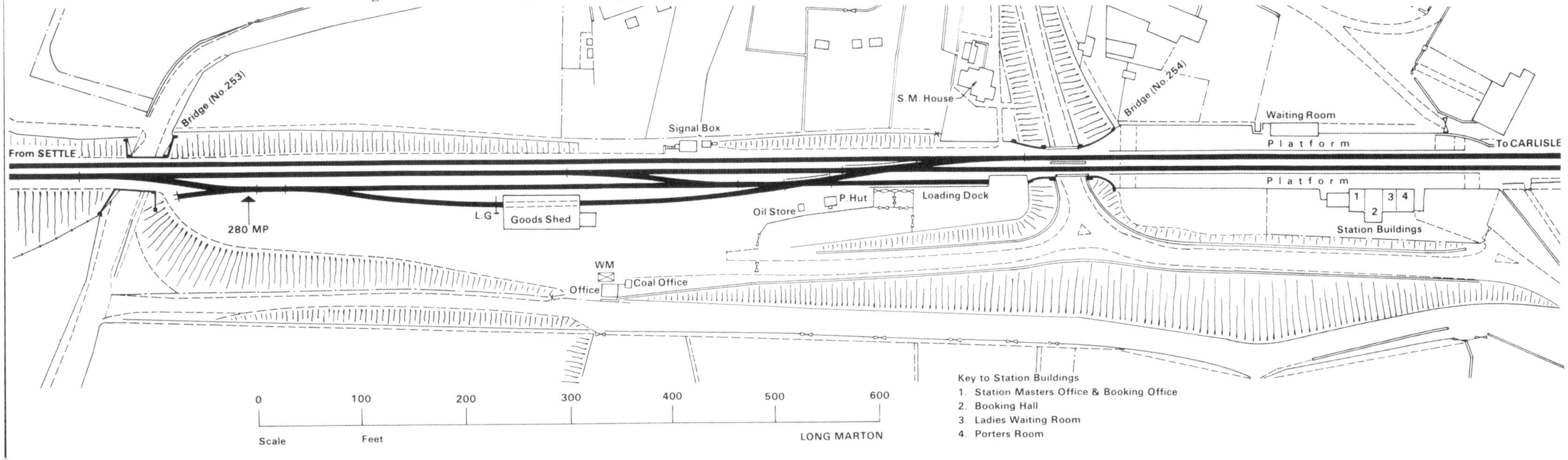

Bridge (No. 253)

From SETTLE

280 MP

L.G Goods Shed

WM
Office Coal Office

S.M. House

Signal Box

Bridge (No. 254)

Oil Store P. Hut Loading Dock

Waiting Room

Platform

Platform

1 3 4
2
Station Buildings

To CARLISLE

| 0 | 100 | 200 | 300 | 400 | 500 | 600 |

Scale   Feet

LONG MARTON

Key to Station Buildings
1. Station Masters Office & Booking Office
2. Booking Hall
3. Ladies Waiting Room
4. Porters Room

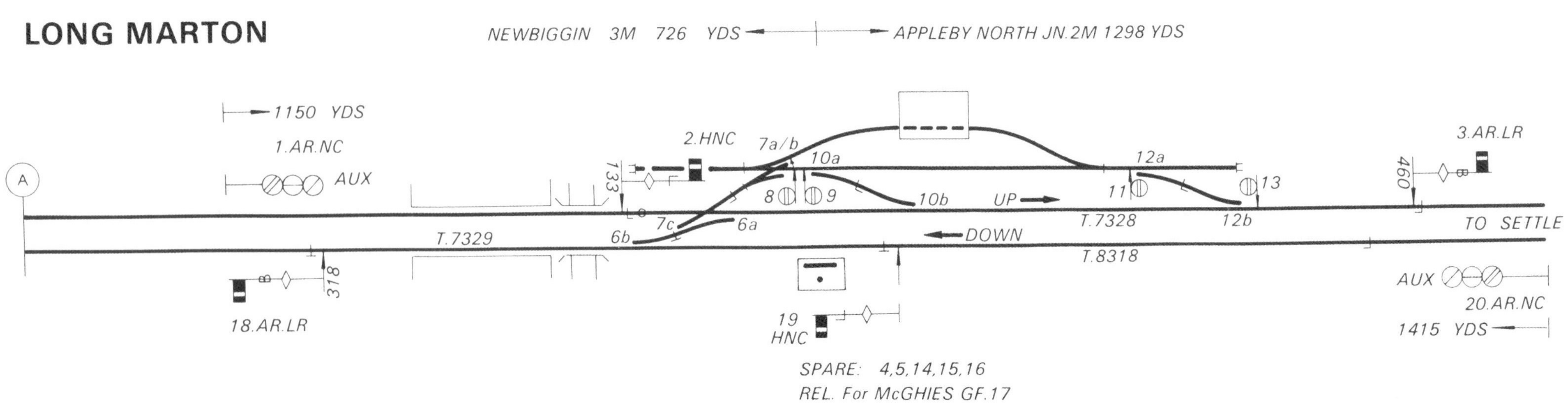

LONG MARTON

NEWBIGGIN 3M 726 YDS ← → APPLEBY NORTH JN.2M 1298 YDS

1150 YDS

1.AR.NC

AUX

2.HNC 7a/b 10a

8 9 10b UP → 12a 11 13

T.7329 6b 7c 6a DOWN ← T.7328 12b T.8318 3.AR.LR TO SETTLE

133 460 AUX 20.AR.NC 1415 YDS

318

18.AR.LR

19 HNC

SPARE: 4,5,14,15,16
REL. For McGHIES GF.17

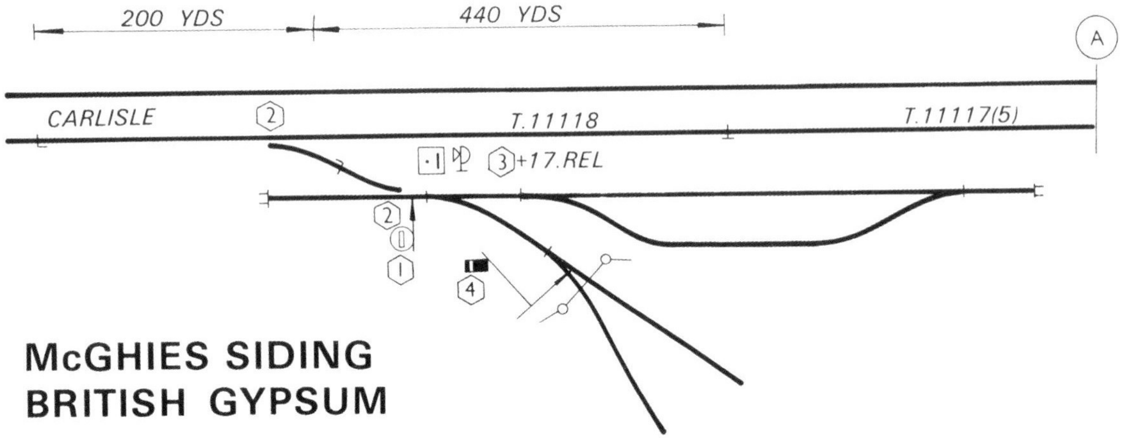

200 YDS 440 YDS

CARLISLE ② T.11118 T.11117(5) (A)

·1 ③ +17.REL

②

①

④

McGHIES SIDING
BRITISH GYPSUM

Figure 51 (above): The signalling diagram for Long Marton and the nearby McGhies Siding, based upon information available for 1961.

Figure 52 (below left): The track plan detailing the additional siding for the Silverband Mine at Long Marton, from a survey by the LMS District Engineer's Office (Leeds) 1941.

Plate 148: Long Marton signal box brought into use on 29th July 1890, was of wood construction, measured 16ft. 6in. x 11ft. 6in. x 8ft., and had a 20 lever tumbler frame. The box closed on 22nd March 1970 when signal arms were removed and all points were secured, pending removal. This action necessitated the transfer of control of the McGhies Siding ground frame to Appleby North.

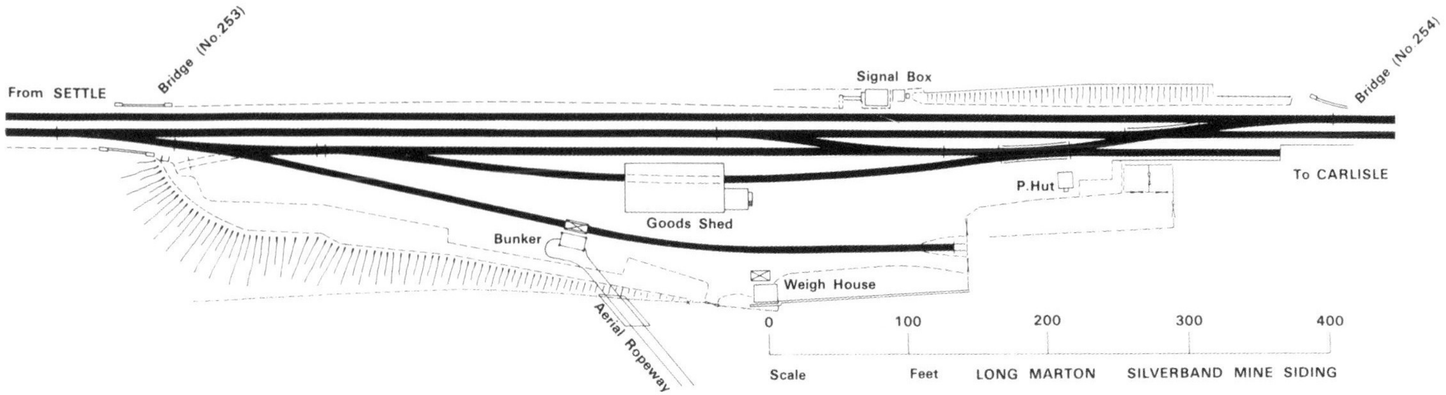

From SETTLE Bridge (No 253) Signal Box Bridge (No 254)

Goods Shed P.Hut To CARLISLE

Bunker

Weigh House

Aerial Ropeway

Scale 0 100 200 300 400

Feet LONG MARTON SILVERBAND MINE SIDING

GOTHAM CO. SIDING

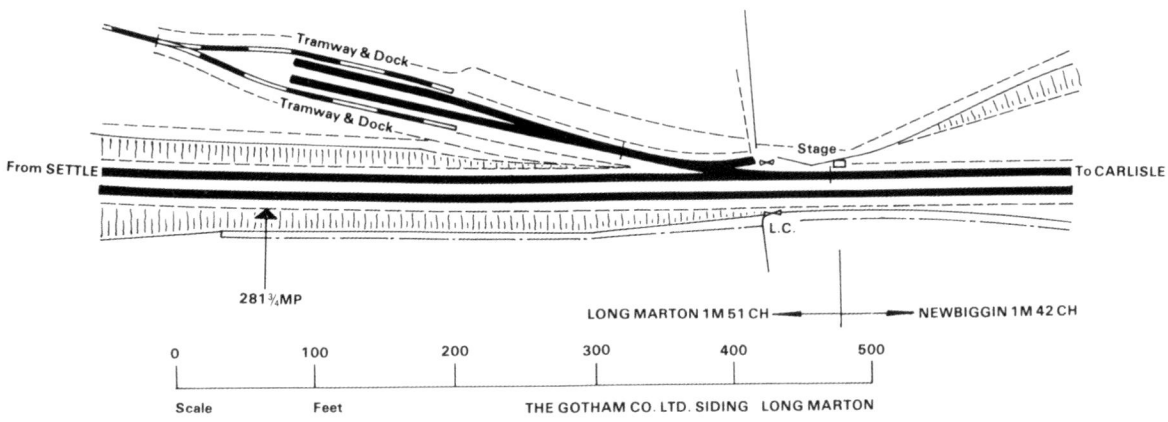

Tramway & Dock

Tramway & Dock

From SETTLE — Stage — To CARLISLE

L.C.

281¾ MP

LONG MARTON 1M 51 CH ←→ NEWBIGGIN 1M 42 CH

| 0 | 100 | 200 | 300 | 400 | 500 |

Scale Feet THE GOTHAM CO. LTD. SIDING LONG MARTON

Figure 53: The Gotham Co. Ltd., Siding at Long Marton, based upon information from an LMS survey for May 1927. An Agreement of 1924 between the Gotham Co. Ltd. and the railway resulted in the provision of rail connection for the transhipment of gypsum. A lever frame was provided, protected by fixed signals. Trains were not allowed to stop between sunset and sunrise, and signal lamps were not lit during the night. The lamps were illuminated during daylight hours if there happened to be fog or falling snow. This siding could not be used as a lie by.

McGHIES SIDING

Figure 54: T. McGhie's Thistle Siding track layout at New Biggin, based upon information from a Midland Railway survey for 1911. The Thistle Alabaster Works of T. McGhie & Co. Ltd. was situated on the west side of the line, adjacent to mile post 282. It was controlled by a 4 lever ground frame which was brought into use in 1906. Operational procedures were similar to those at the Gotham Co. Siding, ¼ mile to the south.

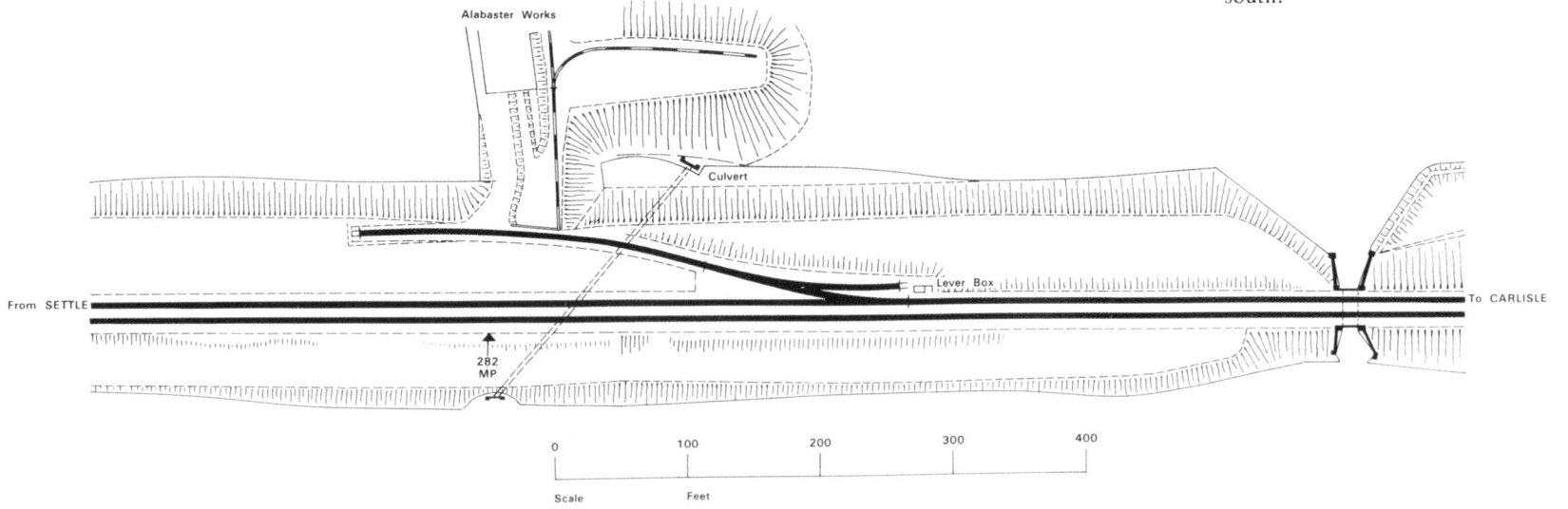

Alabaster Works

Culvert

From SETTLE Lever Box To CARLISLE

282 MP

| 0 | 100 | 200 | 300 | 400 |

Scale Feet

BRITISH GYPSUM SIDING

Figure 55: The track layout of the New Biggin British Gypsum Ltd. Siding, based upon information from a BR survey, circa 1968. The railway continued to call the siding McGhies although British Gypsum had absorbed the undertakings of McGhie's and the Gotham Co. Ltd. The siding developed to combine and extend those shown in **Figures 53 & 54**, removing the southerly rail connection. The remaining rail connection came under the direct control of Long Marton signal box, following replacement of the 1906 ground frame by an open type (4 lever) which was brought into use on 17th September 1947. From this date, it was possible to use this siding as a lie by, thus allowing following trains to pass. This procedure continued until closure of Long Marton box on 22nd March 1970 when control was transferred to Appleby North box. In 1960, a proposal to develop a site on the 'up' side, adjacent to McGhie's, was considered, which would have provided sidings and a signal box. The latter would have been called 'Dunfell Iron Mines' and was to contain a standard 1943 pattern lever frame. The scheme came to naught.

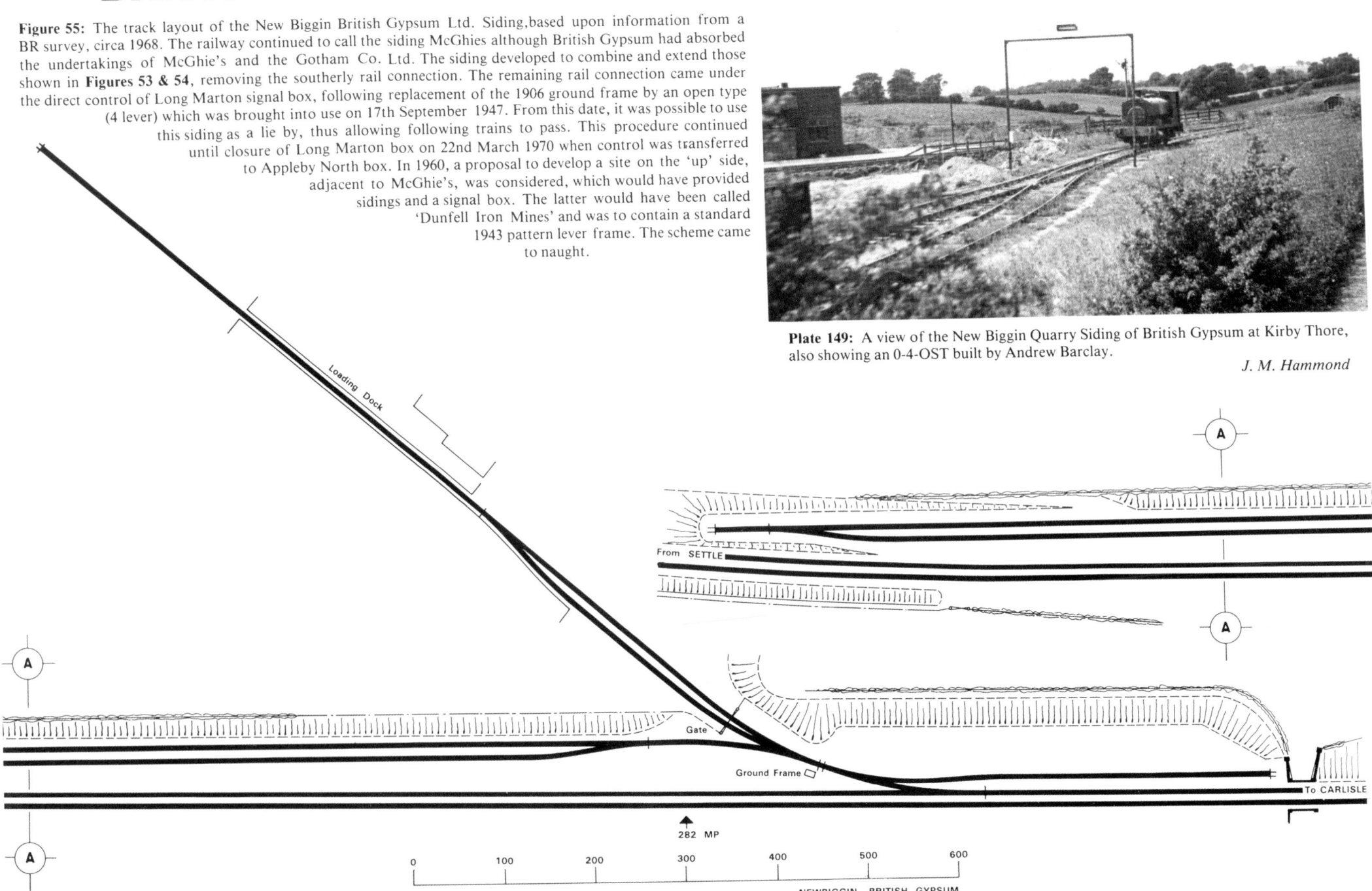

Plate 149: A view of the New Biggin Quarry Siding of British Gypsum at Kirby Thore, also showing an 0-4-0ST built by Andrew Barclay.

J. M. Hammond

Loading Dock

From SETTLE

Gate

Ground Frame

To CARLISLE

282 MP

| 0 | 100 | 200 | 300 | 400 | 500 | 600 |

Scale   Feet

NEWBIGGIN, BRITISH GYPSUM

NEW BIGGIN

Plate 150: New Biggin, looking north, at about the turn of the century. This was another station with a small type of building. The goods facilities here were not extensive; the cattle dock was proposed for five wagons. The tall five-span overbridge in the distance connects the two parts of Park Wood, which was bisected by the coming of the railway.

D. F. Tee Collection

Plate 151: New Biggin, from the north, on 22nd May 1965. Another change of building materials can be seen; local golden-coloured freestone, with red sandstone quoins, plinth and window surrounds. Note the short cast-iron lamp standard carrying an oil lamp. This station became an unstaffed halt in January 1967 and closed to passengers on 4th May 1970. Goods services were withdrawn on 7th November 1966.

D. F. Tee

Figure 56: The signalling diagram for New Biggin, based upon information available for 1956, with amendments added for 1972.

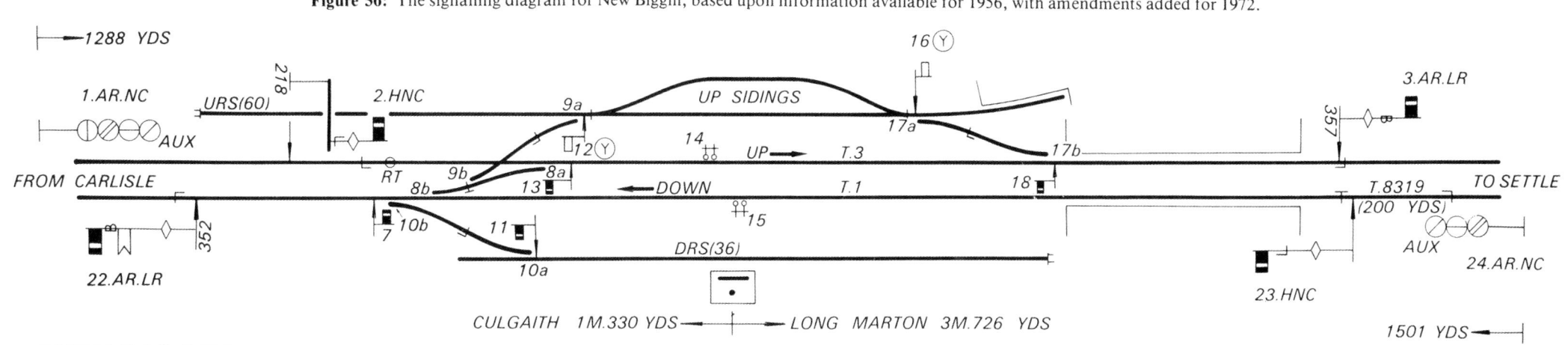

NEW BIGGIN

SPARE: 4,5,6,19,20,21

Detonators added 22.12.72, otherwise as from 24.7.56

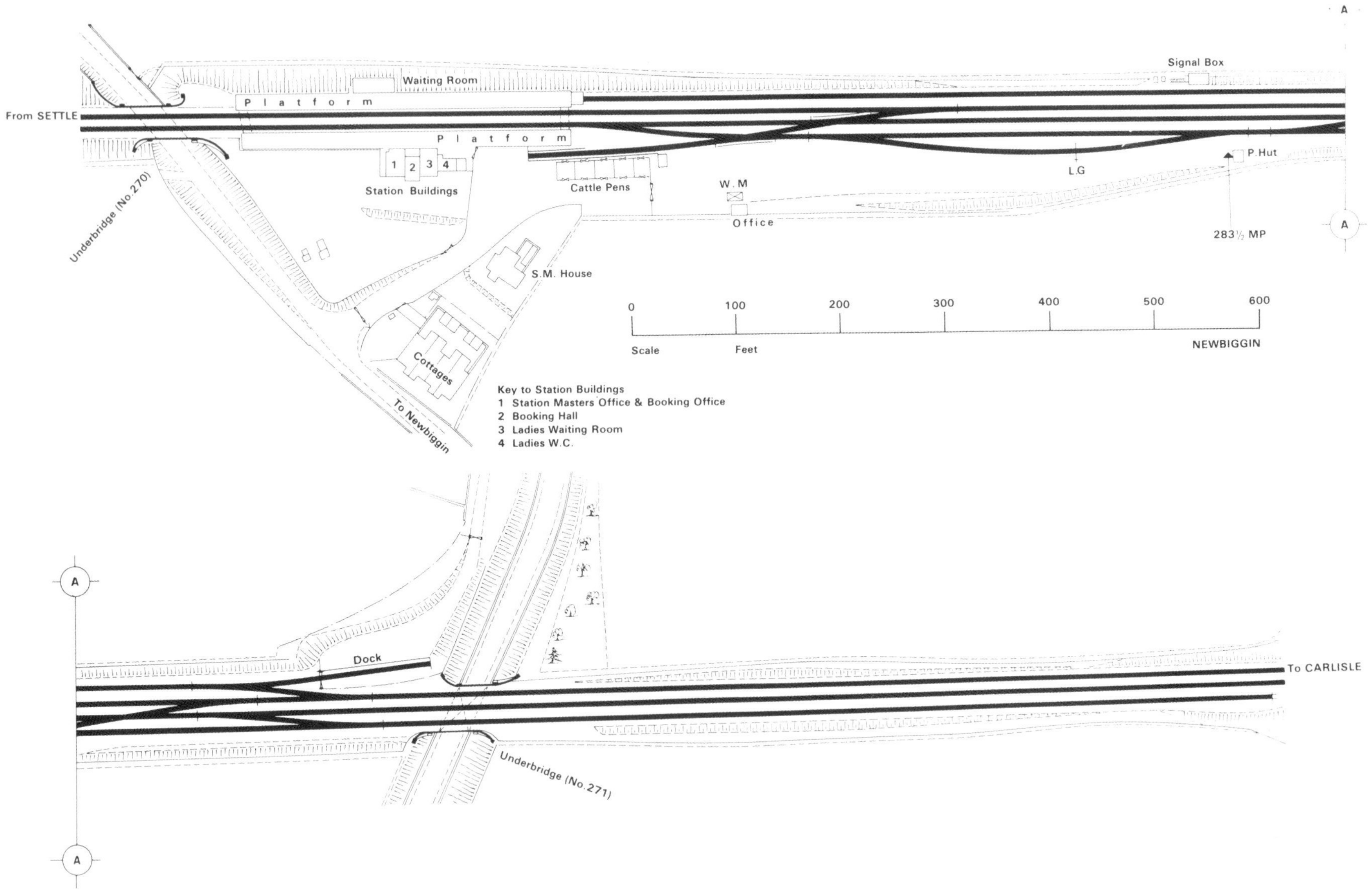

Figure 57: The track layout for New Biggin, based upon a Midland Railway survey for 1911 and an LMS survey for 1931. The loading dock near bridge No. 271 was, by an Agreement of 17th September 1926, sold to Gotham Co. Ltd., who became responsible for the maintenance of this, although, of course, the LMS retained responsibility for the associated trackwork.

Plate 152: New Biggin signal box in 1973. The box was brought into use in 1890, was of wood construction and measured 20ft. x 11ft. 6in. x 12ft. with a 24 lever tumbler frame. It closed on 16th December 1973.

Plate 153 (above): New Biggin, 1962; the first example of a timber waiting shelter. The ground plan closely follows that of the more usual stone-built type. Of note is the diagonal boarding beneath the windows and for the doors, echoing that to be found on the waiting-room screens of the main building. The rustic seat carries the station name. The Midland Railway painted these seats in chocolate brown with the name painted in white on an Oxford blue panel.

D. Jenkinson

Plate 154 (left): Crowdundle Viaduct (No. 272) in 1962 (283 miles 64 chains). Crowdundle Beck, passing 55ft. below the third opening, marked the boundary of the old counties of Westmorland and Cumberland as well as the parishes of New Biggin and Culgaith. The 86 yard long, four arch viaduct, was built entirely of stone.

D. Jenkinson

CULGAITH

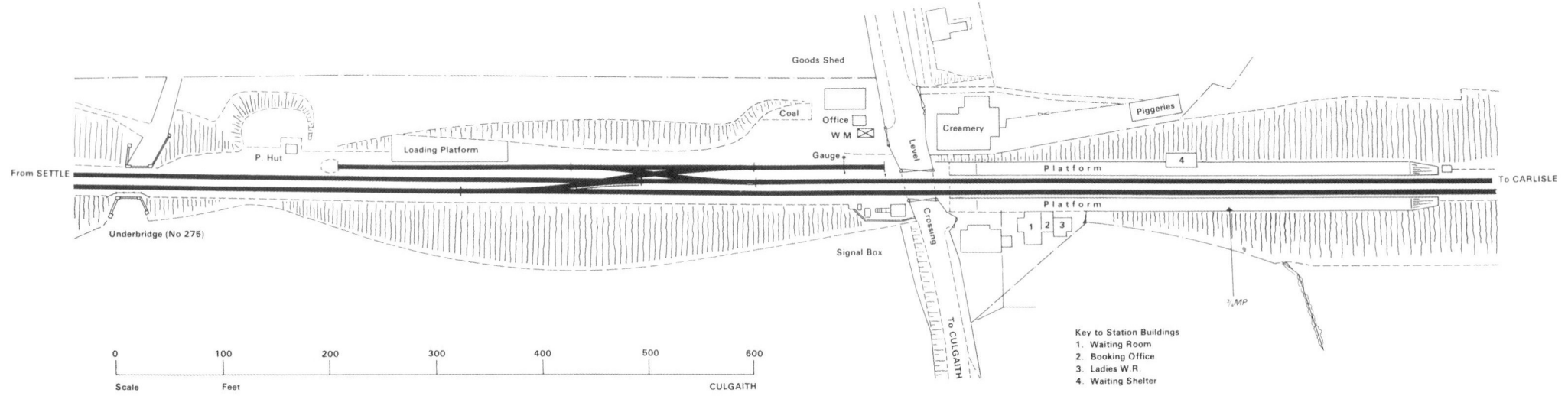

Figure 58 The track layout for Culgaith, from a Midland Railway survey for 1912. Note the simplified track layout to the goods yard. The loading platform was constructed in 1880 to handle potato traffic.

Plate 155: A view of Culgaith, looking south at about the turn of the century. Early plans precluded a station at Culgaith, but the local vicar, Revd G. W. Atkinson, together with some local landowners, wrote to Derby requesting a station. The board at first refused but, as the residents persisted, Crossley was asked to discuss the matter with the vicar. The negotiations must have been favourable, but were dependent upon the local authority constructing and maintaining a suitable road from the village; this they promised to do in 1875, although implementation was obviously delayed. It seems that there was some form of track down the hill from the village, for which a level crossing and crossing keeper's house were provided. Indeed, it was this house that formed the basis of early plans for the station building, although eventually the station that finally opened on 1st April 1880 had the building illustrated here. In this view can be seen the first signal box, which was subsequently replaced in 1908. Official records indicate that, at the new station, ten levers were provided for signalling, etc. but no mention of a signal box was made. For the most part, platforms were of timber construction, unusual for this line. Again there are tall posted oil lamps ranged along the platforms. The fencing was of the vertical paling type, later to be replaced. At the other side of the level crossing the small goods yard can be seen. The local community expected a goods shed, but the Midland Railway declined to provide one.

Lens of Sutton

Plate 156: Culgaith, as seen on 22nd May 1965, an almost identical view to that in **Plate 155**. However, a few changes have taken place, and include a new signal box, new fencing, the ivy has been removed, and the ornate lamp columns have been replaced by lamps on wooden posts. In line with other Settle & Carlisle stations, Culgaith became an unstaffed halt on 2nd January 1967, and was closed to passengers on 4th May 1970. Goods facilities were withdrawn on 5th October 1964.

D. F. Tee

Plate 157: Culgaith, looking north, in June 1961. On the right is the crossing keeper's house, originally intended as the basis of the station building. The structure which was eventually built bears no relation to other Settle & Carlisle structures, although it is an attractive cottage style building. Note the cock's comb ridge tiles and ball finials on the roof.

G. Biddle Collection

Plate 158: Culgaith level crossing and signal box, in April 1971. This signal box brought into use on 4th October 1908, was of wood construction, measured 16ft. 6in. x 11ft. 6in. x 8ft., had a 16 lever tappet frame with 6in. centres, and had a renewal cost of £250 (W & W Committee Minute No. 22118, 2/11/1906). The gates of the road crossing were converted to a manned barrier installation in 1976.

G. Biddle

Plate 159: Culgaith, in 1962, showing an unusual form of timber waiting shelter, more reminiscent of Midland practice elsewhere, particularly in the Derby/Trent area.

D. Jenkinson

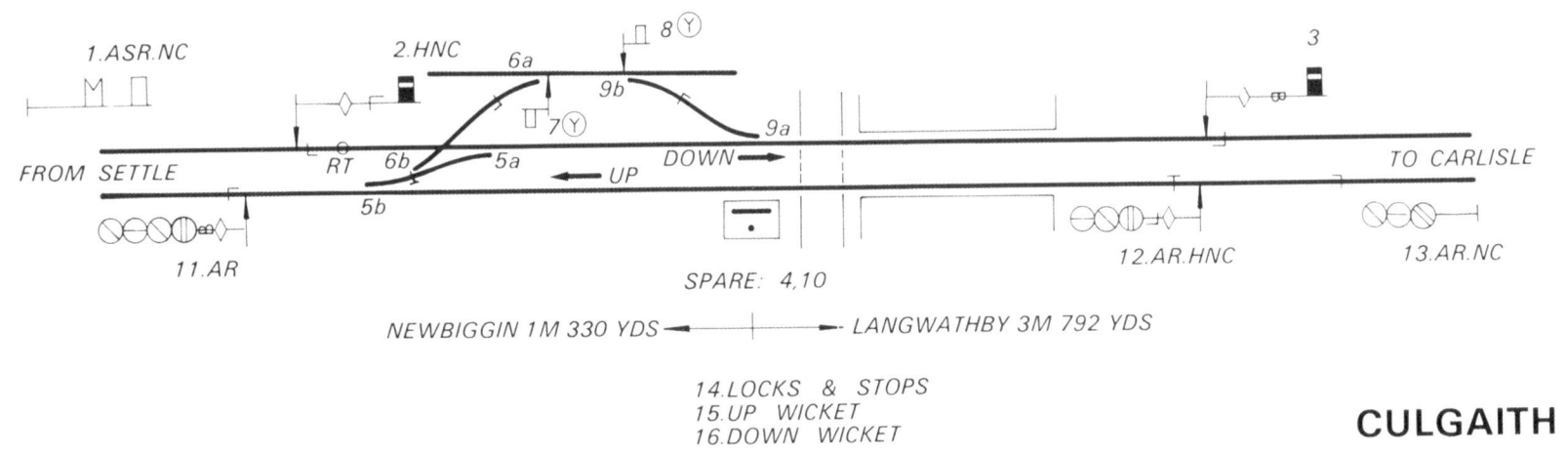

1.ASR.NC 2.HNC 6a 8(Y) 3 9b

7(Y) 9a

FROM SETTLE RT 6b 5a UP DOWN TO CARLISLE

5b

11.AR 12.AR.HNC 13.AR.NC

SPARE: 4,10

NEWBIGGIN 1M 330 YDS ⟵——┼——⟶ LANGWATHBY 3M 792 YDS

14.LOCKS & STOPS
15.UP WICKET
16.DOWN WICKET

CULGAITH

Figure 59: The Culgaith signalling diagram, based upon information available for 1960.

Plate 160: A view of Culgaith Tunnel (No. 276) in October 1984, showing the southern approach from the station (284 miles 77¾ chains). Having been cut through red marl, the 661 yard long tunnel had brick side walls, invert and arch, and stone faces. It was constructed between 1870 and 1873 and had one ventilating shaft which was 74ft. deep.

Plate 161: Culgaith Tunnel, showing the northern end. The short length of level running, the longest section on the line, as the route passes from Culgaith to Waste Bank, holds a position on the side of the valley above the River Eden.

D. Jenkinson

Plate 162: Waste Bank Tunnel (No. 277) showing the southern portal (285 miles 47½ chains). Although a cutting was originally planned, a tunnel was eventually cut through 164yds. of red sandstone. The tunnel has brick side walls, invert and arch, with brick portals trimmed in stone.

D. Ibbotson

Plate 163: Waste Bank Tunnel, from the north, as seen in October 1984. Note the Culgaith distant colour light signal and the 285¾ mile post.

LANGWATHBY

Plate 164: a view of Langwathby, looking north, on 27th August 1966, showing another attractive medium-sized building. Most of the oil lamps are mounted on wooden posts against the fence, and have again replaced lamps on tall cast-iron fluted columns. However, as at New Biggin and Lazonby, one square lamp, mounted on a shortened cast post, has been retained to mark the entrance/exit to the platform.

D. F. Tee

Plate 165: This view of Langwathby, looking south, on 24th September 1966, takes in the whole of the station, goods yard and signal box. The signal box brought into use on 5th July 1903 was of wood construction, measured 16ft. 6in. x 11ft. 6in. x 8ft., with a 20 lever tumbler frame, and had a renewal cost of £250 (W & W Committee Minute No. 19492, 7/11/1902). It closed on 27th October 1968. It will be seen that the waiting shelter on the 'up' platform is of timber construction, and is similar to that at New Biggin. The station closed to passengers on 4th May 1970 after being unstaffed since 1967; closure to goods was on 6th June 1964.

O. F. Carter

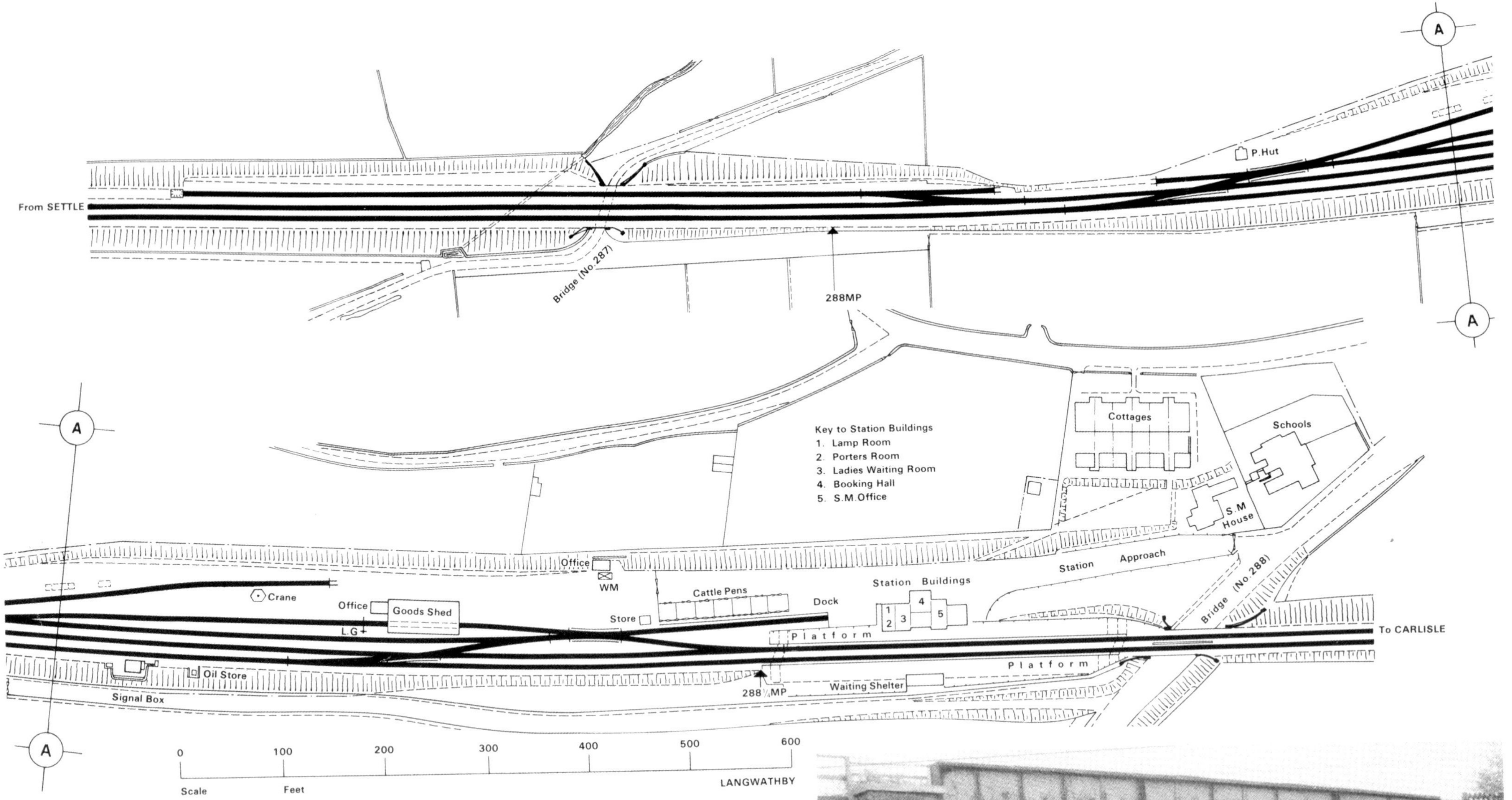

Figure in upper part showing track layout with labels:

From SETTLE · Bridge (No. 287) · 288MP · P.Hut · A

Key to Station Buildings
1. Lamp Room
2. Porters Room
3. Ladies Waiting Room
4. Booking Hall
5. S.M.Office

Cottages · Schools · S.M House · Station Approach · Bridge (No. 288)

Office · WM · Cattle Pens · Dock · Station Buildings
Crane · Office · Goods Shed · Store · 1 4 / 2 3 5 · Platform · To CARLISLE
L.G · Platform
Oil Store · 288 MP · Waiting Shelter · Platform
Signal Box

0 100 200 300 400 500 600
Scale   Feet
LANGWATHBY

Figure 60: The Langwathby track layout, based upon a Midland Railway survey for 1913.

Plate 166: The bridge over the Alston Road (No. 288) at Langwathby (288 miles 26½ chains), photographed in October 1984, was strengthened in 1904 in line with the Midland Railway decision to upgrade the line. The wrought-iron members were supplemented by the addition of a steel centre girder, connected to the cross-girders by steel hanger bolts. This type of bridge is similar to bridge No. 2 at Anley pictured in **Plate 6**, but the need for extensive wing walls with relieving arches does not exist here. Four additional structures in the Langwathby area were strengthened as part of the programme. The contract for bridges Nos. 279 and 286, together with another seven bridges on the route, was awarded to W. Richards, Phoenix Iron Works, Leicester, for the total sum of £830. Bridge No. 287, the fourth, was upgraded in a contract awarded to Messrs Eastwood, Swingler & Co., Derby for £450 8s. 2d. (£450. 41), for this and another four bridges.

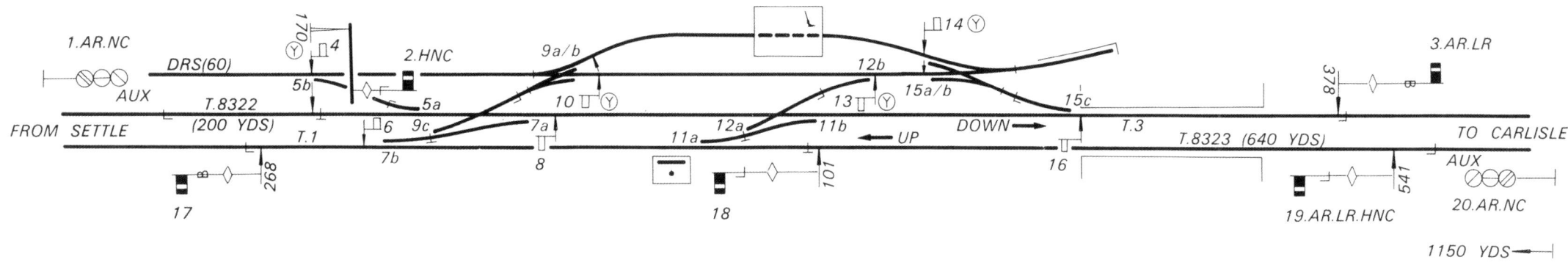

1562 YDS

1.AR.NC

DRS(60)

AUX

T.8322
(200 YDS)

FROM SETTLE

2.HNC

9a/b

12b

14 Y

3.AR.LR

378

10 Y

15a/b

13 Y

15c

UP

DOWN

T.3

T.8323 (640 YDS)

TO CARLISLE

AUX

11a   12a   11b

16

19.AR.LR.HNC

20.AR.NC

17

18

1150 YDS

CULGAITH 3M 792 YDS ← → LITTLE SALKELD 1M 1078 YDS

LANGWATHBY

Figure 61: The signalling diagram for Langwathby, based upon information available for 1960.

Plate 167: Langwathby Station, circa 1900. At first glance, this early view gives the impression of little change over the years, compared with **Plate 165**. However, detailed examination reveals the presence of a Midland angled nameboard, vertical fencing, tall lamp standards, notice-boards, painting schemes, window-boxes, etc. The presence of milk churns reminds us that the farmers moved a considerable volume of milk north from the Eden Valley stations, much of it being sent on to Newcastle.

D. F. Tee Collection

Plate 168: Langwathby, in October 1984, showing the stationmaster's house, standing near to the Alston Road, at the entrance to the station. The style remained the same at all locations, and is detailed in **Figure 88**, at Cumwhinton. As with the stations, the materials used for construction varied, in this case the local red sandstone was used.

END ELEVATION ON A

ROAD SIDE ELEVATION

END ELEVATION ON B

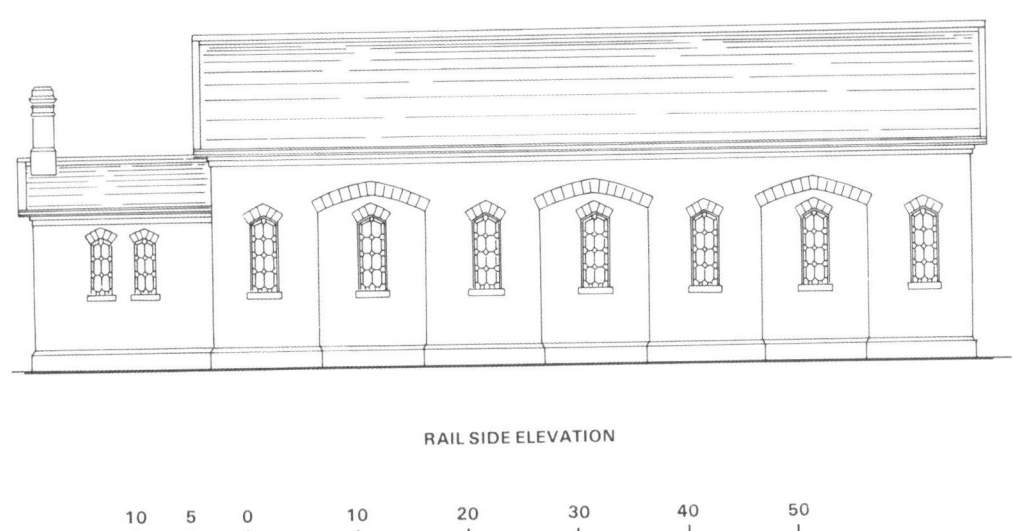

RAIL SIDE ELEVATION

```
10   5   0        10      20      30      40      50
|||||||||||_____|_____|_____|_____|_____|
SCALE  FEET
```

Figure 62: Side and end elevations of a three-wagon goods shed, based upon Midland Railway contract drawing of 1874. The road side elevation was officially termed as the front.

Plate 169: Langwathby Goods Shed, as seen in July 1967. This example of a three-wagon shed was out of railway use when this photograph was taken. The lozenge style windows were a distinctive feature of Settle & Carlisle goods sheds, although the pattern varied at different locations.

G. Biddle Collection

LITTLE SALKELD

Plate 170: Little Salkeld or Dodds Mill Viaduct, (No. 296) over Briggle Beck, (289 miles 39 chains) has seven arches of 44ft. 7in. span, and was built with stone abutments, wings, piers and parapets, and brick arches during the years 1874 and 1875, and is 134 yards long and 60ft. high.

Plate 171: Little Salkeld, photographed on 2nd May 1970, two days before closure to passengers, having been unstaffed for three years. Looking south, this gives yet another fine view of a small type of building.

D. F. Tee

Figure 63: The Little Salkeld track layout, based upon a Midland Railway survey of 1913.

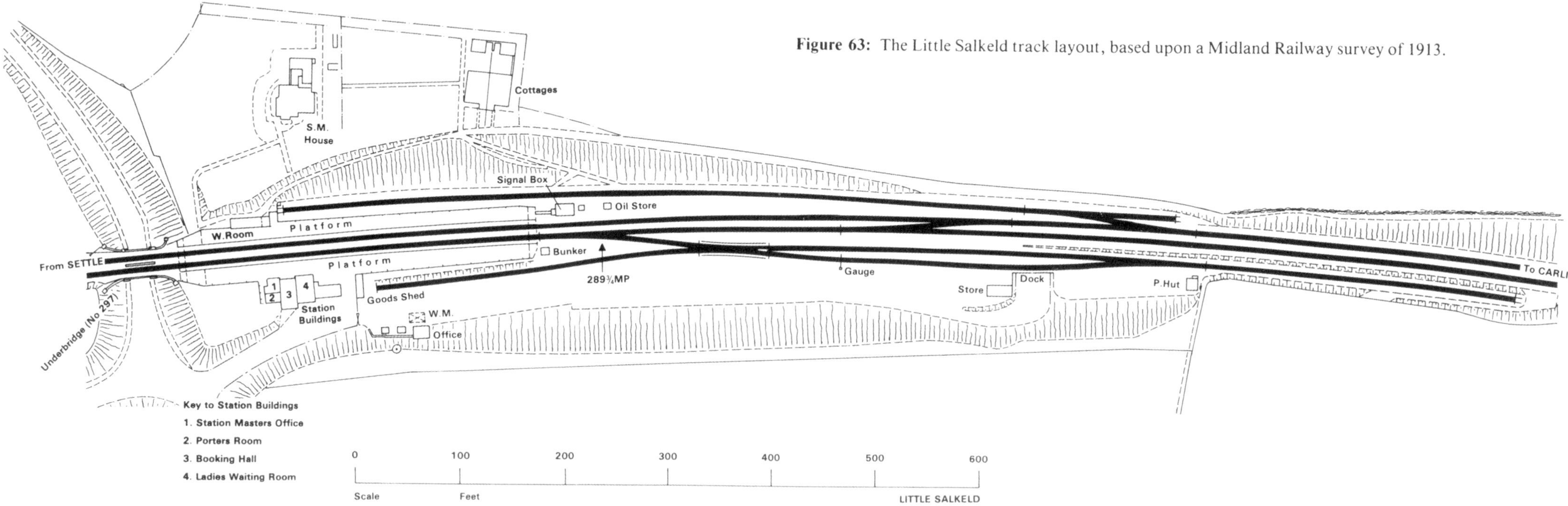

Cottages

S.M. House

Signal Box

Oil Store

W.Room

Platform

Bunker

Platform

From SETTLE

289¾MP

Gauge

To CARLISLE

Store

Dock

P.Hut

1 2 3 4 Station Buildings

Goods Shed

W.M.

Office

Underbridge (No 297)

Key to Station Buildings

1. Station Masters Office
2. Porters Room
3. Booking Hall
4. Ladies Waiting Room

0   100   200   300   400   500   600

Scale   Feet

LITTLE SALKELD

Plate 172: A view of Little Salkeld, looking south. The signal box brought into use on 13th August 1899, was of wood construction, measured 16ft. 6in. x 11ft. 6in. x 8ft., had a 12 lever tumbler frame, and a renewal cost of £230 (W & W Committee Minute No. 17176, 18/5/1899). It closed on 6th July 1964, but the crossover road on the Carlisle side of the signal box and the signals controlling it were removed on 21st July 1963. Well illustrated is the corrugated-iron oil store or lamp room; this was of a Midland Railway design perpetuated by the LMS.

D. F. Tee Collection

Plate 173: Little Salkeld, in May 1963; a repeat of the shelter at New Biggin, but in a better state of repair. The gables of the stationmaster's house can be seen behind the shelter.

D. Jenkinson

Figure 64: The Little Salkeld signalling diagram, based upon information available for 1955.

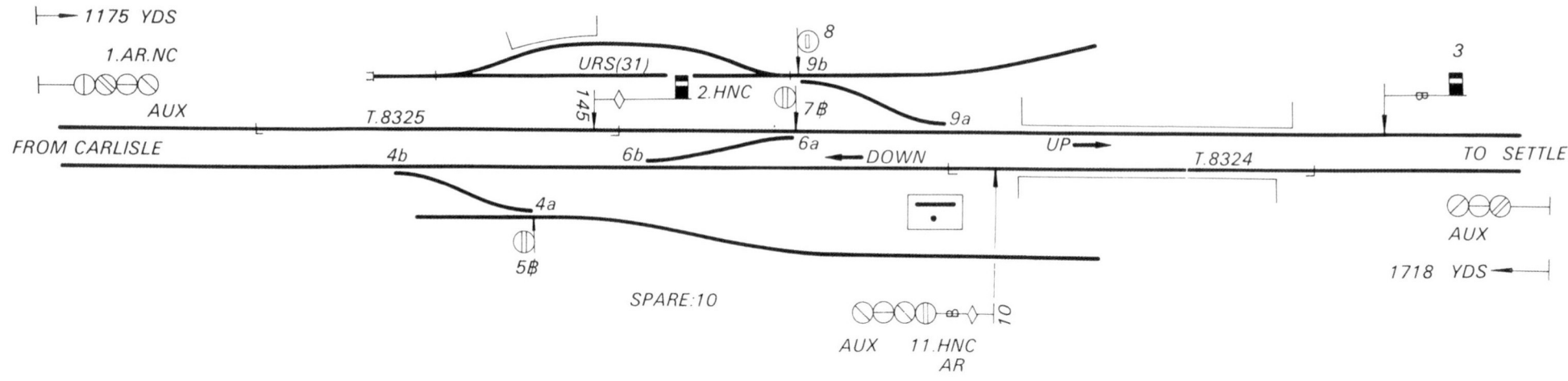

LITTLE SALKELD
APRIL 1955

LONG MEG SDG 1M 83 YDS ⟵——⟶ LANGWATHBY 1M 1078 YDS

LONG MEG SIDINGS

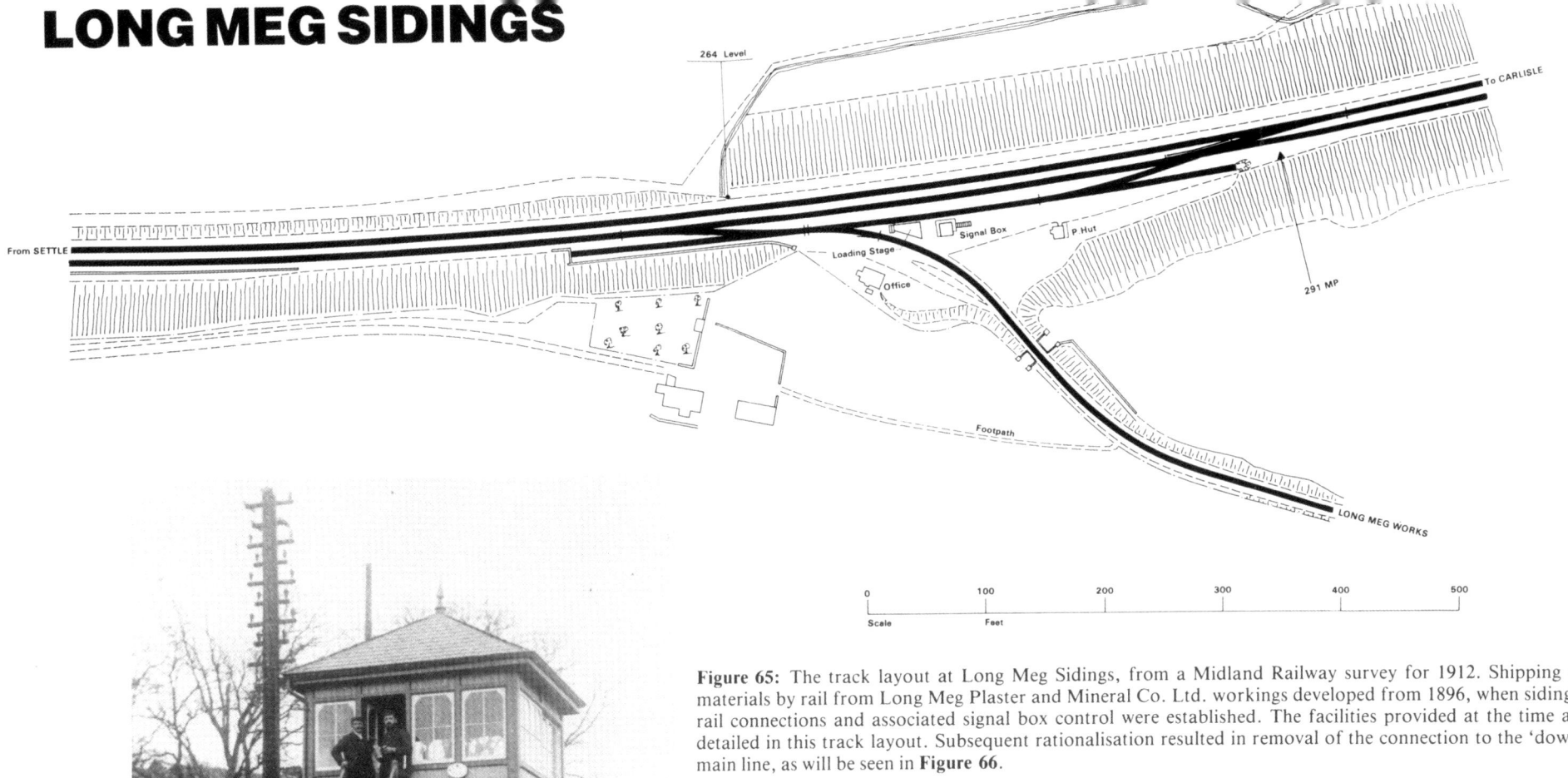

Figure 65: The track layout at Long Meg Sidings, from a Midland Railway survey for 1912. Shipping of materials by rail from Long Meg Plaster and Mineral Co. Ltd. workings developed from 1896, when sidings, rail connections and associated signal box control were established. The facilities provided at the time are detailed in this track layout. Subsequent rationalisation resulted in removal of the connection to the 'down' main line, as will be seen in **Figure 66**.

Plate 174: Long Meg signal box, photographed at about the turn of the century. This is the only example in this book of an early type of Midland signal box, where the 'shorter' windows were fitted to the front of the box as well as to the ends. We have no details of the size of this cabin or the number of levers, but it can be assumed that it was 11ft. 6in. square, and approximately 12ft. to the operating floor from rail level. It was taken out of use from 23rd May 1915.

G. Nicol

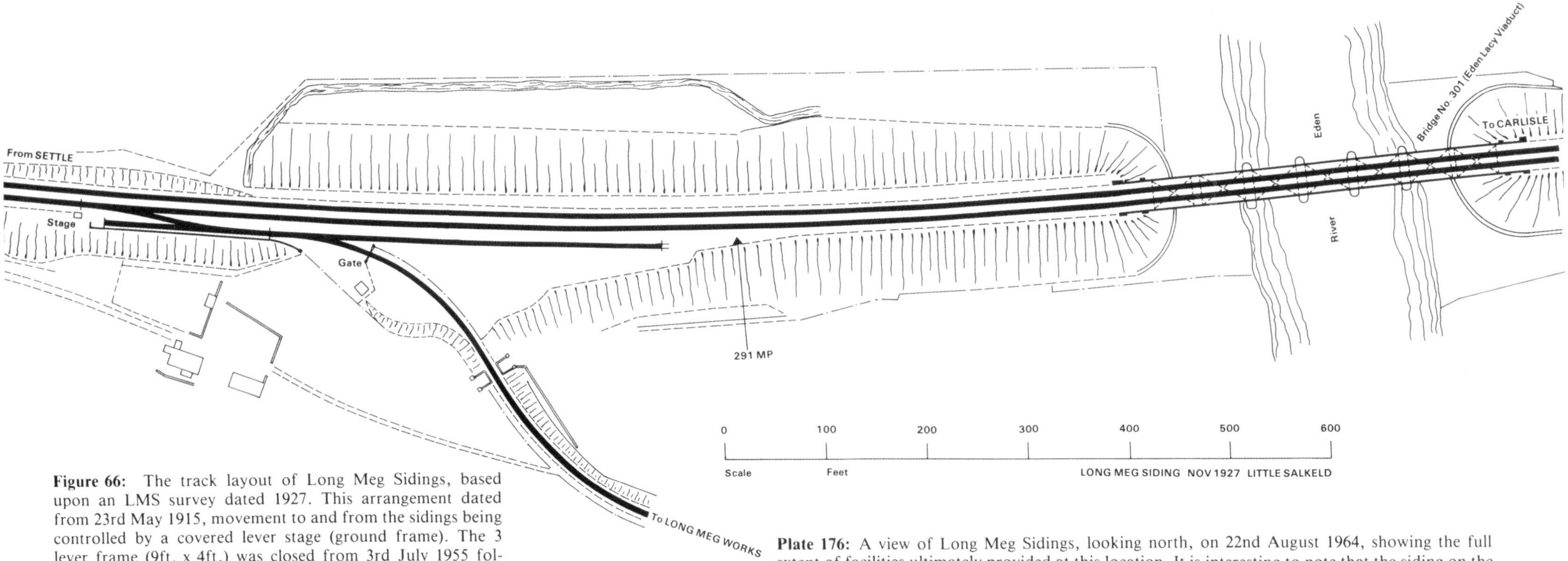

Labels on figure: From SETTLE, Stage, Gate, 291 MP, TO LONG MEG WORKS, Eden, River, Bridge No. 301 (Eden Lacy Viaduct), To CARLISLE

Scale bar: 0 100 200 300 400 500 600 Feet

LONG MEG SIDING NOV 1927 LITTLE SALKELD

Figure 66: The track layout of Long Meg Sidings, based upon an LMS survey dated 1927. This arrangement dated from 23rd May 1915, movement to and from the sidings being controlled by a covered lever stage (ground frame). The 3 lever frame (9ft. x 4ft.) was closed from 3rd July 1955 following the developments shown in **Figure 67**. It is interesting to note the close proximity to Eden Lacy Viaduct.

Plate 176: A view of Long Meg Sidings, looking north, on 22nd August 1964, showing the full extent of facilities ultimately provided at this location. It is interesting to note that the siding on the extreme left, designated 'cripples' on the proposal, is in use for loaded wagons.

P. Baughan

Plate 175: Long Meg, looking north, in 1963, showing the connection from the 'down' to the 'up' main line, and the facing connection from the 'up' main. The 1896 signal box occupied a position near the site of the platelayers' hut and bracketed 'up' home signal. The parapets of the viaduct can also be seen.

D. Jenkinson

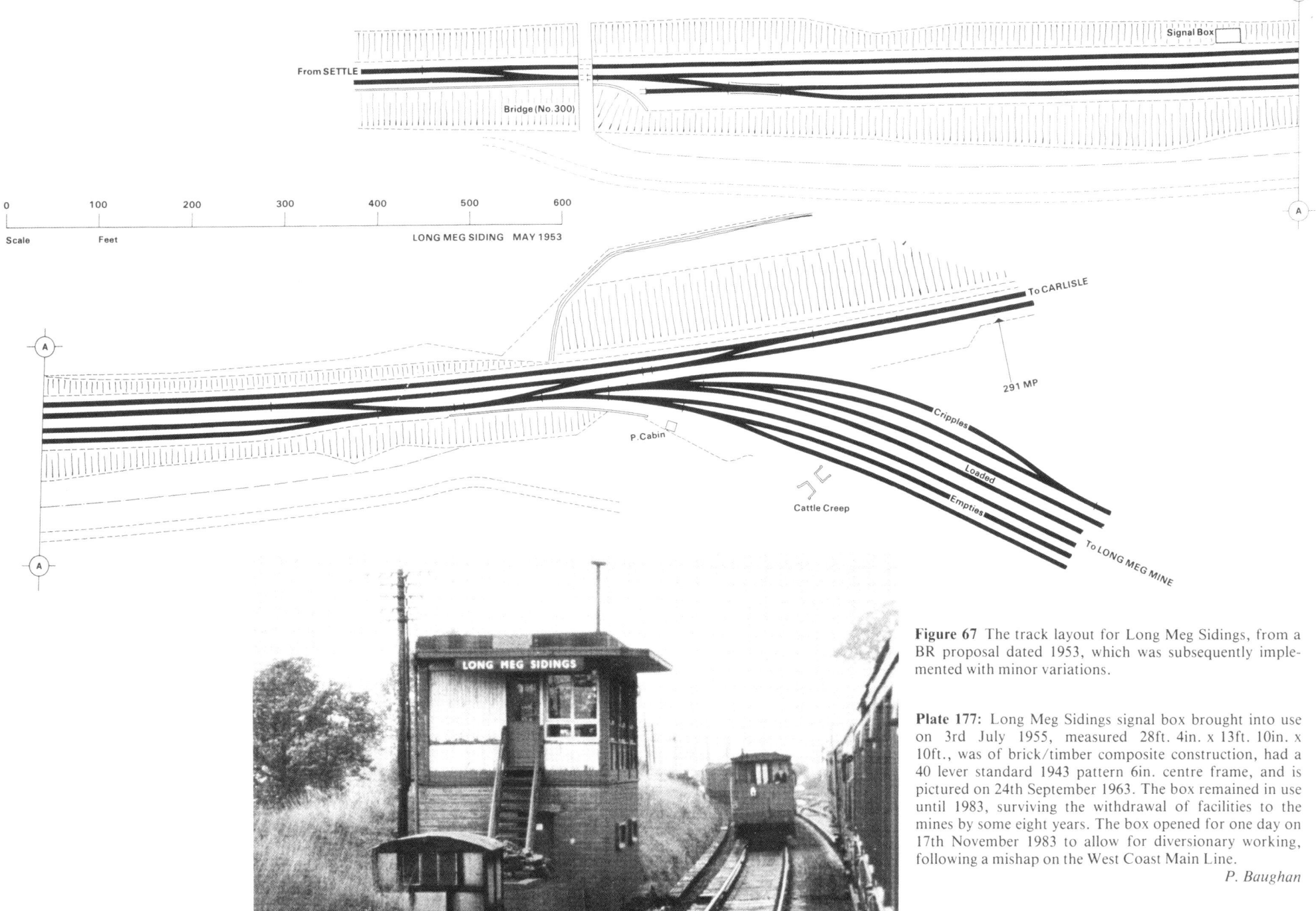

Scale Feet
0 100 200 300 400 500 600

LONG MEG SIDING   MAY 1953

From SETTLE

Bridge (No.300)

Signal Box

To CARLISLE

291 MP

Cripples

Loaded

Empties

To LONG MEG MINE

P.Cabin

Cattle Creep

LONG MEG SIDINGS

Figure 67 The track layout for Long Meg Sidings, from a BR proposal dated 1953, which was subsequently implemented with minor variations.

Plate 177: Long Meg Sidings signal box brought into use on 3rd July 1955, measured 28ft. 4in. x 13ft. 10in. x 10ft., was of brick/timber composite construction, had a 40 lever standard 1943 pattern 6in. centre frame, and is pictured on 24th September 1963. The box remained in use until 1983, surviving the withdrawal of facilities to the mines by some eight years. The box opened for one day on 17th November 1983 to allow for diversionary working, following a mishap on the West Coast Main Line.

P. Baughan

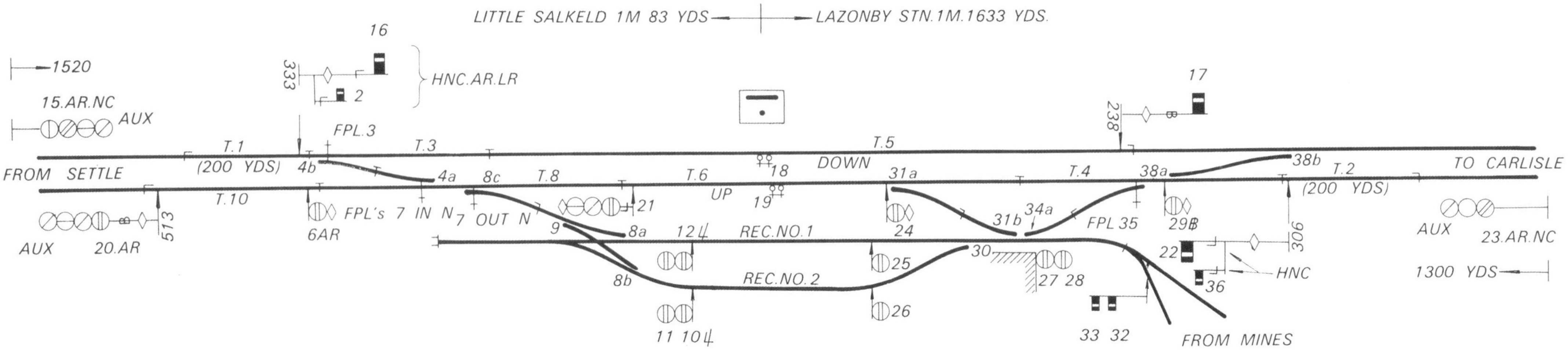

16

333

HNC.AR.LR

2

17

1520

15.AR.NC

AUX

238

T.1
(200 YDS)

FPL.3

T.3

T.5

DOWN

T.4

38b
T.2

FROM SETTLE

4b

4a

8c

T.8

T.6

18

31a

38a

TO CARLISLE
(200 YDS)

T.10

513

FPL's 7 IN N

7 OUT N

21

UP

19

31b

34a

FPL 35

29

306

AUX

AUX

20.AR

6AR

9

8a

12

REC.NO.1

24

22

23.AR.NC

8b

REC.NO.2

25

30

27 28

36

HNC

1300 YDS ⟶

26

33 32

FROM MINES

LONG MEG SIDINGS

SPARE: 1,5,14,37,39,40

Figure 68: The Long Meg Sidings signalling diagram, based upon information available for 1955. Note that the return crossover (31a-31b) is additional to the proposal (**Figure 67**). It can be seen between the trains on **Plate 177**.

Plate 178: A view of Eden Lacy Viaduct (No. 301) — 291 miles 8 chains. This 137 yard long viaduct was constructed entirely of local red sandstone between 1871 and 1875. Four of the six piers are set in the bed of the River Eden, and the nominal diameter of each span is 45ft. The Engineer's Department christened this viaduct Long Meg, and the plaster works of the same name can be seen on the extreme right, behind the viaduct.

Weston Collection

LAZONBY SAND SIDING

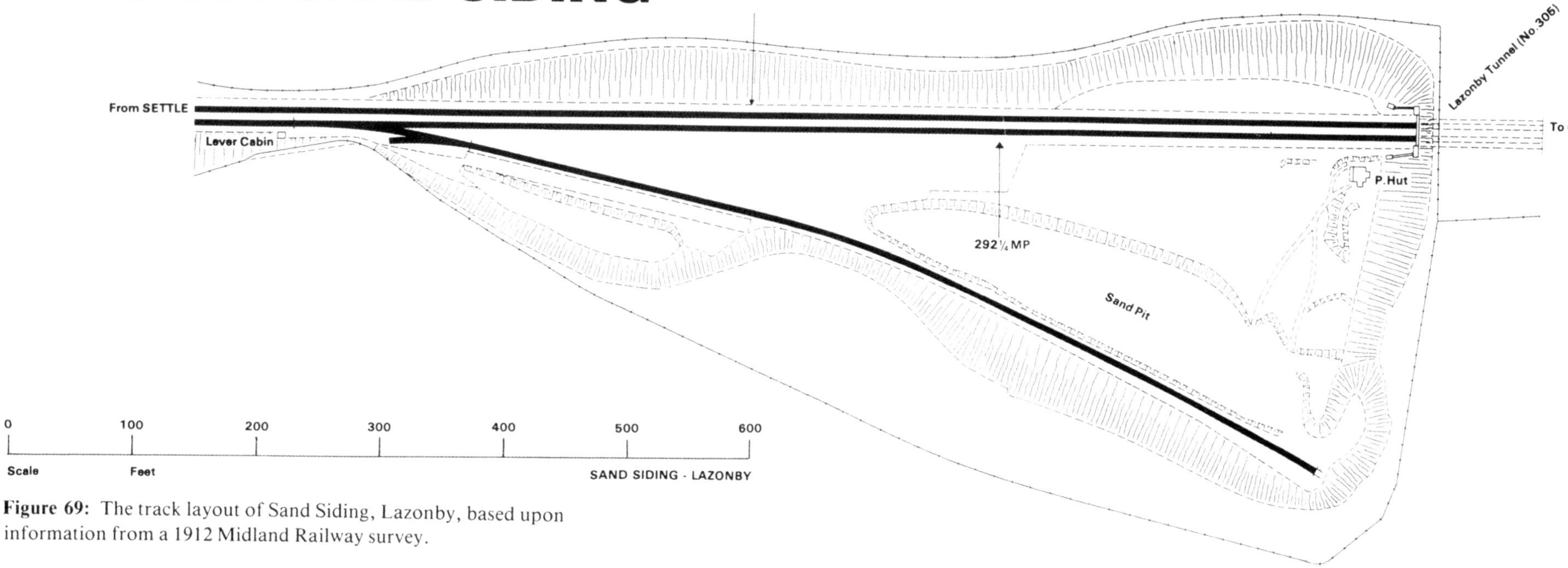

Figure 69: The track layout of Sand Siding, Lazonby, based upon information from a 1912 Midland Railway survey.

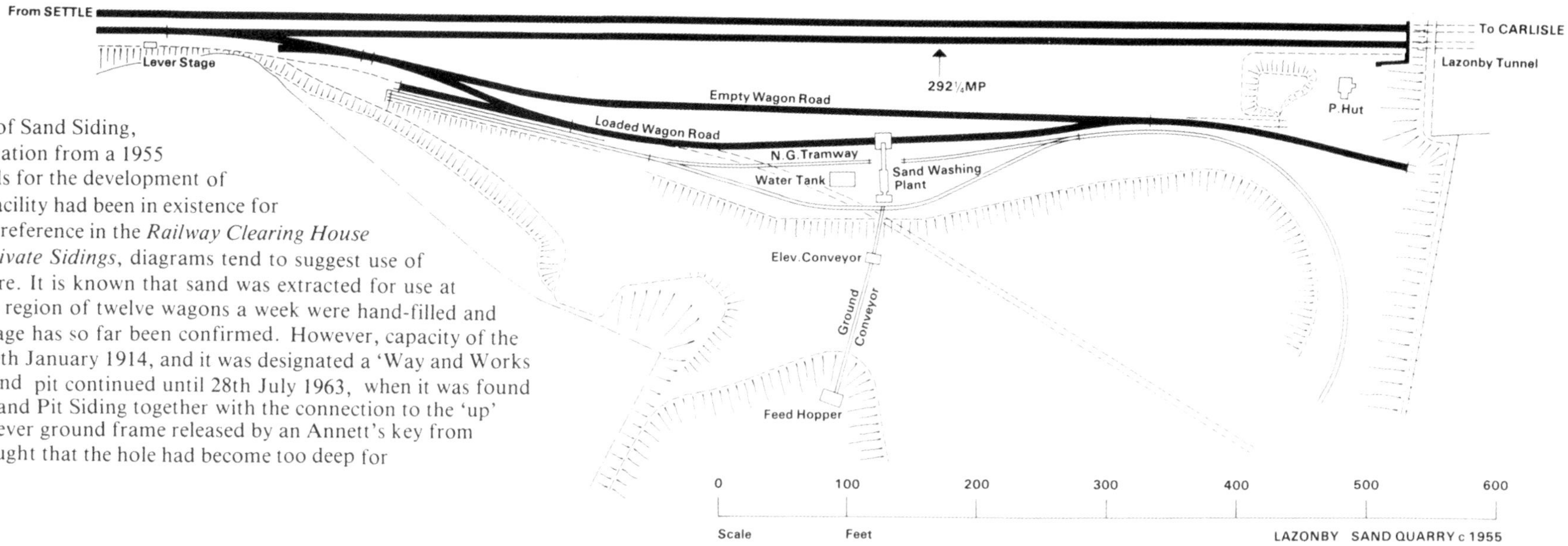

Figure 70: The track layout of Sand Siding, Lazonby, based upon information from a 1955 BR survey, showing proposals for the development of the sand pit. Although this facility had been in existence for many years, omission of any reference in the *Railway Clearing House Handbook of Stations or Private Sidings*, diagrams tend to suggest use of a railway departmental nature. It is known that sand was extracted for use at motive power depots. In the region of twelve wagons a week were hand-filled and despatched, but no other usage has so far been confirmed. However, capacity of the siding was increased from 10th January 1914, and it was designated a 'Way and Works Siding'. Operation of the sand pit continued until 28th July 1963, when it was found necessary to take away the Sand Pit Siding together with the connection to the 'up' main line, worked by a one lever ground frame released by an Annett's key from Lazonby signal box. It is thought that the hole had become too deep for economical use.

LAZONBY

Plate 179: The south end of Lazonby Tunnel (No. 305) — 292 miles 25 chains. The 99 yard long tunnel was constructed with stone side walls, invert, arch and faces. It was originally planned to have a cutting here, but a tunnel resulted, and it was cut during 1871 and 1872. To the right of the picture is the platelayers' hut on the land adjacent to the Sand Siding, and is shown in **Figures 69 & 70**.

D. Ibbotson

Plate 181: Lazonby and Kirkoswald Station, as seen from the north. The photographer is standing alongside the extensive cattle pens for eight wagons, provided for the large volume of livestock traffic generated here. Although the year is 1939, the station is essentially still in its Midland Railway guise. Note, particularly, the fencing, the tall nameboard, and swan-neck water column. The stationmaster's house is seen to the left.

N. Wilkinson

Plate 180: Lazonby, showing the east face of bridge No. 306 (292 miles 44 chains) immediately to the south of Lazonby Station, and carrying the railway over the Lazonby to Kirkoswald road. The bridge was built entirely of stone, each span being 25ft. The parapet on the western side was surmounted by cast-iron railings, provided as a precaution to prevent passengers stepping over the parapet from coaches of trains which were too long to fit the platform.

Plate 182: Lazonby and Kirkoswald Station, pictured from the south on 22nd August 1966, a further fine example of a No. 2 medium-sized station. Kirkoswald was added to the name from July 1895. The station became an unstaffed halt on 2nd January 1967, and closed to passengers on 4th May 1970.

D. F. Tee

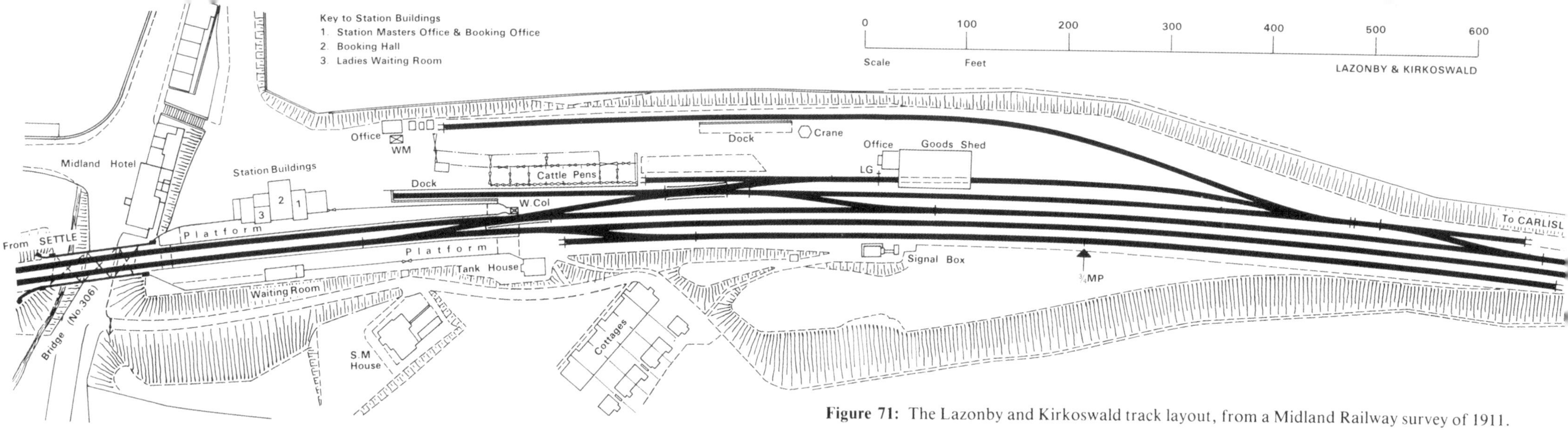

Key to Station Buildings
1. Station Masters Office & Booking Office
2. Booking Hall
3. Ladies Waiting Room

Scale Feet

LAZONBY & KIRKOSWALD

Figure 71: The Lazonby and Kirkoswald track layout, from a Midland Railway survey of 1911.

Plate 183: Lazonby signal box brought into use on 19th July 1895, was of wood construction, measured 16ft. 6in. x 11ft. 6in. x 8ft., had a 16 lever tumbler frame, and a renewal cost of £212 (W & W Committee Minute No. 14316, 7/6/1895). It closed on 25th June 1969. All 'down' side connections had been taken out of use from 29th March 1965, goods faciities having been withdrawn from 2nd November 1964. The concrete chemical toilet near to the signal box is to an LMS design. The handrails to the signal box staircase are of tubular steel, again to LMS designs. The brick-built coal bunker was not, as usually, provided by the Midland Railway and follows LNWR practice. The platelayers' cabin on the 'up' platform is a BR standard feature. The 12,000 gallon water tank of the 1872 proposals is in evidence at the Carlisle end of the 'up' platform. Note the row of six railway cottages.

Plate 184: Detail of the screen to the waiting area, on the platform side of the medium-sized station building at Lazonby, retains all the features of the original design.

Plate 185: One of the typical Midland square oil lamps, as relocated on a short cast standard.

D. Jenkinson

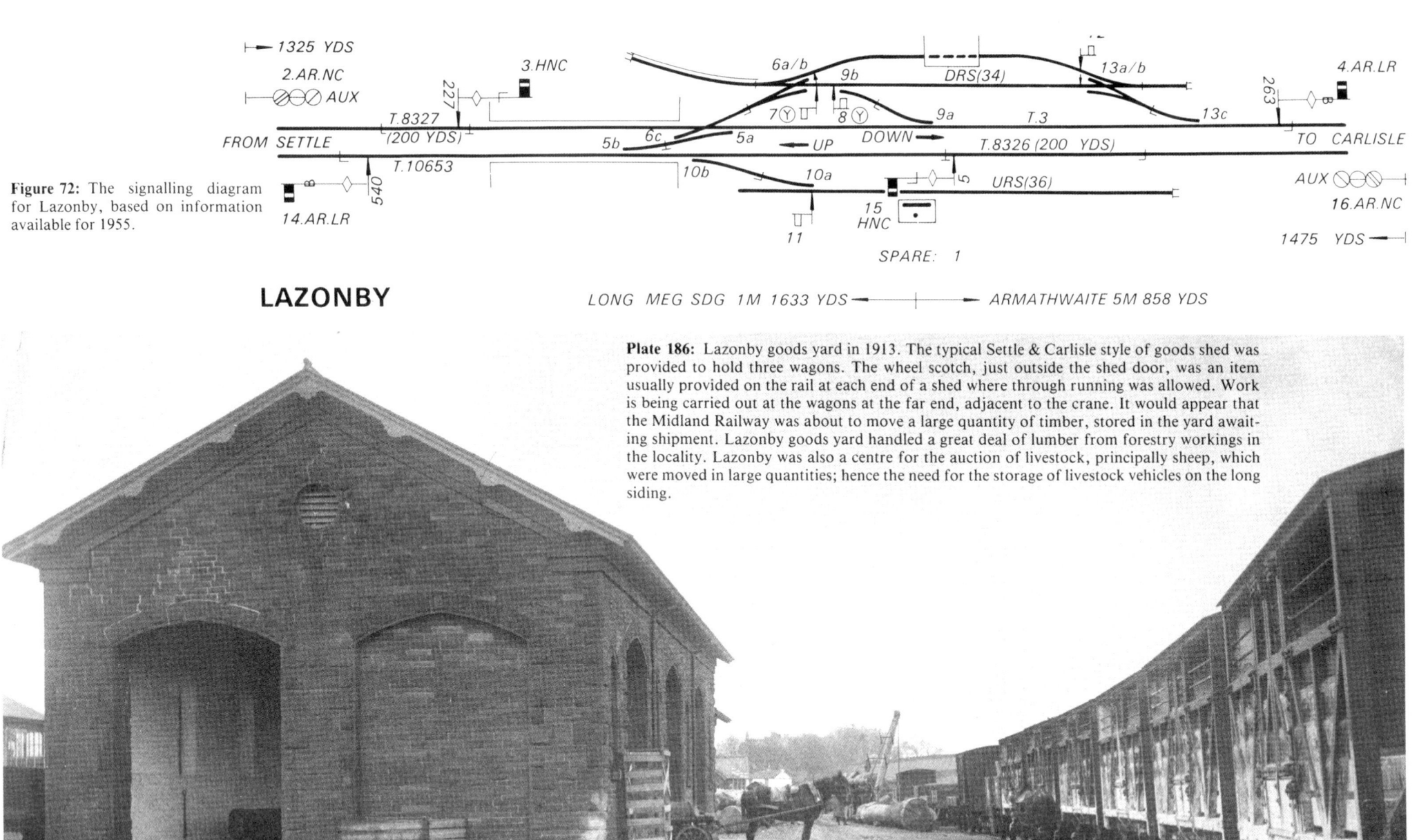

Figure 72: The signalling diagram for Lazonby, based on information available for 1955.

1325 YDS

2.AR.NC
AUX

3.HNC

227

T.8327 (200 YDS)

FROM SETTLE

T.10653

540

14.AR.LR

6a/b

9b

DRS(34)

13a/b

4.AR.LR

263

7 (Y)   8 (Y)   9a   T.3   13c

5b   6c   5a   UP   DOWN   T.8326 (200 YDS)   TO CARLISLE

10b   10a   URS(36)   5

15 HNC

11

AUX

16.AR.NC

1475 YDS

SPARE: 1

LAZONBY

LONG MEG SDG 1M 1633 YDS ———— ARMATHWAITE 5M 858 YDS

Plate 186: Lazonby goods yard in 1913. The typical Settle & Carlisle style of goods shed was provided to hold three wagons. The wheel scotch, just outside the shed door, was an item usually provided on the rail at each end of a shed where through running was allowed. Work is being carried out at the wagons at the far end, adjacent to the crane. It would appear that the Midland Railway was about to move a large quantity of timber, stored in the yard awaiting shipment. Lazonby goods yard handled a great deal of lumber from forestry workings in the locality. Lazonby was also a centre for the auction of livestock, principally sheep, which were moved in large quantities; hence the need for the storage of livestock vehicles on the long siding.

BARON WOOD SIDING

Plate 187: The north end of Baron Wood Tunnel No. 1 (No. 315) — 295 miles 49 chains. The 207 yard long tunnel was cut between the years 1870 and 1873; it was finished with red sandstone side walls, arch and facing, with patches of brickwork to the arch.

D. Ibbotson

Plate 188: Baron Wood Tunnel No. 2 (No. 316) — 295 miles 63 chains — showing the south end. The 251 yard long tunnel is of similar construction to No. 1, and was constructed between 1871 and 1873.

D. Ibbotson

Figure 73: The Baron Wood Sidings track layout, based upon a Midland Railway survey of 1913.

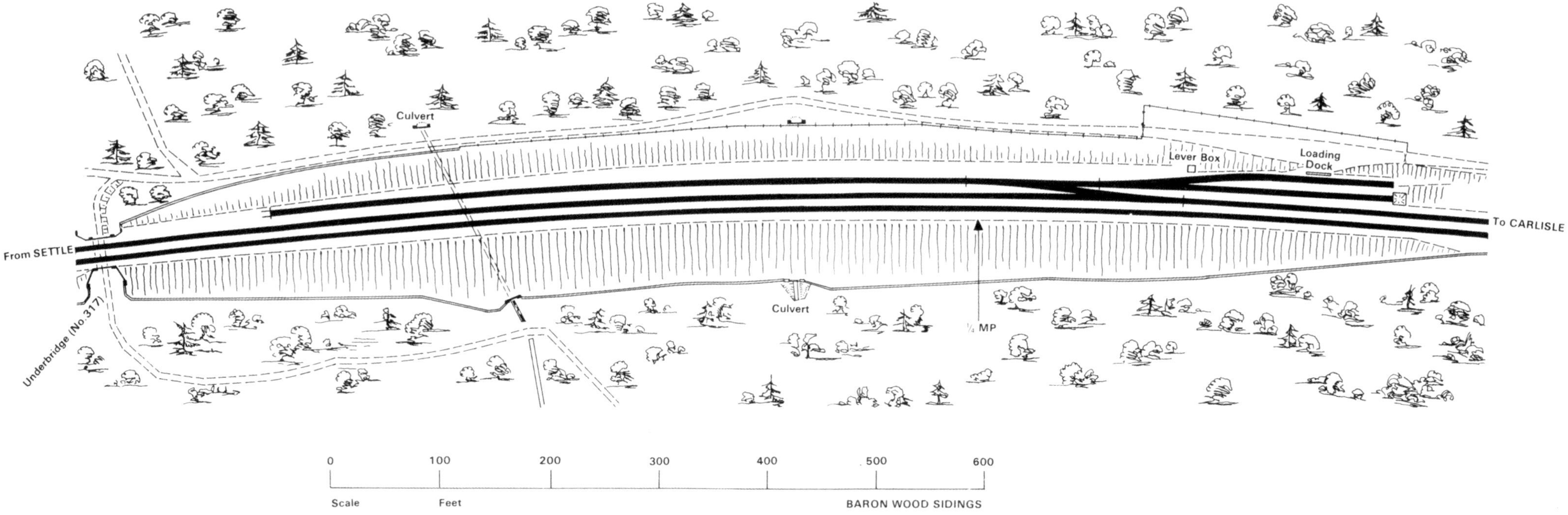

Culvert

From SETTLE

Underbridge (No. 317)

Culvert

Lever Box

Loading Dock

To CARLISLE

¼ MP

| 0 | 100 | 200 | 300 | 400 | 500 | 600 |

Scale   Feet

BARON WOOD SIDINGS

Plate 189: At Baron Wood Sidings, a 5MT 4-6-0 locomotive, No. 44902, with a northbound express freight, passes on 28th May 1960. A private siding was provided at Baron Wood for the use of the Ley family of Lazonby Hall, whose extensive forestry land is traversed between Lazonby and Armathwaite. Pit props were prepared at the local sawmill and transported from Baron Wood Sidings during World War I, sufficient traffic to warrant the provision in 1914 of a covered lever frame of three levers (tumbler type). Perhaps because of handling difficulties, the sidings never reached their full potential. The sidings finally closed in 1951 and main line connections were subsequently removed.

R. Leslie

Plate 191: A Class 5MT 4-6-0, No. 44963, with a Durran Hill to Washwood Heath express freight, emerges from the southern end of Armathwaite Tunnel on 28th May 1960.

R. Leslie

Plate 190: A Carlisle to Skipton goods train, with 'Black Five' No. 44884 in charge, passes the long headshunt of Baron Wood Sidings on 7th November 1967. The small lever stage was protected by fixed signals. The key to the stage was kept at Lazonby signal box, the guard returning it to the signalman at Armathwaite after use.

J. M. Hammond

Plate 192: Armathwaite Tunnel (No. 318) — 296 miles 63 chains. The 325 yard long tunnel was constructed with stone side walls, arch and facings. An alternative name for this tunnel is Cat Clint, a local name for the area through which the tunnel passes. Here we see the 09.50 St. Pancras to Glasgow 'Thames Clyde Express', headed by 'Peak' class diesel No. D23, on 8th September 1967.

J. M. Hammond

ARMATHWAITE

Plate 193 (left: A Class 5 4-6-0 locomotive, No. 44899, heads a northbound freight away from Armathwaite Tunnel, as the line curves to the right over Armathwaite Viaduct and along to Armathwaite Station. The line is still holding a raised position on the valley side as it descends towards Carlisle.

J. M. Hammond

Plate 194 (below left): Armathwaite Viaduct (No. 320) — 297 miles 23 chains. The 176 yard long viaduct was constructed entirely of stone between the years 1871 and 1874. The gently curving viaduct, with nine spans each of 44ft. 7in., stood 80ft. above the valley. 'Black Five' No. 44672, with an evening parcels train, crosses the viaduct on 28th April 1967.

D. F. Tee Collection

Plate 195 (below): Bridge No. 321 (297 miles 31 chains), at Armathwaite. The former turnpike road passes through the embankment approach to Armathwaite Viaduct. This is an example of an atypical bridge formation, pointed arches being an infrequent occurrence. It is quite possible that the bridge was constructed prior to the embankment being formed. The slightly skewed bridge was built entirely of stone, in 1871, predating the viaduct.

Plate 196: An unidentified Class 2P heads an 'up' express through Armathwaite Station in 1938. The engine is passing over Station Road bridge (No. 324) — 298 miles 4 chains. Illustrated here is an example of iron railings on the bridge parapet near to a station platform. The bridge numberplate is a standard LMS fitment.

N. Wilkinson

Plate 198: Armathwaite Station some 25 years after opening of the line. The oil lamps are still on their tall standards, and each lamp carries the station name. Note the rustic seats with the name painted on the backrest and the angled nameboard again. This station closed to passengers from 4th May 1970 after being an unstaffed halt for three years.

Lens of Sutton

Plate 197: A view of Armathwaite, circa 1930. This unusual scene illustrates many details to be found in the vicinity of stations, but not frequently photographed. The four cattle pens are larger than those found elsewhere, and the dock was scheduled to have a capacity for five wagons. The small brick building, adjacent to the cattle dock, behind the buffer stops, was designated as a 'saw dust house', a facility provided at other places but not pinpointed on the surveys. Small structures were erected near to many other cattle docks, and the saw dust found use in cattle wagons. The large angled nameboard, which appears to be newly-painted, for some reason was not repeated on the 'down' platform **(cf. Plate 196)**. Note the heavy timber buffer stops, marking the end of the headshunts. In the foreground is the weighbridge and weigh office.

D. F. Tee Collection

Plate 199: A view of Armathwaite Station, looking south from the 'up' platform, and showing the main station building. **Plates 198, 199, 200 & 201** form a sequence to add detail to the drawing of this No. 2 (medium) style of building **(Figures 75 & 76)**. Note the gradient post set near to the waiting area screen.

J. M. Hammond

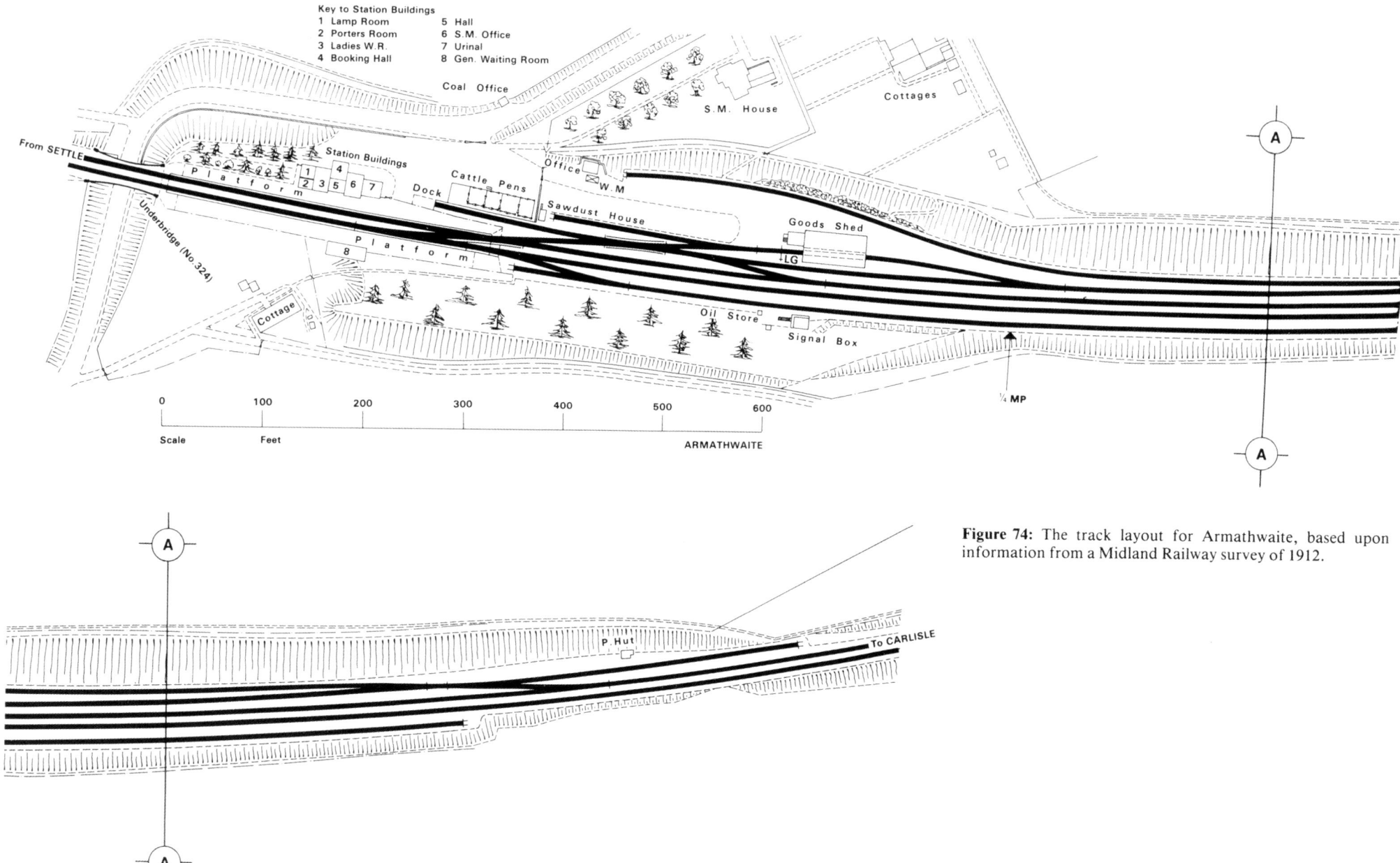

Figure 74: The track layout for Armathwaite, based upon information from a Midland Railway survey of 1912.

Key to Station Buildings
1 Lamp Room
2 Porters Room
3 Ladies W.R.
4 Booking Hall
5 Hall
6 S.M. Office
7 Urinal
8 Gen. Waiting Room

Coal Office

S.M. House

Cottages

From SETTLE

Station Buildings

Platform

Underbridge (No.324)

Cattle Pens

Dock

Office
W.M

Sawdust House

Goods Shed

LG

Platform

Cottage

Oil Store

Signal Box

¼ MP

0 100 200 300 400 500 600

Scale   Feet

ARMATHWAITE

A

P. Hut

To CARLISLE

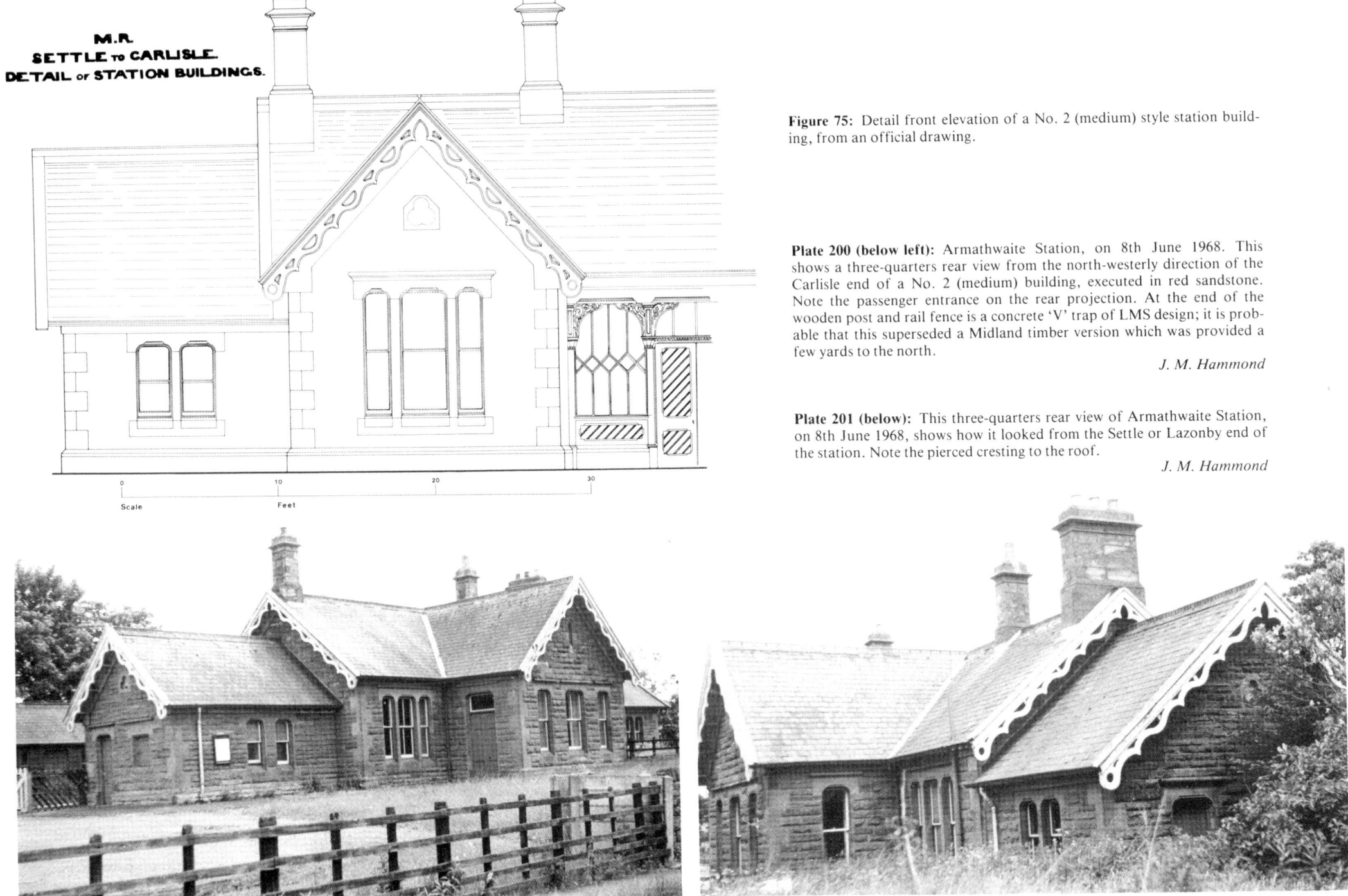

M.R.
SETTLE to CARLISLE.
DETAIL of STATION BUILDINGS.

Scale ... Feet
0 ... 10 ... 20 ... 30

Figure 75: Detail front elevation of a No. 2 (medium) style station building, from an official drawing.

Plate 200 (below left): Armathwaite Station, on 8th June 1968. This shows a three-quarters rear view from the north-westerly direction of the Carlisle end of a No. 2 (medium) building, executed in red sandstone. Note the passenger entrance on the rear projection. At the end of the wooden post and rail fence is a concrete 'V' trap of LMS design; it is probable that this superseded a Midland timber version which was provided a few yards to the north.

J. M. Hammond

Plate 201 (below): This three-quarters rear view of Armathwaite Station, on 8th June 1968, shows how it looked from the Settle or Lazonby end of the station. Note the pierced cresting to the roof.

J. M. Hammond

ELEVATION NEXT APPROACH ROAD

END ELEVATION ON A

| COALS | | |
| DUST | W.C | URINAL |

STATION MASTERS OFFICE

WAITING SHED

LADIES WAITING ROOM

PORTERS ROOM

LAMP ROOM

WAITING HALL

LOBBY   W.C

END ELEVATION ON B

GROUND PLAN

SCALE   FEET

10 5 0 10 20 30 40 50

Figure 76: A plan and elevations of a No. 2 (medium) style of station building for the Settle & Carlisle Railway, taken from an official drawing. The front elevation has been omitted, as details can be found by utilising **Figure 75** and the right-hand end of the drawing of the larger No. 1 style shown in **Figure 5** at Settle.

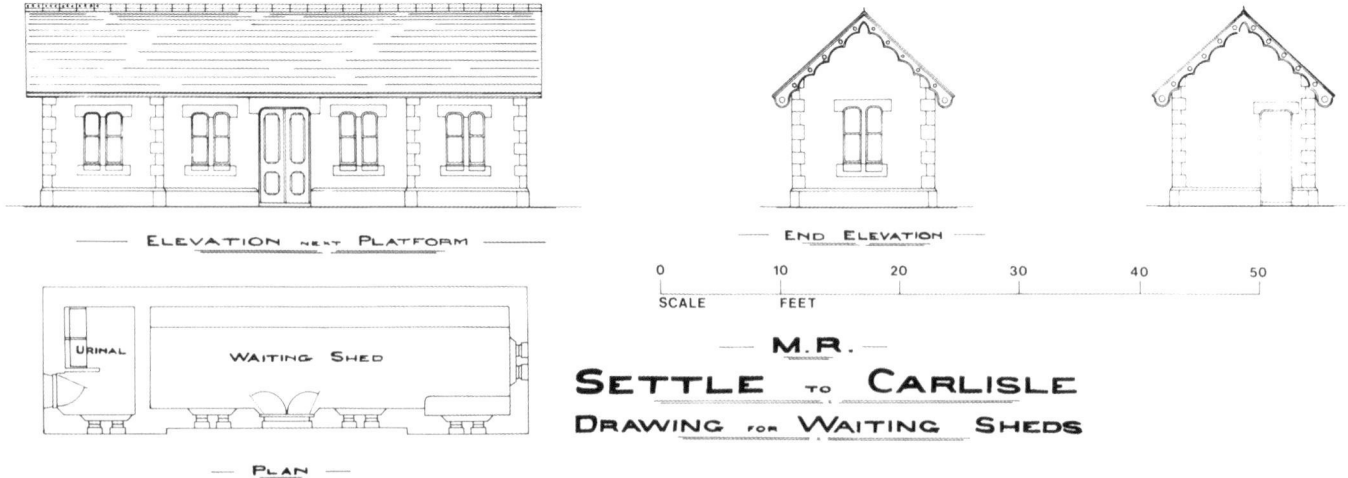

ELEVATION next PLATFORM

END ELEVATION

0   10   20   30   40   50
SCALE   FEET

URINAL   WAITING SHED

PLAN

M.R.
SETTLE to CARLISLE
DRAWING for WAITING SHEDS

Figure 77: The plan and elevations for the stone-built type of shelter, from an official drawing.

Plate 202: A fine example of a stone waiting shelter; that of Armathwaite, pictured on 8th June 1968. Note the diagonally-boarded panels to the doors, the pierced cresting to the roof, and the bargeboards, all echoing those to be found on the main building. Compare this shelter barge boarding with that at other locations, often being to an alternative design.

J. M. Hammond

Plate 203: Armathwaite goods shed, as seen in 1963. A two-wagon shed was proposed for this site, although a larger one was ultimately provided. Note the lozenge windows, the wheel scotches at each end, and the location of the loading gauge. A concrete bin of LMS design was provided near the shed door, to hold sand. The stationmaster's house can be seen on the hillside behind the goods shed. Armathwaite closed to goods from 6th April 1964.

D. Jenkinson

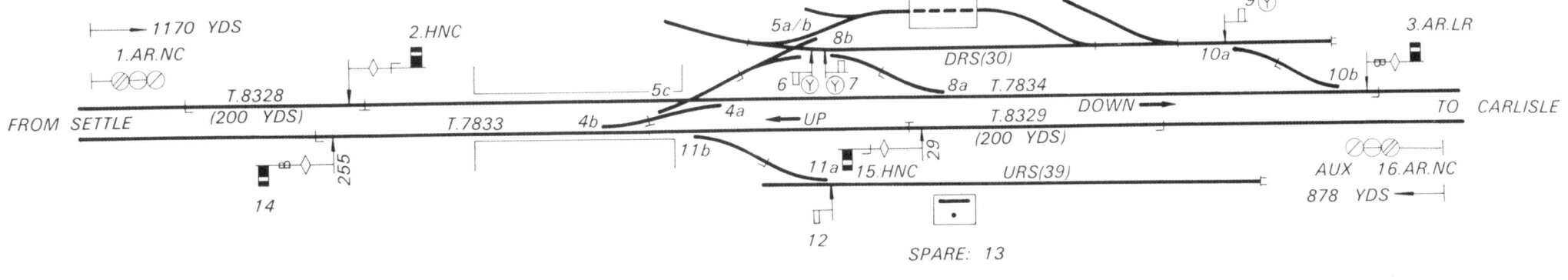

1170 YDS →
1.AR.NC
2.HNC
5a/b
8b
DRS(30)
9 (Y)
3.AR.LR
10a
10b
T.8328
(200 YDS)
5c
6 (Y) (Y) 7
8a T.7834
TO CARLISLE
FROM SETTLE
T.7833
4b
4a
← UP
T.8329
DOWN →
255
11b
11a
29
(200 YDS)
14
15.HNC
URS(39)
AUX 16.AR.NC
878 YDS →
12
SPARE: 13

ARMATHWAITE

LAZONBY STN. 5M 858 YDS ← | → LOW HOUSE CROSSING 1M 836 YDS

Figure 78 (above): The Armathwaite signalling diagram, based upon information available for 1955.

Plate 204 (left): 'Jubilee' class 5XP, No. 45714, *Revenge* passes Armathwaite signal box with the 'up' 'Waverley' on 20th July 1957.

R. Leslie

Plate 205 (below): Armathwaite signal box, brought into use on 16th July 1899, was of wood construction, measured 16ft. 6in. x 11ft. 6in. x 12ft., had a 16 lever tumbler frame, and a renewal cost of £260 (W & W Committee Minute No. 17176, 18/5/1899). It closed on 15th January 1983. A Midland corrugated-iron oil store is again in evidence.

J. M. Hammond

Plate 206: Dry Beck Viaduct, Armathwaite (No. 326), in 1919 (299 miles 5 chains). This interesting view shows maintenance in progress to the 139 yard long viaduct of seven 44ft 4in. spans, constructed with stone abutments, wings, piers and parapets. In this view, repairs are being carried out to the brick arch rings, and the use of timber scaffolding and platforms should be compared with modern methods. Note the timber chute used to transfer material to the base of the 80ft. high structure. Careful investigation will reveal the Midland Railway boundary markers; one being to the left of the second pier, and another to the left of the fourth pier, numbering from the left.

LOW HOUSE CROSSING

LOW HOUSE CROSSING

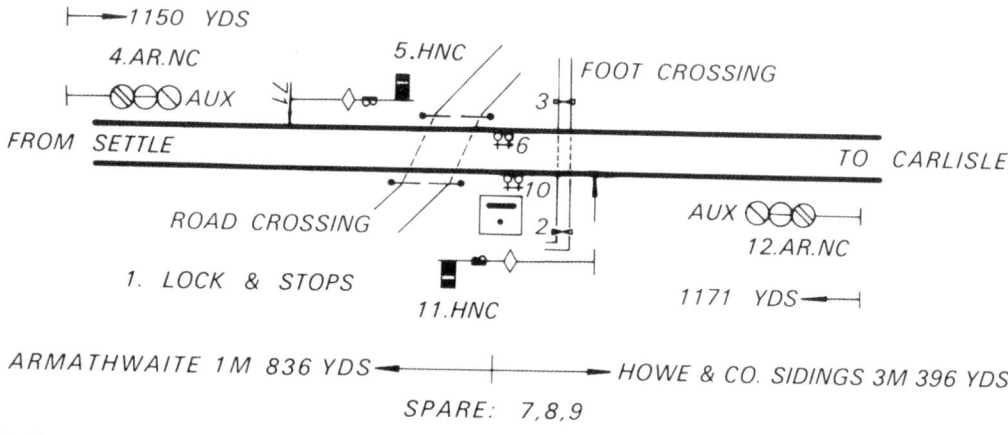

Plate 208 (above): Low House Crossing, as seen from the north. Information regarding both the box and the frame is inconclusive, but it appears that the box was constructed on 14th October 1890, and that the present frame was brought into use from 12th October 1900; this latter date would coincide with Way and Works Committee Minute No. 18026, 6/7/1900, for a renewal cost of £250. The crossing gates were removed and lifting barriers were provided in 1975. Although the road crosses the railway on the skew, the pedestrian footway crosses the rails at right angles.

J. M. Hammond

Plate 207 (above left): Low House Crossing, and the signal box, as seen from the south, on 21st October 1967.

J. M. Hammond

Figure 79: The signalling diagram for Low House Crossing, based upon information available for 1955.

LOW HOUSE CROSSING

COTEHILL

Key to Station Buildings

1. General Waiting Room
2. Ladies Waiting Room
3. Booking Hall
4. Porters Room
5. Station Masters Office

Figure 80: The track layout for Cotehill, based upon information from a Midland Railway survey of 1912.

Plate 209: Cotehill Viaduct (No. 333) — 301 miles 3 chains. A comparatively short viduct of 91yds. in length utilises construction techniques not previously seen. Stone was used for the abutments, piers, spandrel walls and parapet coping. The brick used for the arch rings was unusually not faced with stone. Brick was also used for the parapet wall on the string course above the spandrel. The openings are on a slight skew; three being 46ft. 10in., and one 46ft. 6in. The viaduct stands 60ft. above High Stand Gill, one of the alternative names often used for this structure, the other being Knothill. Here we see a Caprotti Class 5MT 4-6-0, No. 44754, with a southbound evening freight on 1st May 1958.

R. Leslie

Plate 210: A view looking north over Cotehill Viaduct on 23rd October 1958. Note the placing of the LMS bridge numberplate at the end of the western parapet. It is just possible to make out the painted numbers of the Midland sign on the eastern side capstone, the end stone of the coping.

BR/OPC

Plate 212: Cotehill Station, shortly before complete closure on 7th April 1952. This is our last view of a No. 3 (small) style of building. The connection to the 'down' sidings can be seen on the left, and the track layout diagram **(Figure 80)** shows two double slips, but these were replaced by plain turnouts in 1942. Cotehill signal box, although not shown here, stood on the 'up' side, between the station and the viaduct. It was brought into use in 1890 but was provided with a replacement 16 lever Midland tumbler frame in 1904. The box measured 16ft. 6in x 13ft. 6in. x 8ft. and closed at about the same time as the station.

D. Thompson

Plate 211: Cotehill, as seen in 1984. A view of the stationmaster's house and the row of four cottages. The private line to the Robinson's Knott Hill plaster works originally passed across the field in the foreground, but all evidence has disappeared in the forty or so years from the removal of the siding in 1940.

Plate 213: An 'up' freight, with ex-LMS 4F No. 44183, passes the site of Cotehill Station on the evening of 10th December 1960. The station was completely removed very soon after closure.

D. F. Tee

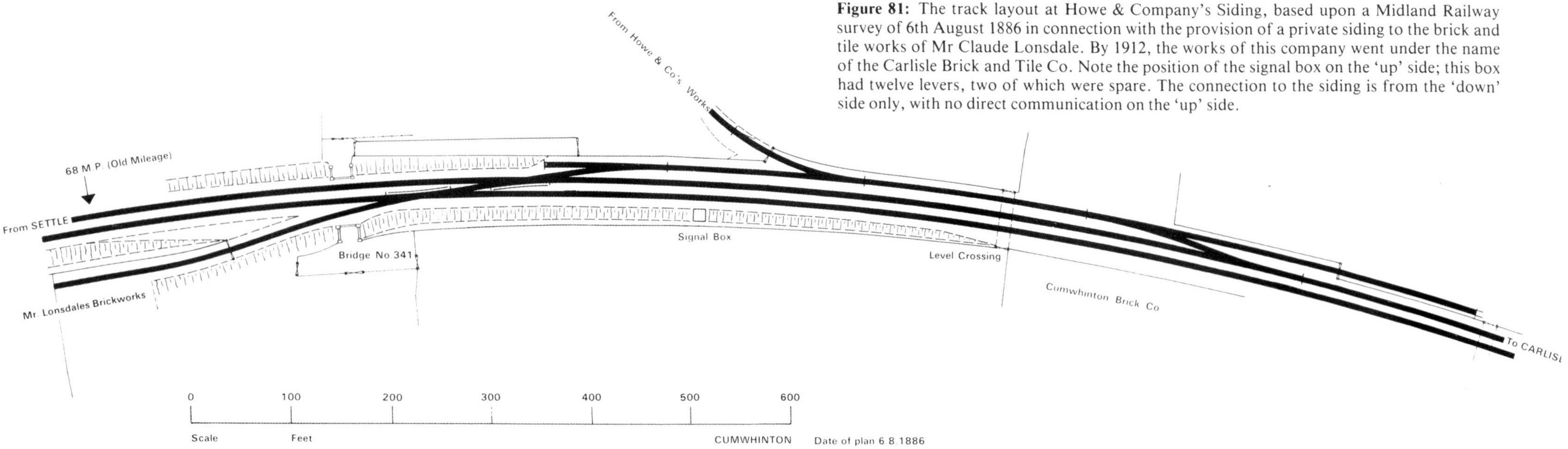

Figure 81: The track layout at Howe & Company's Siding, based upon a Midland Railway survey of 6th August 1886 in connection with the provision of a private siding to the brick and tile works of Mr Claude Lonsdale. By 1912, the works of this company went under the name of the Carlisle Brick and Tile Co. Note the position of the signal box on the 'up' side; this box had twelve levers, two of which were spare. The connection to the siding is from the 'down' side only, with no direct communication on the 'up' side.

From Howe & Co's Works

68 M P (Old Mileage)

From SETTLE

Mr Lonsdales Brickworks

Bridge No 341

Signal Box

Level Crossing

Cumwhinton Brick Co

To CARLISLE

| 0 | 100 | 200 | 300 | 400 | 500 | 600 |

Scale   Feet

CUMWHINTON   Date of plan 6.8.1886

Figure 82: The track layout at Howe & Company's Siding, based upon information from an LMS survey of 1927. By the time this survey was carried out, the Gotham Company of Nottingham had taken over interest in the Cocklake's alabaster works (previously Howe & Co.). This change appeared in amendments for 1921, although there was an Agreement with the LMS, dated from 14th November 1924. The signal box was replaced, to the position shown here, in 1916. The private siding for the Thomas Hamilton Company, shown on the Midland Railway map, was an extension of the northerly Howe & Co. Siding headshunt. Hamilton Company changed its name to Messrs Wright in 1918. The siding was taken out of use in 1924.

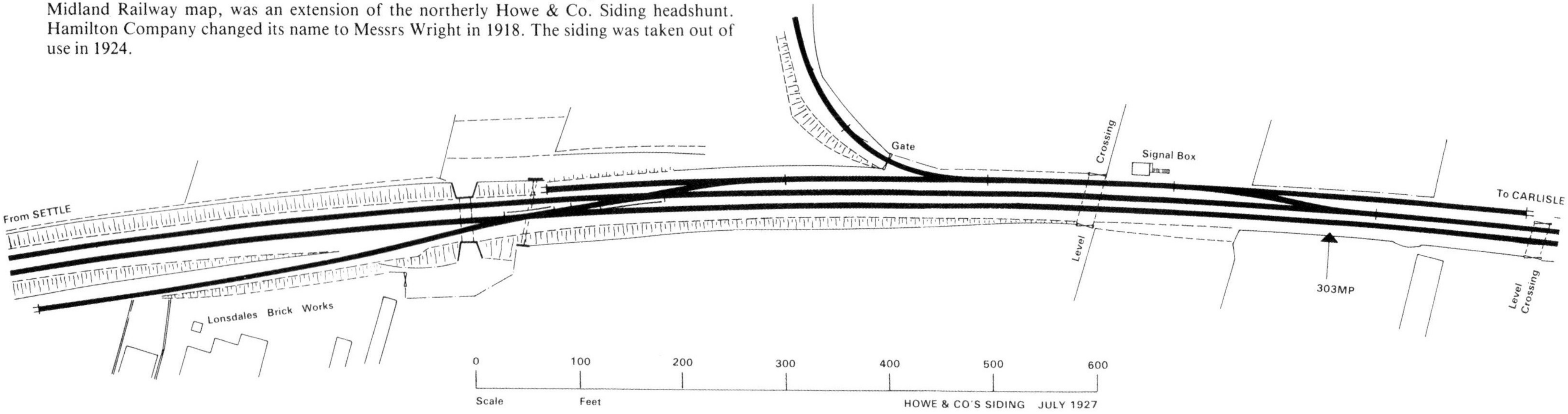

HOWE & CO. SIDINGS

From SETTLE

Gate

Crossing

Signal Box

To CARLISLE

Lonsdales Brick Works

303MP

Level Crossing

Level

| 0 | 100 | 200 | 300 | 400 | 500 | 600 |

Scale   Feet

HOWE & CO'S SIDING   JULY 1927

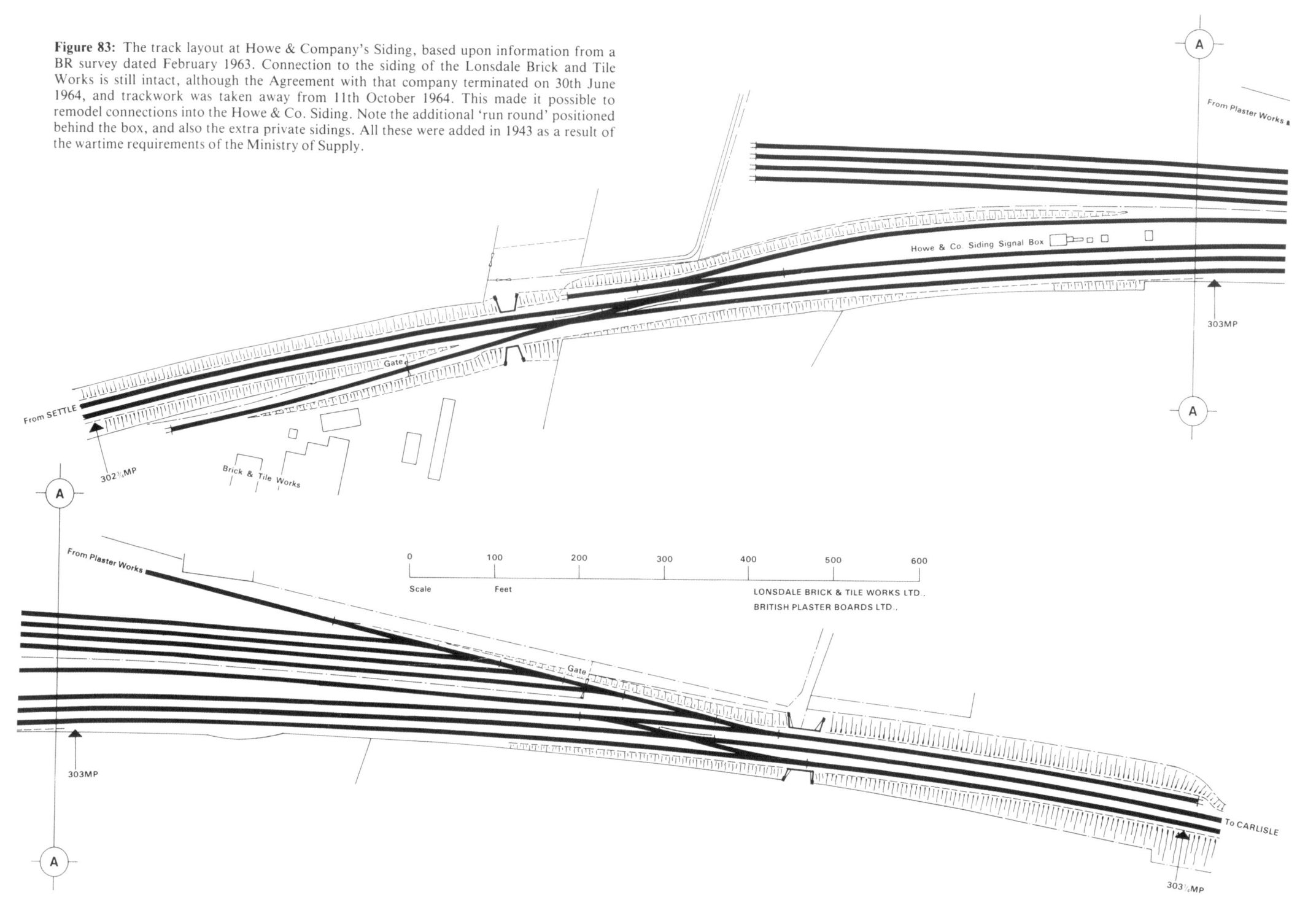

Figure 83: The track layout at Howe & Company's Siding, based upon information from a BR survey dated February 1963. Connection to the siding of the Lonsdale Brick and Tile Works is still intact, although the Agreement with that company terminated on 30th June 1964, and trackwork was taken away from 11th October 1964. This made it possible to remodel connections into the Howe & Co. Siding. Note the additional 'run round' positioned behind the box, and also the extra private sidings. All these were added in 1943 as a result of the wartime requirements of the Ministry of Supply.

From Plaster Works

A

Howe & Co. Siding Signal Box

303MP

Gate

From SETTLE

302¾MP

A

Brick & Tile Works

From Plaster Works

A

Scale   Feet

0   100   200   300   400   500   600

LONSDALE BRICK & TILE WORKS LTD.,

BRITISH PLASTER BOARDS LTD.,

Gate

303MP

To CARLISLE

A

303¾MP

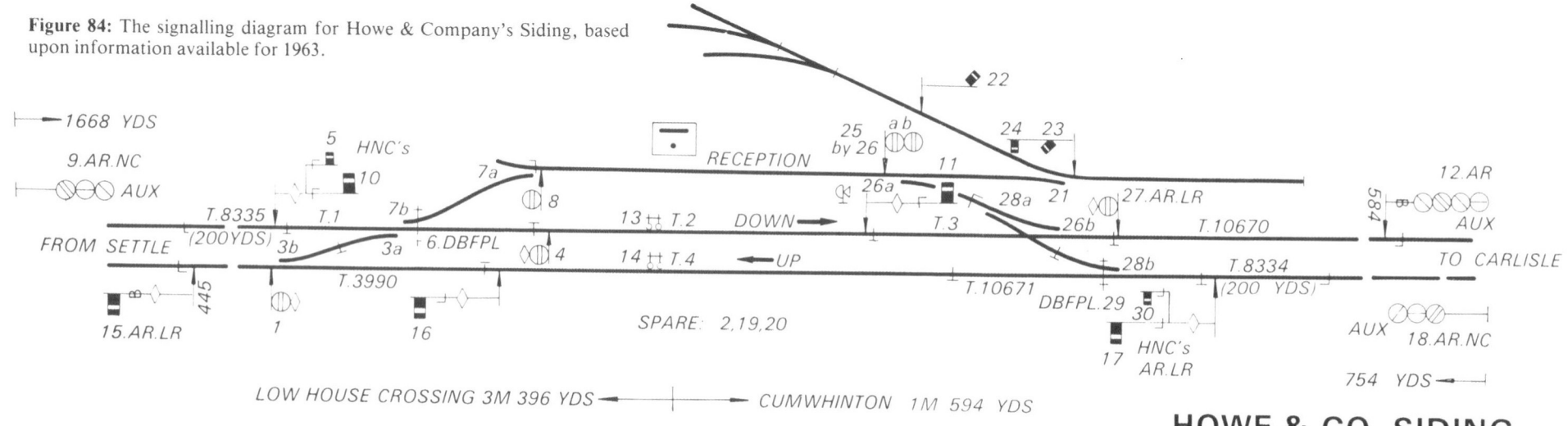

Figure 84: The signalling diagram for Howe & Company's Siding, based upon information available for 1963.

HOWE & CO. SIDING

Plate 214: Howe & Company's Siding signal box, viewed from the north-east, brought into use in 1916, was of wood construction, measured 16ft. 6in. x 11ft. 6in. x 10ft.,and had a 20 lever Midland tappett frame with 6in. centres (W & W Committee Minute No. 27529, 5/10/1916). The lever frame was replaced in 1943 to coincide with additional siding accommodation, when a pre-1943 standard 30 lever frame (4½in. centres) was installed.

BEATYS SIDING

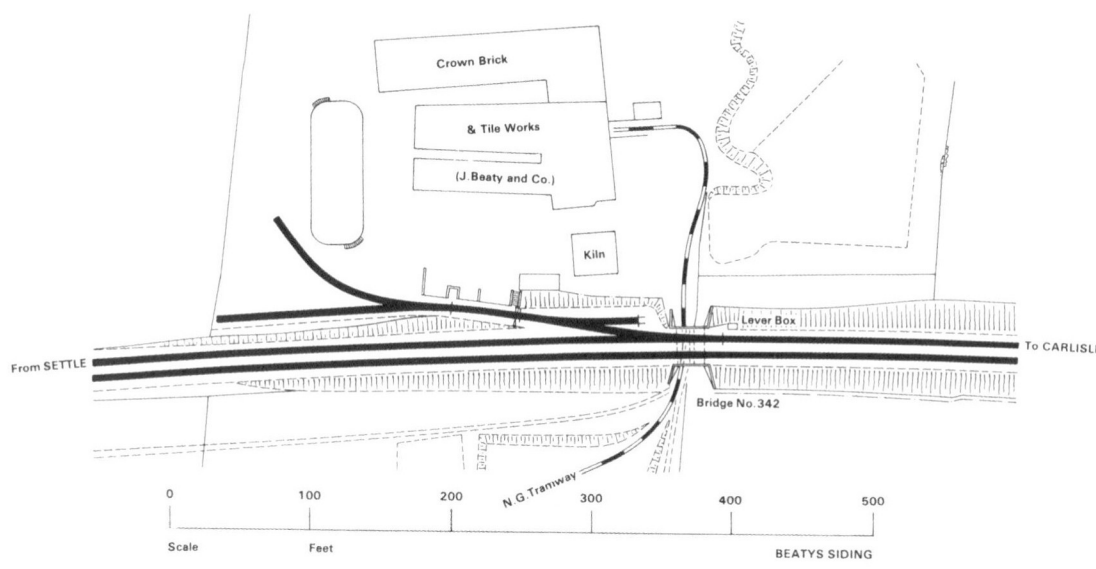

Figure 85: The track layout at Beaty's Siding, based upon information from a Midland Railway survey of 1912. This is another example of a small private siding controlled from a small lever frame. On this occasion, the key to the frame was kept at the Howe & Company's Siding cabin, and the siding was for the use of the Crown Brick and Tile Co. We have no details of the closure of this facility, but it was out of use in 1932 and recovered in 1935. The narrow gauge tramway passing beneath bridge No. 342 connected the brickworks to the clay pit.

Figure 86: The track layout for Cumwhinton, based upon information from a Midland Railway survey of 1911.

CUMWHINTON

Cottages

S M House

Key to Station Buildings
1 Ladies Waiting Room
2 Booking Hall
3 Station Master

Station Buildings

WM

P. Hut

Oil Store

Level Crossing

To CARLISLE

Platform

Sand

From SETTLE

Bridge (No. 346)

Platform

Waiting Room

Signal Box

MP

Scale   Feet

0   100   200   300   400   500   600

CUMWHINTON

Plate 215: A view of Cumwhinton, circa 1955. Pictured from the public overbridge, south of the station, it shows a medium-sized building, well-maintained, and complete with all fretted bargeboards. The goods facilities here were more in keeping with those provided at the smaller stations. Note the position of the signal box.
N. Wilkinson

Plate 216: Ex-LMS 'Crab' 2-6-0 No. 42790 climbs through Cumwhinton with an 'up' freight from Durran Hill to Stourton on 16th July 1955. Note the well-tended gardens and the poster boards still bearing the legend LMS. This station closed completely on 5th November 1956.
R. Leslie

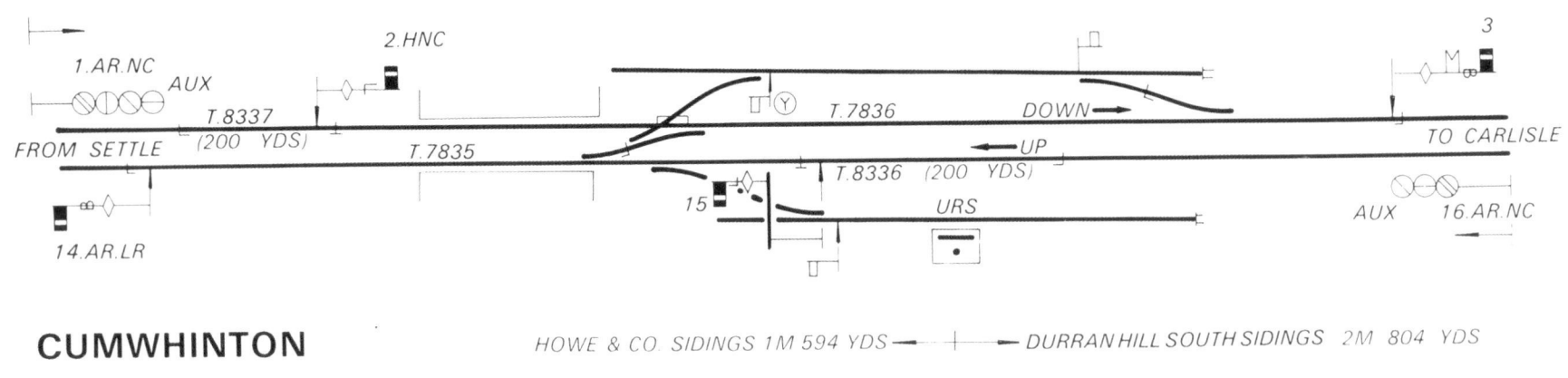

CUMWHINTON

HOWE & CO. SIDINGS 1M 594 YDS ———|——— DURRAN HILL SOUTH SIDINGS 2M 804 YDS

Figure 87: The signalling diagram for Cumwhinton, based upon information available for 1955. The signal box brought into use in 1897, was of wood construction, measured 16ft. 6in. x 11ft. 6in. x 8ft., had a 16 lever tumbler frame, and a renewal cost of £224. (W & W Committee Minute No. 15695, 20/5/1897). It closed on 1st March 1958.

Plate 217: Cumwhinton stationmaster's house, built of red sandstone and standing above the station approach.

Plate 218: Cumwhinton, showing a row of four cottages built for employees.

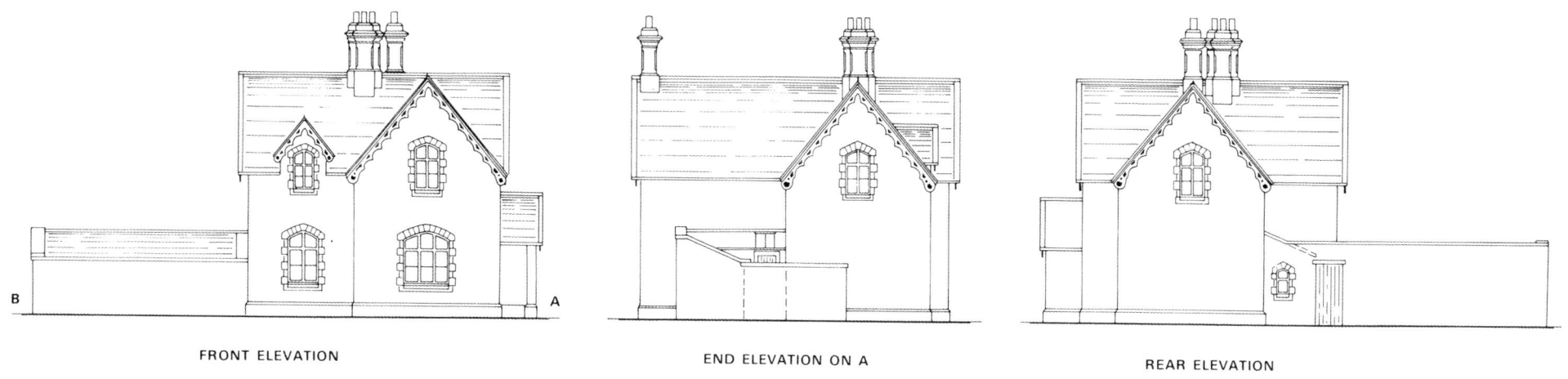

FRONT ELEVATION   END ELEVATION ON A   REAR ELEVATION

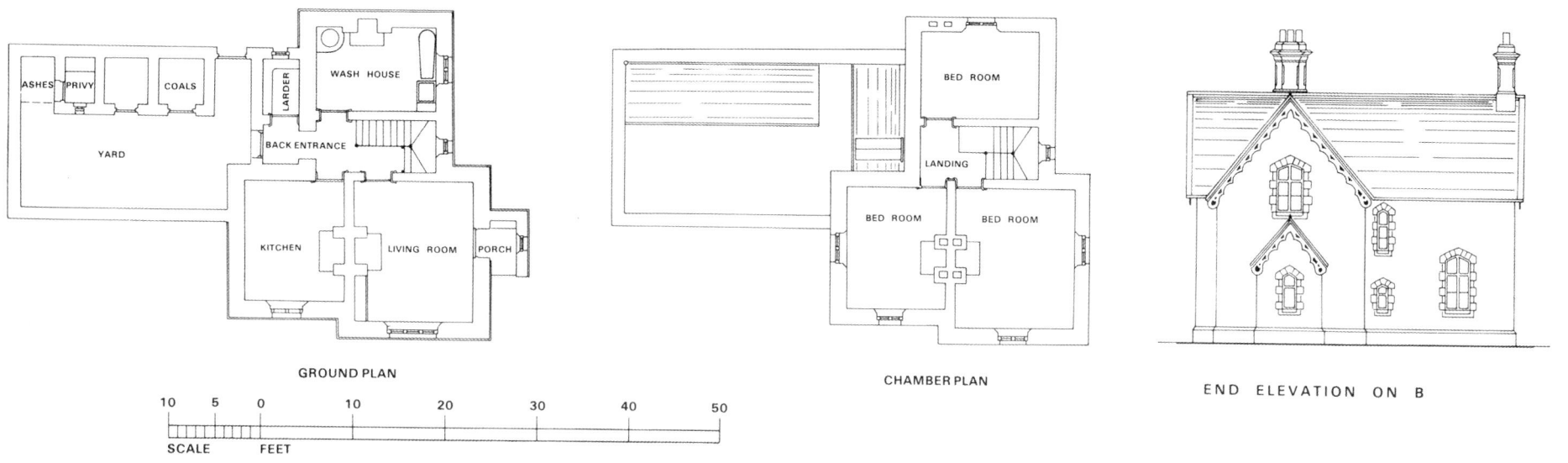

GROUND PLAN   CHAMBER PLAN   END ELEVATION ON B

SCALE FEET
10 5 0 10 20 30 40 50

Figure 88: A typical stationmaster's house for the Settle & Carlisle Railway, from an official drawing.

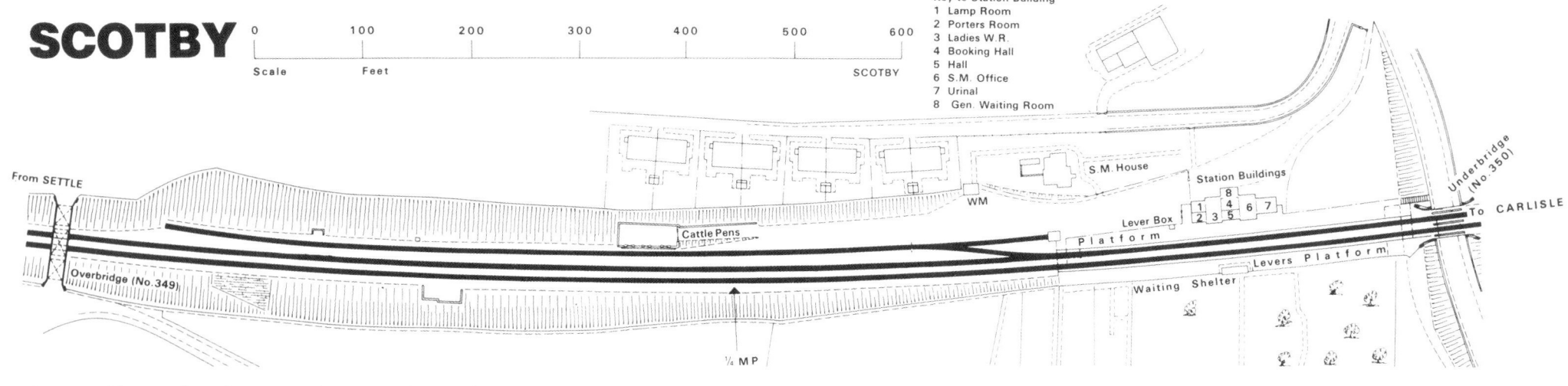

SCOTBY

Scale   Feet   0   100   200   300   400   500   600   SCOTBY

Key to Station Building
1 Lamp Room
2 Porters Room
3 Ladies W.R.
4 Booking Hall
5 Hall
6 S.M. Office
7 Urinal
8 Gen. Waiting Room

From SETTLE

Overbridge (No.349)

Cattle Pens

WM

S.M. House

Lever Box

Platform

Station Buildings
8
1 4 6 7
2 3 5

Underbridge (No.350)

To CARLISLE

Levers Platform

Waiting Shelter

¼ M P

Figure 89: The track layout at Scotby, based upon information from a Midland Railway survey of 1912.

Plate 219: Scotby was the most northerly Midland Railway station, and served a village quite near to the city of Carlisle. This may account for its early demise, on 1st February 1942. A medium-sized building was provided here. The waiting shelter on this the 'up' platform, although of a design to be found elsewhere on the Midland system, was uncharacteristic of the Settle & Carlisle line. The station nameboards appear to be much less tall than others we have come across, but utilise the cast letters as seen on the larger angled boards. On this occasion the tall lamps utilise gas for illuminations, and the tall posts are to the same design as used elsewhere. A new signal box had been provided in 1897, and occupied a position set in the embankment where the permanent way hut can be seen. However, Way & Works Committee Minute No. 23768, 4/6/1909, authorised removal of the box, and the provision of a covered lever frame on the 'down' platform (to the left of the station building) and levers on the 'up' side (next to the waiting shelter). One siding only was provided as goods facilities, although this did have a small cattle dock and the services of a crane.

Lens of Sutton

MIDLAND STATION, SCOTBY   2127

DURRAN HILL & PETTERIL BRIDGE

Plate 221 (above): An earlier view of Durran Hill South Sidings in 1935, photographed from bridge No. 360, situated immediately south of Durran Hill Junction box.

D. F. Tee Collection

Plate 220 (left): Durran Hill South Sidings, on 1st June 1963, as viewed from the windows of the signal box (of the same name) shortly after closure. This box, brought into use on 8th November 1891, was of wood construction, measured 22ft. x 11ft. 6in. x 12ft., received a replacement 30 lever tappett frame (6in. centres) in 1921, and closed on 12th May 1965. This view, looking towards Carlisle, shows the sidings, incorporating improvements implemented during World War II, and so should be compared with the track layout in **Figure 91**. Durran Hill Junction signal box can be seen in the distance, and the larger of the cluster of buildings in the centre is the telegraph office.

D.F. Tee

Figure 90: The signalling diagram for Durran Hill South Sidings signal box, based upon information available for 1958.

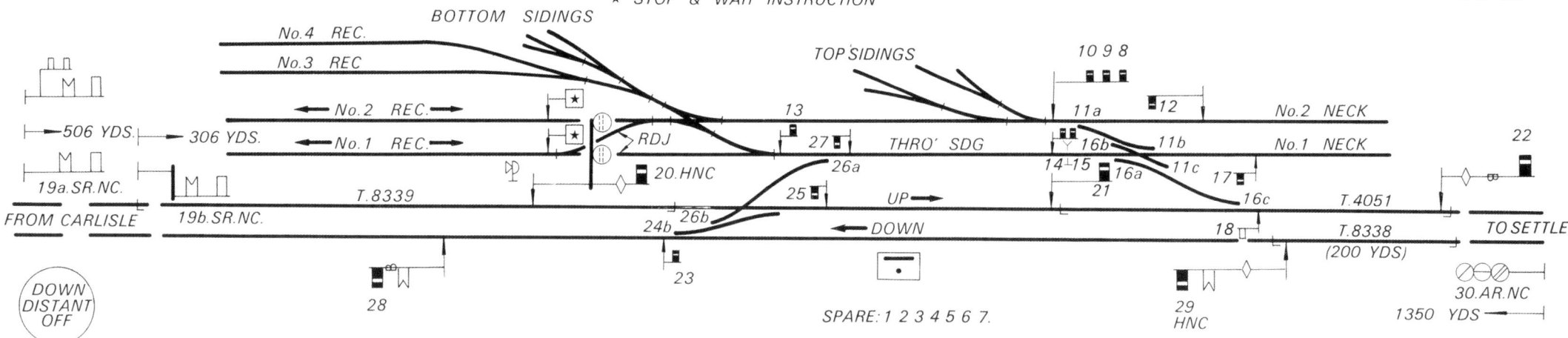

DURRAN HILL SOUTH SIDINGS

DURRANHILL JN. 638 YDS ⟵ ⟶ CUMWHINTON 2M 804 YDS

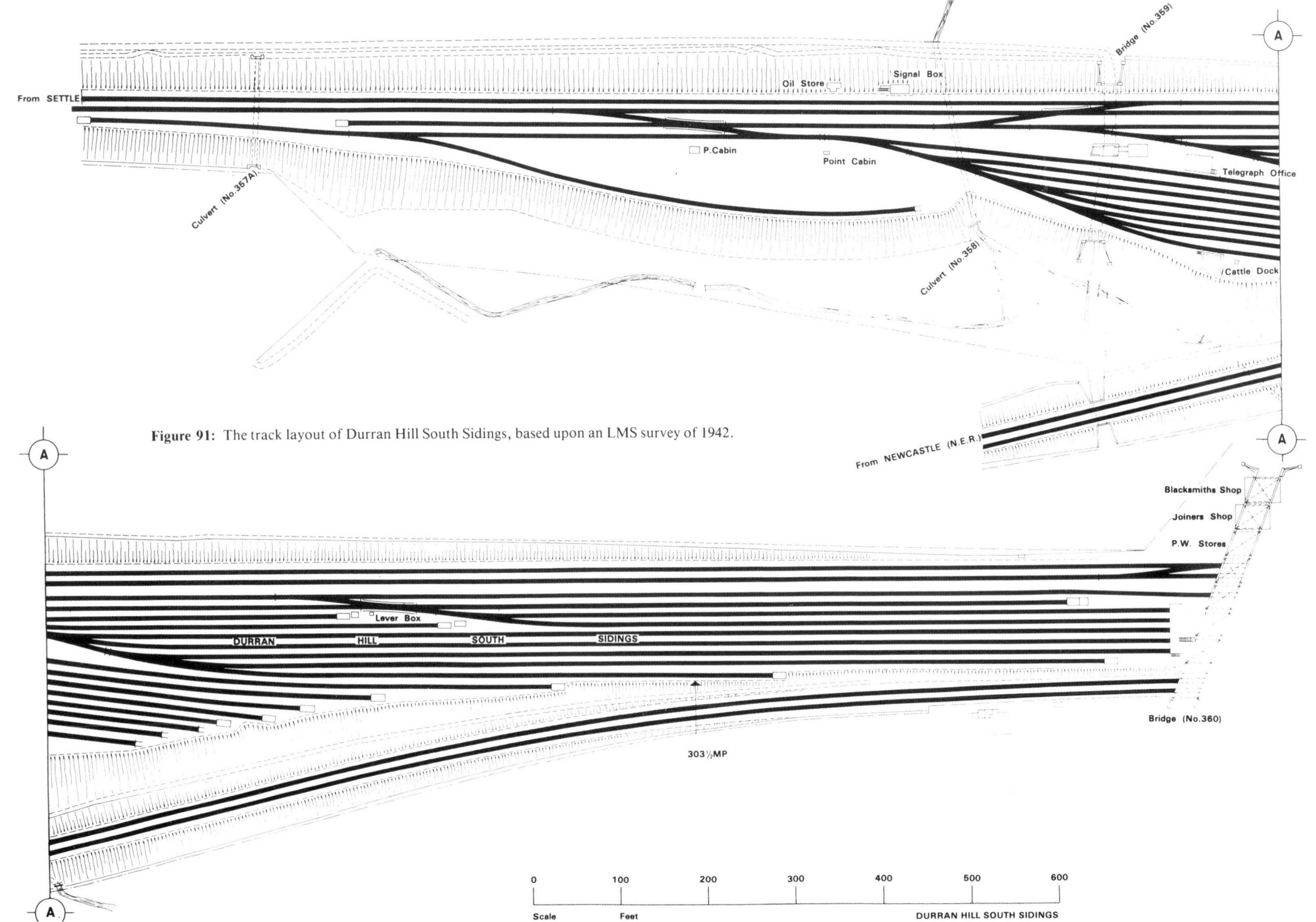

Figure 91: The track layout of Durran Hill South Sidings, based upon an LMS survey of 1942.

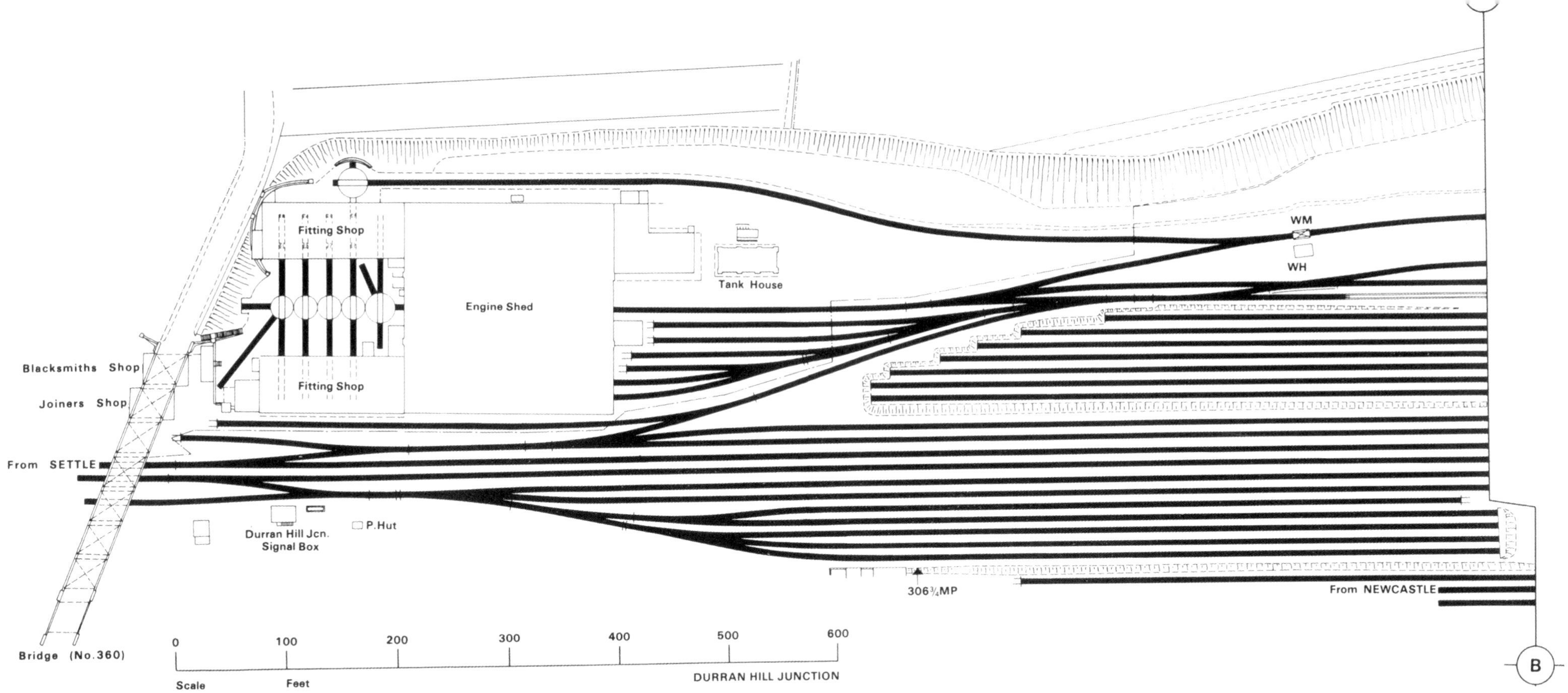

Fitting Shop

Fitting Shop

Blacksmiths Shop

Joiners Shop

Engine Shed

Tank House

WM

WH

From SETTLE

Durran Hill Jcn.
Signal Box

P.Hut

306¾MP

From NEWCASTLE

Bridge (No.360)

| 0 | 100 | 200 | 300 | 400 | 500 | 600 |

Scale   Feet

DURRAN HILL JUNCTION

B

Figure 92: The track layout of Durran Hill Junction, based upon an LMS survey of 1942. The engine shed closed on 16th February 1936, but reopened as a wartime measure in 1943 for stabling of engines for fire, ashpan and smokebox cleaning, and for coaling. After the war, it was used for engine storage until November 1959.

Plate 222: A view of Durran Hill, circa 1930, photographed from bridge No. 360 but now looking north, towards Petteril Bridge and Carlisle. The Durran Hill Junction signal box is to the right, and the fitting shops and engine shed to the left. The lines and yards to the right are those of the ex-North Eastern Railway Company.

D.F. Tee Collection

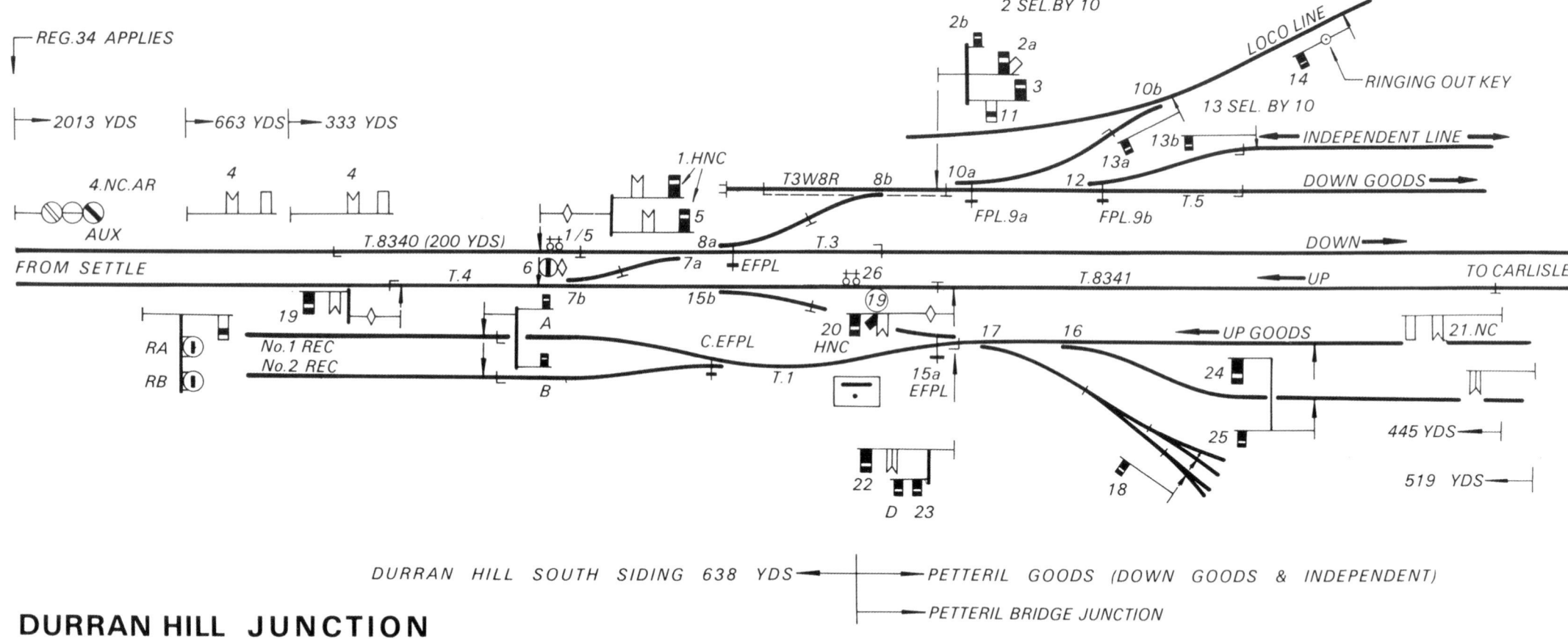

DURRAN HILL JUNCTION

Figure 93: The signalling diagram for Durran Hill Junction, based upon information available for 1958.

Plate 223: Durran Hill Junction signal box is being passed by Class 8F No. 48104, as it commences the run south with an 'up' freight on 7th June 1963. The signal box brought into use from 7th November 1895, was of wood construction, measured 22ft. x 15ft. x 7ft. and had a renewal cost of £290 (W & W Committee Minute No. 14562, 17/10/1895).

D. F. Tee

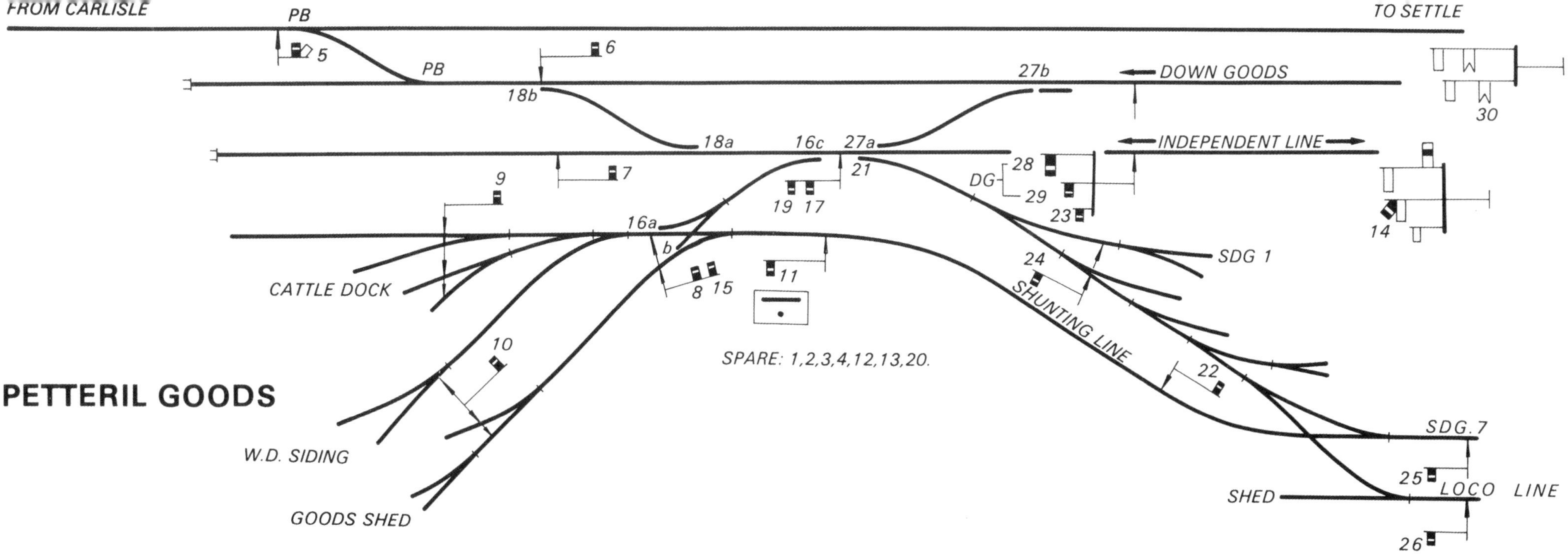

TO SETTLE

PB
5
6
PB
27b
DOWN GOODS
18b
18a
16c
27a
INDEPENDENT LINE
9
7
28
29
23
DG
21
19 17
16a
b
8 15
11
24
SDG 1
30
14
22
CATTLE DOCK
SPARE: 1,2,3,4,12,13,20.

PETTERIL GOODS

10
SHUNTING LINE
SDG. 7
25
W.D. SIDING
SHED
LOCO LINE
GOODS SHED
26

Figure 94: The signalling diagram for Petteril Goods, based upon information available for 1957.

Plate 224 (left): Petteril goods yard, looking south, from the Petteril Goods signal box, circa 1935. The Durran Hill locomotive depot is to the right. In the distance can be seen bridge No. 360 from which the views in **Plates 221 & 222** were photographed. Petteril Goods signal box brought into use on 18th October 1891, was of wood construction, and measured 25ft. x 11ft. x 12ft. (W & W Committee Minute No. 11649, 16/7/1891). A replacement tappet frame was fitted in 1920 containing 30 levers at 6in. centres. The box was replaced by a ground frame of two levers following closure on 16th July 1965 after the recovery of redundant sidings in 1964. The ground frame subsequently closed on 25th April 1971.

D. F. Tee Collection

Plate 225 (below): The wagon repair shop at Petteril Goods, photographed on 28th April 1962.

D. F. Tee

Plate 226: Twenty four houses for employees were constructed in two blocks of twelve at Petteril Bridge by the Midland, in response to the recommendations of the 1873 report.

D. F. Tee

Figure 95: The track layout at Petteril Bridge Junction and Petteril Goods, based upon an LMS survey of 1942.

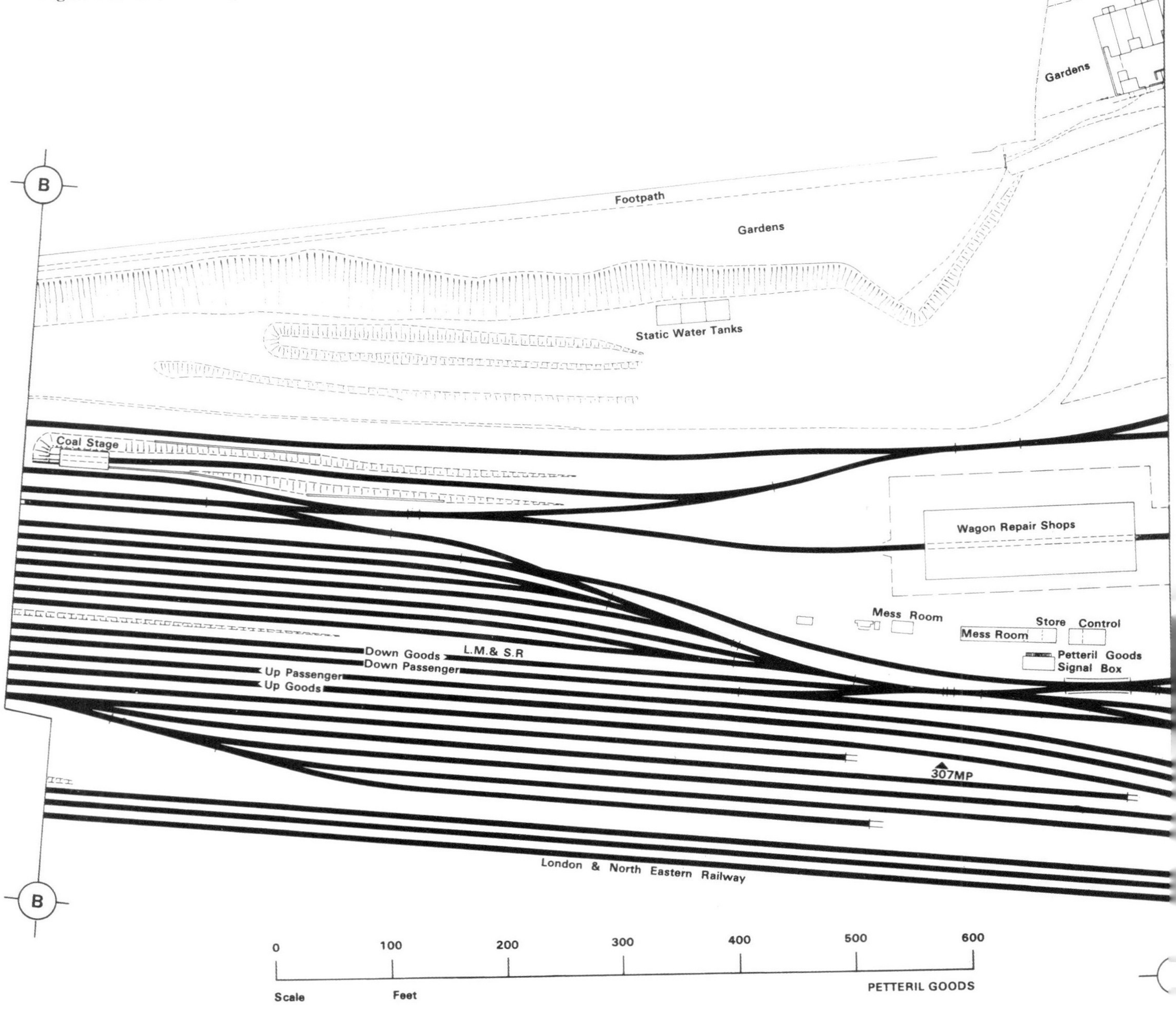

C

Gardens

B

Footpath

Gardens

Static Water Tanks

Coal Stage

Wagon Repair Shops

Mess Room

Store   Control

Mess Room

Down Goods   L.M.& S.R
Down Passenger

Petteril Goods
Signal Box

Up Passenger
Up Goods

▲307MP

London & North Eastern Railway

B

| 0 | 100 | 200 | 300 | 400 | 500 | 600 |

Scale   Feet

PETTERIL GOODS

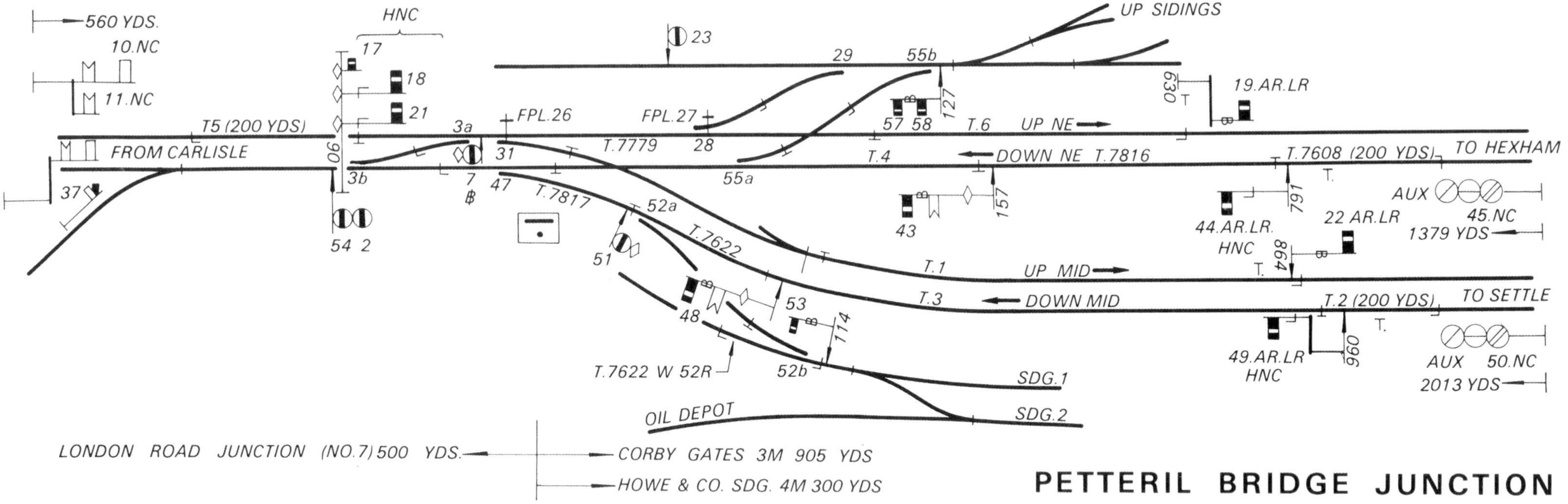

PETTERIL BRIDGE JUNCTION

Diagram labels:
- 560 YDS.
- HNC
- UP SIDINGS
- 10.NC
- 11.NC
- 17
- 18
- 21
- 23
- 29
- 55b
- 19.AR.LR
- T5 (200 YDS)
- 3a
- FPL.26
- FPL.27
- 28
- 57 58
- T.6 UP NE
- 630 T
- FROM CARLISLE
- 31
- T.7779
- 55a
- DOWN NE T.7816
- T.7608 (200 YDS) TO HEXHAM
- 37
- 3b
- 7
- 47
- 52a
- T.7817
- T.7622
- 43
- 157
- 44.AR.LR. HNC
- 22 AR.LR
- AUX 45.NC
- 54 2
- 51
- 48
- T.1 UP MID
- 864
- 1379 YDS
- 53
- 114
- T.3 DOWN MID
- T.2 (200 YDS) TO SETTLE
- T.7622 W 52R
- 52b
- SDG.1
- 49.AR.LR HNC
- 990
- AUX 50.NC
- OIL DEPOT
- SDG.2
- 2013 YDS
- LONDON ROAD JUNCTION (NO.7) 500 YDS.
- CORBY GATES 3M 905 YDS
- HOWE & CO. SDG. 4M 300 YDS

Figure 96: The Petteril Bridge Junction signalling diagram, based upon information available for 1973.

Plate 227: Petteril Bridge Junction signal box. At this point Midland line trains came under the control of NER signalmen. This composite brick and timber NER box contained a Stevens frame of 66 levers. The box closed on 2nd June 1973 following implementation of the Carlisle power signal box.

Plate 228: The Settle & Carlisle Railway ended at Petteril Bridge Junction, from whence running was over the metals of the NER. However, Midland influence did extend further north into the goods yards at Dentonholme, west of Carlisle (Citadel) Station. Numbering of structures in the Midland sequence continued into Dentonholme goods yard ending at the bridge over the River Caldew to the right of this photograph. Dentonholme goods yard was, to a large extent, under the control of a number of Midland signal boxes.

LNER 'A4' No 4498 *Sir Nigel Gresley* crosses the River Ribble at Sheriff Brow on 8 June in 1985. W. A. SHARMAN

BR '9F' No 92220 *Evening Star* heads north over the skew bridge at Sheriff Brow beside the Ribble on 21 April 1984. W. A. SHARMAN

Brush Type 4 No 47488 draws into Horton in Ribblesdale station on 19 June 1988 with a down passenger train. Both the double gable station building on the up side and the shelter on the down side have lost their original bargeboards but the station building retains its entrance porch and screen to the waiting area. The quatrefoil freestone inset in the station gables and trefoil inset in the shelter gable are a consistent feature of all the station buildings on the Settle & Carlisle. Having been closed to passengers in May 1970, it was reopened in July 1986 and enjoys six trains a day in each direction. MARK B. WARBURTON

LMS 'Black Five' No 5305 in full flight crossing Ribblehead Viaduct on 20 September 1980. W. A. SHARMAN

Blea Moor signal box, 21st June 1965. ONLINE TRANSPORT ARCHIVE, A. S. CLAYTON

MR Compound No 1000 and LMS 'Jubilee' No 5690 *Leander* are seen at a wintry Blea Moor on 5 February 1983. J. H. COOPER-SMITH

Looking northwest from the Dales Way road we look along Dentdale with, in the foreground, Denthead Viaduct across the Fell End Gill on 16 August 1984. The railway has just emerged from Blea Moor Tunnel and can be seen against the hillside on the far right for the three miles or so to Dent station. On the skyline is the mass of East Baugh Fell and in front and to the left Rise Hill and Aye Gill Pike, with the high ground of Langshaw Wold nearer to us forming the left side of Dentdale.
MARK B. WARBURTON

Dent Head Viaduct in the distance and the northern portal of Blea Moor Tunnel, on 21 June 1965.
ONLINE TRANSPORT ARCHIVE, A. S. CLAYTON

LMS 'Princess Coronation' No 46229 *Duchess of Hamilton* leaves Blea Moor Tunnel on 12 March 1983. J. H. COOPER-SMITH

Mixed freight on Arten Gill Viaduct, *c*1967. ONLINE TRANSPORT ARCHIVE, A. S. CLAYTON

SR No 850 *Lord Nelson* crosses Arten Gill Viaduct on 29 July 1981. DR L. A. NIXON

LMS Class 5 MT4-6-0 No 44852 swings through Dent station with an up Class H freight train on 16 May 1967. Dent station was nearly five miles from the settlement of Dent and over 500 feet higher – on the Great Western Railway it would have been called Dent Road! This view of the southern end of the station shows the stationmaster's house on the left and the small double-gabled station building with the exhaust from the locomotive obscuring the overbridge carrying the Coal Road just to the north of the station. Unusually, the locomotive retains its upper lamp iron at the top of the smokebox; most of the other engines had had it removed to the smokebox door to avoid problems with overhead electric conductors. MARK B. WARBURTON

An unidentified BR Type 4 1Co-Co1 (later Class 45 or 46) hauls the up Thames-Clyde Express through Dent station on 16 May 1967, seen from the Coal Road bridge. The two lines of snow fences were erected as the exposure to the north and east here causes snow to fill the area. As we look back in a southerly direction, the Arten Gill Viaduct can be seen directly above the locomotive and Denthead Viaduct just to the right of the station building chimney stack. On the left skyline we see the flat top of Wold Fell and straight ahead Blea Moor and the lower slopes of Whernside. MARK B. WARBURTON

An unidentified Class 40 hauls a mixed freight through Dent station on 4 July 1980. W. A. SHARMAN

LMS Class 5MT 4-6-0 No 44899 restarts its down Class D freight train having dropped the pilotman at Garsdale station on 5 October 1967 when there was an occupation of the down line between Dent and Garsdale. On the up line BR Class 9F 2-10-0 No 92249 waits with another Class D freight with steam to spare. Between the two engines can be seen the up sidings, to the right of which ran the Hawes branch. Behind the down starter signal is the site of the famous stockaded turntable. Behind the up freight can be seen the arches of Moorcock Viaduct across Dandry Mire. MARK B. WARBURTON

Garsdale station looking north on 5 October 1967 during a brief sunny interval. The station buildings date back to the opening of the line but have lost their ornate bargeboards. The right-hand platform was an island, with the Hawes branch trains using the other face, and between about 1900 and 1950 sported a 'ridge and furrow' awning. On the near end of the left-hand building can be seen one of the cast-iron drinking fountains. The signal box was brought into use in 1910 as Hawes Junction, replacing two smaller boxes, and its 40-lever frame required three 'modules'. MARK B. WARBURTON

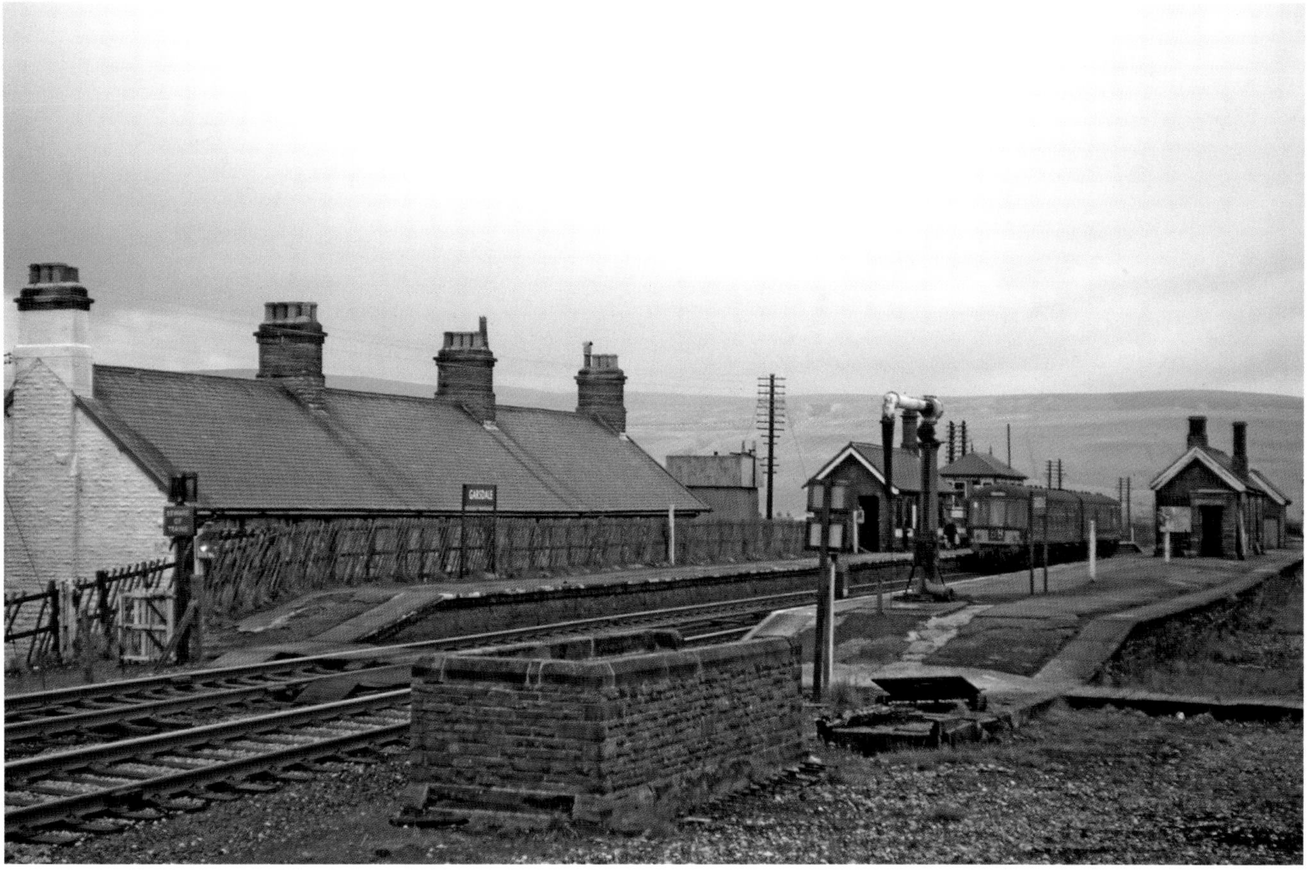

DMU at Garsdale station, *c*1967. ONLINE TRANSPORT ARCHIVE, A. S. CLAYTON

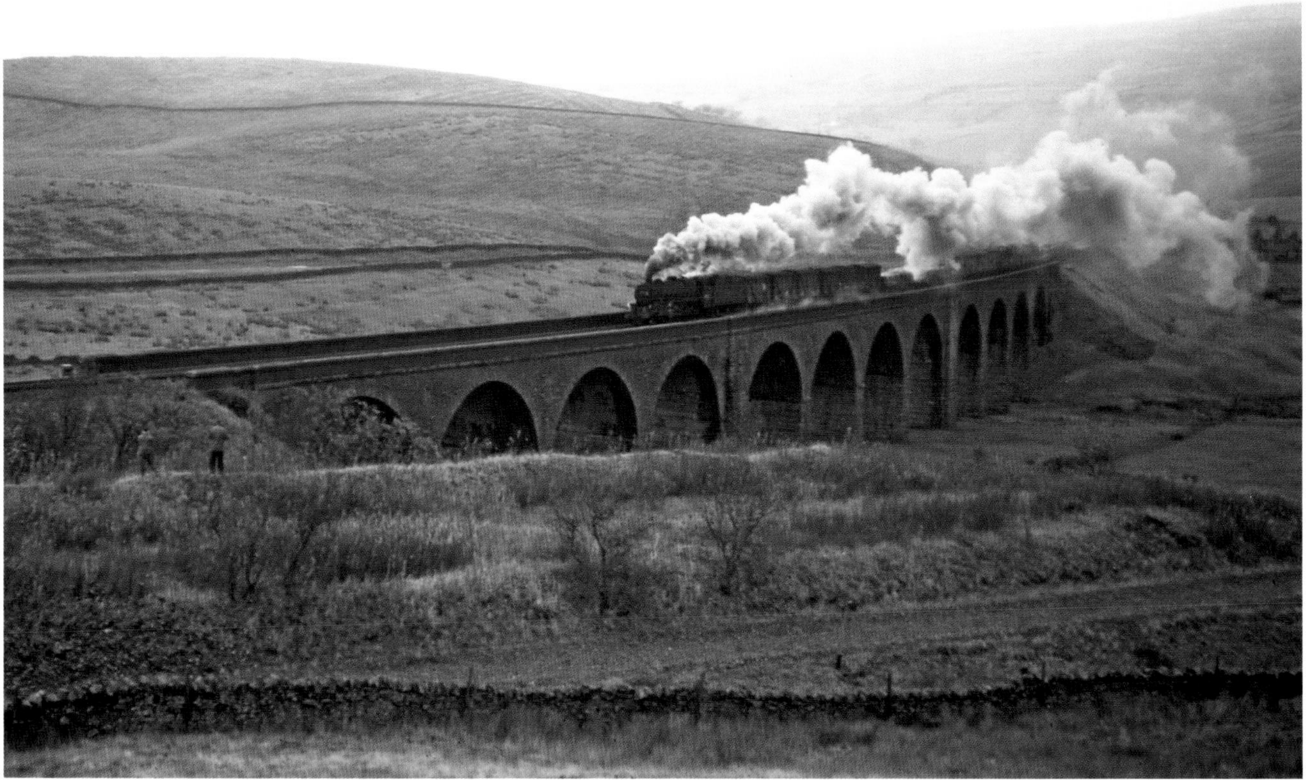

Moorcock/Dandry Mire Viaduct, *c*1967. ONLINE TRANSPORT ARCHIVE, A. S. CLAYTON

Class 47 No 47543 crosses Moorcock/Dandry Mire Viaduct, approaching Garsdale, on the 10.40 ex-Carlisle to Leeds service on 23 August 1986. W. A. SHARMAN

LMS 'Jubilee No 5690 *Leander* comes off Moorcock/Dandry Mire Viaduct on 26 August 1980, heading towards Ais Gill summit.
W. A. SHARMAN

There has been much discussion over why Shotlock Hill Tunnel was built. As the notice proclaims it was only 106 yards long and the ground level over it was less than 20 feet. The ground here is composed of boulder clay which was one of the most difficult materials to manage in the construction of the railway, being solid one moment and liquid the next. The tunnel is fully lined and was justified on the grounds of the avoidance of landslips. The plaque on the pediment has the date 1875. This photograph of the southern (up) portal was taken on 5 October 1967. MARK B. WARBURTON

BR Type 4 1Co-Co1 No D188 (later 46051) on the down Thames-Clyde Express approaches Ais Gill summit and signal box on 17 August 1967. The handrail in the foreground was on the rail-side of the footpath from the road to the signal box. The maintenance of telegraph wires was not a problem on a fine day such as this but the weather is notoriously changeable at an altitude of 1,170 feet above sea level. MARK B. WARBURTON

LMS Class 5MT 4-6-0 No 45061 on an unfitted up ballast train has just crossed Ais Gill Viaduct on 5 October 1967. To the right can be seen Ais Gill Farm and the broad valley of the River Eden and behind the locomotive Mallerstang Common rising up to Wild Boar Fell. The line here is climbing the western side of the valley at 1 in 100 and can be seen clinging to the hillside. MARK B. WARBURTON

An unidentified named Brush Class 47 diesel on a down train is about to enter the southern end of Birkett Tunnel on 19 June 1988. The dry stone wall in the foreground is on the verge of the Tommy Road. The ruined platelayer's hut to the right of the locomotive and the 20 years of tree growth since the demise of steam traction is a reminder of the work that was done by the permanent way gangers to keep cuttings clear of vegetation as well as inspect and maintain the track. The geology of this area is complicated by a major fault causing contorted strata and engineering challenges. MARK B. WARBURTON

Turning round from the previous photograph, we see LMS Class 5MT 4-6-0 No 45268 and the fitted vans at the head of its down Class D freight passing through the deep cutting through Wiseber Hill to the northwest of Kirkby Stephen station. The shallow angle of the cutting show that the underlying rock here was not stable and the area bare of grass shows where there has been a landslip. In building the line, deep cuttings were not necessarily a problem as the civil engineers would balance the need for embankments with adjacent cuttings to provide the material. MARK B. WARBURTON

Kirkby Stephen goods shed with the station in the distance, looking north, 31 May 1967. ONLINE TRANSPORT ARCHIVE, A. S. CLAYTON

LMS Class 5MT 4-6-0 No 45268 rolls through Kirkby Stephen West with a down Class D freight on 17 August 1967. All the buildings in this picture were built by the Midland Railway: from left to right are the two-storey buildings of Midland Terrace, the station weighbridge house, the station buildings and signal box and, on the right, the single storey buildings of Midland Cottages. The main settlement of Kirkby Stephen was some 1½ miles north, 300 feet lower and more conveniently served by Kirkby Stephen East station on the North Eastern Railway's Stainmore line. MARK B. WARBURTON

The station buildings at Kirkby Stephen are seen in more detail in this rail-level view on 17 August 1967. This was one of the three larger station buildings with two large gables and one smaller gable (the others were at Settle and Appleby). However, even here the platforms were only 300 feet long, ie could only accommodate five-coach trains. At the time of this photograph the 1st Class waiting room had been adapted for use as an office by the Engineers' Department who had erected the porch seen under the nearest gable. In the distance High Pike Hill to the left marks the northern limit of Mallerstang Edge which dominates the eastern side of the River Eden valley as far as Ais Gill. MARK B. WARBURTON

Kirkby Stephen West station buildings looking north, 31 May 1967. ONLINE TRANSPORT ARCHIVE, A. S. CLAYTON

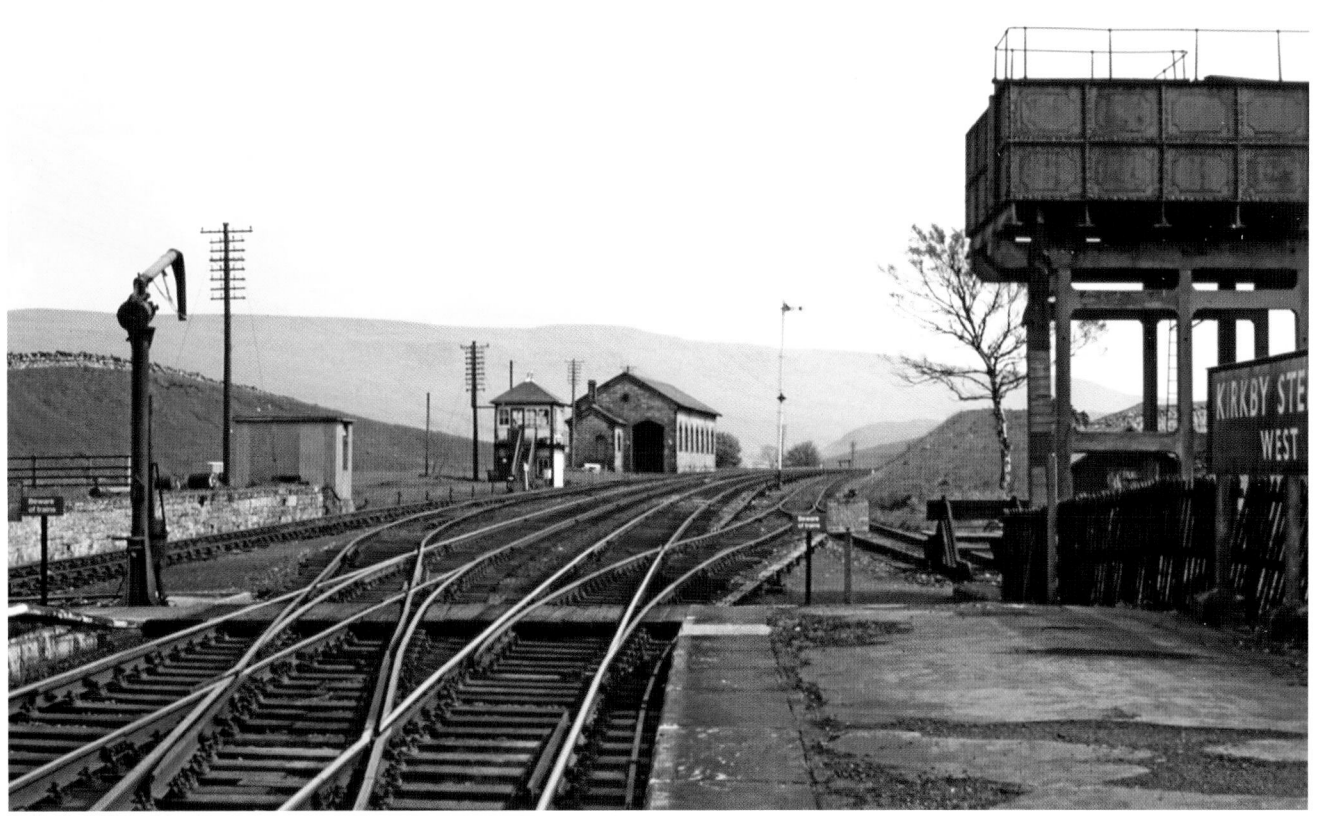

Kirkby Stephen West looking south on the same day, 31 May 1967, showing watertower, signal box and goods shed.
ONLINE TRANSPORT ARCHIVE, A. S. CLAYTON

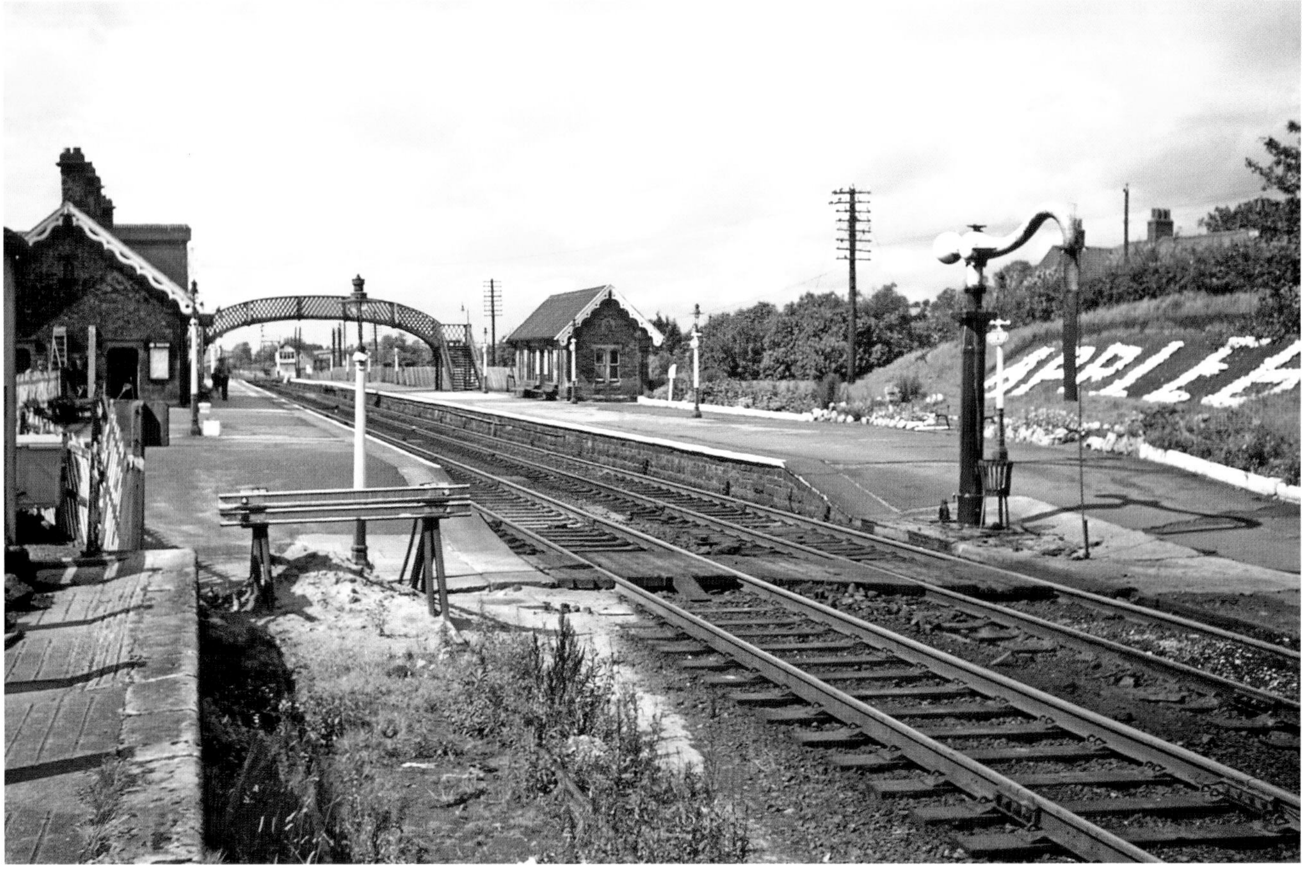

Appleby station looking north on 16 August 1967 exhibits the same style of buildings seen previously but now executed in brick with stone dressings rather than the stone construction in the high hills. At this time the station name totems still proclaim 'Appleby West' and will do so for another six months despite the closure of the ex North Eastern station in 1962. This was the only station provided with a passenger footbridge and station lighting is by gas, showing that civilisation has been reached! MARK B. WARBURTON

The station footbridge provides a vantage point to photograph BR Class 9F 2-10-0 No 92137 and an up Class E train of anhydrite from Long Meg passing through Appleby West on 16 August 1967. The bridge plate is prominent on the occupation underbridge No 237. Above the rear unsheeted wagons of the train can be seen Appleby North Junction signal box in the fork of the connecting line to the ex North Eastern Railway line to Penrith. The platforms here were nearly 600 feet long and could accommodate a 10-coach train. They are noticeably wider in this photograph than other stations on the line. Appleby had a weekly stock auction and the livestock and milk traffic here was considerable into the 1950s. MARK B. WARBURTON

The waitning room on the 'up' platform at Appleby West station, 31 May 1967. ONLINE TRANSPORT ARCHIVE, A. S. CLAYTON

Appleby West station looking north on 31 May 1967. ONLINE TRANSPORT ARCHIVE, A. S. CLAYTON

This time looking south on 31 May 1967. Appleby West was the only station on the line provided with a passenger footbridge.
ONLINE TRANSPORT ARCHIVE, A. S. CLAYTON

Long Marton signal box 31 May 1967. ONLINE TRANSPORT ARCHIVE, A. S. CLAYTON

Long Marton Viaduct also photographed on 31 May 1967. ONLINE TRANSPORT ARCHIVE, A. S. CLAYTON

Classes 25 and 31 pass Culgaith station heading north on 5 November 1983. J. H. COOPER-SMITH

Class 45 No 45142 heads south with the 16.45 ex-Carlisle to Leeds service near Long Meg sidings on 21 April 1984. W. A. SHARMAN